Grammar for First Certificate

with answers

Second edition

Self-study grammar
reference and practice

LOUISE HASHEMI and
BARBARA THOMAS

CAMBRIDGE
UNIVERSITY PRESS

CAMBRIDGE UNIVERSITY PRESS
Cambridge, New York, Melbourne, Madrid, Cape Town,
Singapore, São Paulo, Delhi, Tokyo, Mexico City

Cambridge University Press
The Edinburgh Building, Cambridge CB2 8RU, UK

www.cambridge.org
Information on this title: www.cambridge.org/9780521690874

First published 2003
Second edition 2008
6th printing 2011

Printed in Dubai by Oriental Press

A catalogue record for this publication is available from the British Library

ISBN 978-0-521-69087-4 Edition with answers and Audio CD
ISBN 978-0-521-69104-8 Edition without answers

Acknowledgements

The authors would like to thank their editors, Alison Sharpe, Anna Teevan and Lynn Townsend, and also the following people for their comments and advice: Shahla Hashemi, Neca Huntic and Christina Wylie.

The authors and publishers would also like to thank the following teachers from around the world who commented on the material in its draft form:
Roger Scott, Bournemouth, UK; Mairi Beaton, Lyon, France; Elisabeth de Lange, Beckum, Germany, Helen Gialias, Bournemouth, England; Mechthild Hesse, Bad Homburg, Germany; Diana Hopkins, Bath, England; Scott Lusher, Izmir, Turkey; Mark Nettle, Bath, England; Graham Palmer, Royston, England; Martin Parrott, London, England; Dmitris Primolis, Archanes, Greece; Susan Rastetter-Gies, Aschaffenburg, Germany; Nick Shaw, A Coruna, Spain; Anna Sikorzynska, Warsaw, Poland; Sylvia Sommer, Lyon, France; Roy Sprenger, Troyes, France.

The authors and publishers are grateful to the following for permission to reproduce copyright material. It has not always been possible to identify the sources of all the material used and in such cases the publishers would welcome information from the copyright owners:

p.23: text adapted from 'Me and my glad rags' by Liz Gill, *Financial Times 'How to spend it'*, December 2002; p.32: adapted extract from 'Hurled through the door' by Max Wooldridge, *Observer*, 6 February 2000 © Max Wooldridge, reproduced with permission of Max Wooldridge; p.198: adapted text from *The Language of Clothes* by Alison Lurie, published by Henry Holt and Company (Owl Books) © Alison Lurie, reproduced with permission of A. P. Watt Ltd on behalf of Alison Lurie; p.213: adapted extract from 'World Standard English', *The Cambridge Encyclopaedia of the English Language*, 1997, by David Crystal, reproduced with permission of Cambridge University Press.

Photographs: p. 6: Powerstock Zefa; p. 11: Picture Desk/Kobal; p. 12: Powerstock Zefa; p. 13: Jaimie Duplass/Shutterstock; p. 21: Stockbyte; p. 31: Art Directors and Trip; p. 32: Robert Harding Picture Library Ltd/Alamy; p. 56.1: Network Photographers; p. 56.2: Robert Harding Picture Library Ltd; p. 56.3: Digital Vision Ltd./SuperStock; p. 56.4: inmagine/digital vision; p. 64: Alamy.com; p. 70: Robert Harding Picture Library; p. 77: Corbis UK Ltd; p. 84: Simon Heaton/Alamy; p. 87: Anthony Blake Picture Library; p. 88: f1 online/Alamy; p. 91a: Greg Evans Picture Library; p. 91b: Greg Evans Picture Library; p. 91c: Robert Harding Picture Library Ltd; p. 91d: Rex Features; p. 100: Art Directors and Trip; p. 104: JUPITERIMAGES/ Brand X/Alamy; p. 125: Art Directors and Trip; p. 135: JUPITERIMAGES/ PHOTOS.COM /Alamy; p. 153: Popperfoto; p. 182a: Juha Tuomi/Shutterstock; p. 182b: Rex Features; p. 182c: Powerstock Zefa; p. 182d: Robert Harding Picture Library Ltd; p. 187: Charles Taylor/Shutterstock; p. 196: Art Directors and Trip; p. 197: Rex Features; p. 216: Mandy Godbehear/Shutterstock; p. 222: Rex Interstock.

Produced by Kamae Design, Oxford

Contents

iv

To the student

Who is this book for?

This book is for anyone preparing for the Cambridge First Certificate in English exam and covers the grammar needed for the exam. You can use it with a general English language course for extra grammar practice or with practice tests as part of a revision programme. You can use it in class or for self-study.

How do I use this book?

There are two ways to use this book. You can either start at Unit 1 and work through to the end of the book, or you can do the Entry test on p.ix to find out which units you need most practice in and begin with those.

What is in this book?

This book contains 25 units. Each unit is in four parts:

A: Context listening This introduces the grammar of the unit in context. This will help you to understand the grammar more easily when you study section B. It also gives you useful listening practice. Listen to the recording and answer the questions. Then check your answers in the Key before you read the Grammar section.

B: Grammar Read through this section before you do the exercises. For each grammar point there are explanations with examples. You can also refer back to this section when you are doing the exercises.

C: Grammar exercises Write your answers to each exercise and then check them in the Key.

D: Exam practice Each unit has a writing task and one other exam task. These have been designed to give you practice in the grammar for that unit as well as helping you to get to know the different parts of the exam. The Use of English tasks test the grammar presented in that unit, but they also test other areas of grammar (which are presented in the rest of the book). In the actual First Certificate exam, each question would test a different grammatical point.

The Key

The Key contains:

- answers for all the exercises. Check your answers at the end of each exercise. The Key tells you which part of the Grammar section you need to look at again if you have any problems.
- sample answers for exercises where you use your own ideas to help you check your work.
- sample answers for all the writing tasks in the Exam practice section. Read these after you have written your own answer. Study the language used and the way the ideas are organised.

The Recording scripts

There are recording scripts for the Context listening in each unit, and for the Exam practice listening tasks. Do not look at the script until after you have answered the questions. It is a good idea to listen to the recording again while you read the script.

Note on contractions

This book generally uses contractions, for example *I'm* for *I am*, *wasn't* for *was not*, because these are always used in speech and are common in written English. The full forms are used in formal written English.

To the teacher

This book offers concise yet comprehensive coverage of the grammar students need for the Cambridge First Certificate in English exam. It can be used for self-study or with a class. It will be particularly valuable for revision, for students retaking the exam and for candidates in classes where some students are not entered for the exam. Sections A, B and C are designed to be useful for all students, whether entered for the First Certificate exam or not.

The Entry test

The entry test can be used diagnostically as a means of prioritising the language areas to be covered, either for a class, or for individual students.

A: Context listening This section is suitable for classroom use. Many of the tasks can be done in pairs or small groups if appropriate.

B: Grammar This section is designed for private study, but you may wish to discuss those parts which are particularly relevant to your students' needs.

C: Grammar exercises This section can be done in class or set as homework. Students can be encouraged to check their own work and discuss any difficulties they encounter.

D: Exam practice This section can be used to familiarise students with the exam task types while offering further practice in the grammar for each unit. Each task is followed by a Grammar focus task, designed to raise students' awareness of a particular language point covered in that unit. The book contains at least one task from each part of the Reading, Writing, Use of English and Listening papers. There are more tasks from the Use of English paper than the others because it is a grammar-based paper. The writing tasks cover the full range of tasks which students may come across in the exam, including emails, articles, essays, short stories and letters. The Writing hints offer extra support in the form of useful words and expressions.

In classes where only some of the students are entered for the First Certificate exam, you might prefer to set exam tasks as extra work for exam candidates only. Alternatively, you could set the tasks for all students, as a further opportunity to practise the grammar of each unit.

Entry test

You can do this test before using the book to help you choose what to study. Choose the correct answer, **A**, **B** or **C**, for each question. When you have finished, check your answers on p.224. The Key tells you which units are most important for you.

1 Teresa .... Russian at evening classes this term.
   A is studying
   B studies
   C study

2 I don't know what this sentence ....
   A is meaning
   B means
   C mean

3 Clive was driving into town when he .... out of petrol.
   A was running
   B run
   C ran

4 I don't enjoy computer games now, but I .... like them when I was younger.
   A was used to
   B used to
   C would

5 We expected George at 7.30 but he .... yet.
   A hasn't arrived
   B has arrived
   C didn't arrive

6 The film started .... so you've missed quite a lot.
   A for half an hour
   B half an hour ago
   C since half an hour

7 When .... the picnic, they went for a swim in the lake.
   A they'd been eating
   B they'd eaten
   C they've eaten

8 .... my sister three times today but her number's always engaged.
   A I'd phoned
   B I've been phoning
   C I've phoned

9 Anna: Shall I ring you at one o'clock?
   Ben: No, my lunch hour is earlier tomorrow so .... my lunch in the canteen then. Ring me at about one-thirty.
   A I'm eating
   B I'll be eating
   C I eat

10 .... to the dentist after college so I can't play squash with you.
   A I'm going
   B I'll go
   C I go

11 I'll write to you as soon as .... my exam results.
   A I know
   B I'll know
   C I'm going to know

12 The builders .... the house by the end of this month.

   A have finished

   B will have finished

   C will have been finishing

13 This dictionary is .... useful than that one.

   A less

   B as

   C so

14 I keep my grammar notes in a .... folder.

   A plastic big red

   B red big plastic

   C big red plastic

15 Until last week, he .... a motorbike before.

   A had never ridden

   B never had ridden

   C had ridden never

16 The day before the holiday, the men worked .... than usual.

   A hardly

   B hardest

   C harder

17 Doesn't your brother .... discos?

   A enjoy

   B enjoys

   C enjoying

18 Let's take a break soon, ... ?

   A is it

   B will you

   C shall we

19 Most of the houses in this country have ....

   A a garden

   B the garden

   C garden

20 My father normally reads the paper while eating ....

   A a breakfast

   B the breakfast

   C breakfast

21 The first thing they did when they met after twenty years was to hug ....

   A each other

   B someone else

   C themselves

22 .... the children look like their mother.

   A Either

   B Both

   C Neither

23 My manager says we .... take more than ten minutes for our break and, if we do, he'll make us work extra hours.

   A don't have to

   B don't need to

   C mustn't

24 I ran all the way to the station but when I got there I realised that .... because all the trains were delayed.

   A I didn't need to hurry

   B I needn't have hurried

   C I didn't have to hurry

25 .... to take a spare T-shirt as you'll probably get really hot playing tennis.
A You'd better
B You should
C You ought

26 You look really busy. .... I put the shopping away for you?
A Would
B Shall
C Will

27 When I got home I looked at the bill and realised the restaurant .... added it up wrong so I'd paid too much.
A must have
B should have
C could have

28 That bicycle .... belong to Judy – it's much too big for her.
A mustn't
B mightn't
C can't

29 While my car .... I wandered round the city centre.
A be repaired
B was repairing
C was being repaired

30 Katie .... her hair cut short when she left school.
A had
B did
C made

31 Gareth .... he was never going to lend Robert anything again.
A informed
B said
C told

32 I asked Ruth where .... her coat.
A did she buy
B had she bought
C she had bought

33 I always avoid .... on the bus because it makes me feel ill.
A to read
B reading
C read

34 My grandfather remembers .... into this house when he was a very small boy.
A moving
B move
C to move

35 If you don't know a word, you can look .... in your dictionary.
A it up
B up it
C it

36 I've never really got .... my neighbour, probably because we're so different.
A up to
B through
C on with

xi

37 I'll book seats for the concert, if there
.... any good ones available.
   A   will be
   B   were
   C   are

38 Liam would have saved a lot of money, if
he .... to my advice.
   A   would listen
   B   had listened
   C   was listening

39 We'll go for a walk .... it's foggy –
I hate walking in the fog.
   A   if
   B   in case
   C   unless

40 I wish I .... a good memory – it
would make learning English much easier.
   A   had had
   B   had
   C   would have

41 Philip wears an old coat .... his suit
when he walks to work.
   A   on
   B   above
   C   over

42 We're having a party .... the last day
of term.
   A   in
   B   on
   C   at

43 As we can't agree .... this subject,
we won't discuss it again.
   A   about
   B   in
   C   with

44 All the nurses were very kind ....
me when I was ill.
   A   with
   B   to
   C   of

45 I enjoyed .... last week.
   A   the book you lent me
   B   the book which you lent it to me
   C   the book, that you lent me

46 This is the room in .... the famous
poet died.
   A   which
   B   where
   C   that

47 I left the cinema .... I had a
headache and the film was very noisy.
   A   as
   B   so that
   C   therefore

48 I'm .... tired to work tonight. I'll
finish my homework in the morning.
   A   very
   B   too
   C   so

49 .... Martin could easily afford to go
on holiday, he never does.
   A   Although
   B   Despite
   C   In spite of

50 Since .... school, Sandra has had
several interesting jobs.
   A   left
   B   leaving
   C   to leave

A   Context listening

1 You are going to hear Millie talking on her mobile phone to her friend Lisa. It's Saturday morning. Before you listen, answer these questions.

1 Where is Lisa? ....

2 Where is Millie? ....

3 Why do you think Millie is phoning Lisa? ....

Millie

Lisa

2 [1a] Listen and check if you were right.

3 [1a] Listen again and answer these questions. Write complete sentences.

1 What's Millie doing this morning? *She's looking round the shops.* ....

2 What does she do nearly every Saturday? ....

3 What's she looking for? ....

4 What's Lisa wearing? ....

5 What's she doing this morning? ....

6 What does she do whenever she goes to town? ....

7 What's Millie looking at right now? ....

8 What does Lisa want Millie to do now? ....

4 Look at your answers to Exercise 3 and answer these questions.

1 Look at answers 2 and 6. What tense are they? ....

2 Look at answers 1, 3, 4, 5 and 7. What tense are they? ....

3 Which sentences are about regular actions? ....

4 Which sentences are about actions at or around the time of speaking? ....

5 Look at answer 8. Does it fit the pattern? ....

1

B Grammar

1 Present simple

+	verb / verb + -s	She **works** in London.
−	do / does not + verb	He **doesn't work** in London.
?	do / does ... + verb?	Where **do** you **work**?

We use the **present simple**:

- to say when things happen if they take place regularly:
  *They **eat lunch at two o'clock**.*

- to talk about permanent situations:
  *I **work** in London.*

- to state general truths:
  *Those bags **sell** really fast.*
  *The moon **goes** round the earth.*

- to talk about habits and how often they happen:
  *You **buy** new clothes **every Saturday**.*

- to describe the plots of books and films:
  *The story **begins** and **ends** in Spain. The year **is** 1937.*

2 Present continuous

+	am / is / are + verb + -ing	He's **working** in London this week.
−	am / is / are not + verb + -ing	I'm **not working** in London this week.
?	am / is / are ... + verb + -ing?	Are you **working** in London this week?

We use the **present continuous**:

- to talk about the present moment:
  *I'm **wearing** a pair of old jeans.*
  *I'm **looking** at a blue bag right now.*

- to suggest that an action is temporary, often with words like *now, at the moment, at present* or *just*:
  *They're **eating** lunch **at the moment**.*
  *I'm **working** in London **this week**. (= I don't usually work in London)*

- for an action around the time of speaking, which has begun but is not finished:
  *I'm **cleaning** my room.*
  *I'm **looking** round the shops. (Millie isn't looking round at this moment – she has stopped to talk to Lisa – but she plans to continue looking round later.)*

- for changing or developing situations:
  *Blue bags **are getting** really fashionable.*
  *The earth's temperature **is rising**.*

- with a word like *always* or *continually*, if we want to criticise or complain:
  *You're **always buying** new clothes! (= you buy too many)*
  *He's **always complaining** about everything.*

- with *always* when something unexpected happens several times:
  *I'm **always meeting** my neighbour John near the station. I guess he works somewhere near there.*

2

3 State verbs

These verbs are nearly always used in a simple rather than a continuous tense. They are mostly about thoughts, feelings, belonging and the senses:

*... that leather bag **you want** to get.* (**not** *you are wanting to*)
*You **don't deserve** to hear it.* (**not** *you aren't deserving to*)

The following are some important **state verbs**:

- thoughts: *believe, know, mean, realise, recognise, remember, suppose, understand, feel* (= believe), *think* (= believe):
  *I **think** you're wrong.*
  *We **feel** this decision is right.*

- feelings: *adore, dislike, despise, hate, like, love, want, wish, prefer*:
  *They **despise** me because of the way I'm living.*

- belonging: *belong, have / have got* (= possess), *own, possess*:
  *It **belongs** to my father.*
  *The manager **has** the biggest company car.*

- senses: *smell, taste, hear, see*:
  *This sauce **tastes** great.*
  *I **hear** what you're saying to me, but I don't agree.*
  ***Do** you **see** anything you want to buy here?*

  We use *can* with these verbs to show we are talking about this moment:
  *I **can see** you are tired.*
  *I **can hear** someone in the next room.*

- other state verbs: *contain, deserve, fit, seem, look* (= seem), *look like, matter, weigh*:
  *This medicine **contains** aspirin.*
  *Mark **weighs** 70 kilos.*

⚠ *Feel* and *think* are not state verbs when they mean the action:
*I'm **thinking** about my holiday.*
*We're **feeling** cold.*

⚠ *Have* can be continuous when it does **not** mean 'possess':
*Steve's **having** a difficult time at college this term.*
*Can I phone you back later? We're **having** lunch right now.*

⚠ *Taste* and *smell* can be continuous when they mean the action:
*I'm **tasting** the sauce.*

⚠ *Listen to, watch* and *look at* are not state verbs and can be continuous:
*I'm **listening to** music and Diane **is watching** a DVD upstairs.*

⚠ *See* can be continuous when it means 'meet':
*Are you **seeing** Tom today?*

⚠ *Weigh* can be continuous when it means the action:
*The shop assistant's **weighing** the cheese.*

1

C Grammar exercises

1 Choose the correct sentence from each pair.

1 a My brother lives with us until he can find a flat of his own.
  b My brother is living with us until he can find a flat of his own. ✓

2 a Megan goes to Hong Kong every January.
  b Megan's going to Hong Kong every January.

3 a I don't have enough money for a long holiday this year.
  b I'm not having enough money for a long holiday this year.

4 a Everyone needs a break from work sometimes.
  b Everyone is needing a break from work sometimes.

5 a What period of history do you study this term?
  b What period of history are you studying this term?

2 Fill in the gaps with the correct form of the verb in brackets, present simple or present continuous.

1 My father ....knows.......... (know) all about mending cars, but nothing about bicycles.

✗ 2 Alex: Why .... (you wear) my coat?
  Ben: Oh, I'm sorry. It .... (look) like mine in this light.

3 This pie .... (smell) a bit odd. What's in it?

4 I .... (like) the jacket of this suit, but unfortunately the trousers
  .... (not fit) me any more.

⊦ 5 You're very quiet this evening. What .... (you think) about?

6 Carl: I .... (have) no idea what this sentence ....
  (mean). Can you translate it?
  Donna: No, sorry. I .... (not understand) it either.

⊦ 7 Eddie: .... (you see) those men near the door? They ....
  (look) at us very strangely.
  ✗ Fergus: Yes. You're right. .... (you recognise) them from anywhere?
  ⊦ Eddie: No, but they certainly .... (seem) to know us. They
  .... (come) across to speak to us.

8 Gina: What .... (you do) in the kitchen?
  Hamid: I .... (just make) some coffee.
  Gina: Well, go away. I .... (not want) your help. Our guests
  .... (wait) for their dessert, and you .... (get)
  in my way!   are getting

4

3 Fill in the gaps with the correct form of the verbs in the box.

> behave   come   cost   eat   enjoy   feel   ~~go~~   have   have   have
> like   love   realise   say   serve   show   smile   stay   take   visit

---

Dear Stephanie,

How are you? We're fine. Our trip round the States ....is going............ (**1**) well and we
.... (**2**) ourselves very much. One good surprise is that things
.... (**3**) less here than back home. For example, this weekend we
.... (**4**) in a motel beside a lake. We .... (**5**) a room with a ✗
beautiful view for only $35 per night.

The only thing we .... (not) (**6**) much is the food. Restaurants
.... (**7**) dinner rather early. We .... (never) (**8**) at six o'clock at ⟩
home so we .... (not) (**9**) hungry then and Americans .... (**10**) ✗
very big meals. Apart from that, we .... (**11**) a wonderful time. We
.... (**12**) lots of interesting little towns and we .... (**13**) the scenery.

People here .... (**14**) in a very friendly manner towards strangers, all the shop ✗
assistants .... (**15**) at us, and everyone .... (**16**) 'Have a nice day!'

At home, the TV .... (always) (**17**) us bad news stories about the States, but in fact,
when you .... (**18**) here, you .... (**19**) it's a really great place. ✗

We .... (**20**) lots of photos to show you.

Much love,

Mick and Mary

---

4 Write six true sentences about yourself, using the words in the box and a suitable verb in the correct form.

> at the moment   before breakfast   every day
> most weekends   once a year   ~~right now~~   this term

1 I'm doing my homework right now, and I'm listening to a CD. ....

2 ....

3 ....

4 ....

5 ....

6 ....

7 ....

1

D Exam practice

Listening Part 4

🎧 1b You will hear an interview with a university student. For questions **1–7**, choose the best answer (**A**, **B** or **C**).

1 Today's edition of Study Talk is about an unusual
   A university.
   B course.
   C hobby.

   | 1 |

2 What is the subject that Ellis Graham is studying for his degree?
   A surfing
   B mathematics
   C computing

   | 2 |

3 What does Jed suggest about most people who enjoy surfing?
   A They waste time when they should be studying.
   B They know a lot of unimportant information.
   C They are not very intelligent.

   | 3 |

4 Ellis says the course he is doing at university
   A is extremely popular.
   B accepts people who failed on other courses.
   C attracts applications from other universities.

   | 4 |

5 What does Ellis make Jed understand?
   A Jed needs to practise seriously to be a good surfer.
   B Jed had the wrong idea about Ellis's studies.
   C Jed does not have to work as hard as the students.

   | 5 |

6 What plans does Ellis say he has for the future?
   A to travel to other countries
   B to join a research project
   C to start a business

   | 6 |

7 Ellis has problems with Jed's last question because
   A it involves discussing something secret.
   B he is unsure of the facts.
   C it's hard to find uncrowded beaches.

   | 7 |

These are some extracts from the first part of the interview. Underline the tenses that the speakers used.

1 And today, someone *sits / is sitting* beside me to give us some info ...
2 ... there are some people who *think / are thinking* it's not really a subject for serious study ...
3 ... *he actually does / he's actually doing* a degree ...
4 ... in something I *enjoy / am enjoying* from time to time ...
5 ... you're a mathematician who *goes / is going* surfing in his free time ...
6 So what *do you do / are you doing*? You have classes on the beach?
7 We learn about ... how waves *form / are forming* ...

Writing Part 2

You have received this letter from your English-speaking penfriend. Read the letter and write your reply.

... and now I'm doing a project about how people in different parts of the world spend their holidays. Please write and tell me where people from your country usually go, and what they do.

I know you're already on holiday, so what are you doing?

Write your **letter** in **120–180** words.

This task gives you a chance to practise:
using the present simple for what people usually do.
using the present continuous for what you're doing on your holiday.

Useful words and expressions
to spend time, to stay with, to go abroad, to relax, to explore
traditional, typical, sightseeing, adventurous

> See also the email in section C, Exercise 3.

2 Past tenses

past simple; past continuous; *used to* (and *to be used to*); *would*

A Context listening

1 You are going to hear Jack talking to his grandmother about something he did last week. Before you listen, look at questions 1–5. Guess which things Jack, his mother and his grandmother did. Write J or M or G.

1 go to London? ..J..
2 see a famous footballer? ....
3 go up to town alone? ....
4 worry about school work? ....
5 go to a club? ....

2 (⊕ 2) Listen and check if you were right.

3 Listen again and answer these questions.

1 Which things did Jack do last Saturday? ....
2 What does he say about (a) a coach? ....
   (b) a film? ....
3 What tense does he use? ....
4 Which things did Gran do when she was young? ....
5 What does Gran say about (a) autographs? ....
   (b) pop concerts? ....
6 Does she do these things now? ....
7 Did she do them regularly in the past? ....

4 (⊕ 2) Listen again and complete these sentences.

1 We did some revision for our exams while we ....
2 When we .... for the cinema, we saw a really famous footballer.
3 He .... a burger and all the crowds .... past but nobody noticed him except me.

5 Which tense is in the gaps in Exercise 4? ....

B Grammar

1 Past simple

+	verb + -ed*	*I **wanted** it.*
–	did not + verb	*I **didn't want** it.*
?	did ... + verb?	*What **did** you **want**?*

*Regular verbs add -ed or -d to the verb: *want → wanted; hope → hoped*
Many common verbs are irregular: *think → thought; make → made* ➢See Appendix 2
To be is irregular: *am, is (not) → was (not); are (not) → were (not)*

We use the **past simple**:

● for completed actions and events in the past:
  *We **had** an exam on Thursday.*
  *We **caught** the coach.*

● for a sequence of actions or events:
  *I **went** round the shops, then I **went** to the cinema.*

● for permanent or long-term situations in the past:
  *I really **enjoyed** myself when I was a teenager.*

● for repeated events:
  *Jack's grandmother **went** to lots of concerts.*
  *She always **asked** for an autograph when she **met** someone famous.*

➢See also Unit 3 for further uses of the past simple.

2 Past continuous

+	was/were + verb + -ing	*They **were waiting**.*
–	was/were not + verb + -ing	*She **wasn't waiting**.*
?	was/were ... + verb + -ing?	***Were** you **waiting**?*

We use the **past continuous**:

● for an activity beginning before a past action and continuing until or after it.
  The action is usually in the past simple:
  *We **did** some revision while we **were travelling**.*
  *When we **were queuing** for the cinema, we **saw** a really famous footballer.*

we were travelling
we did some revision

we were queuing
we saw a famous footballer

● for two things happening at the same time:
  *He **was buying** a burger and all the crowds **were walking** past.*

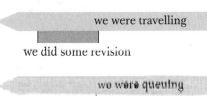

he was buying a burger
the crowds were walking past

- for repeated events, with a word like *always* or *continually*, especially if the speaker is criticising the activity:
  *Your mother **was always doing** her homework.* (= She did her homework regularly and often. Jack's grandmother thinks she worked too hard!)

- for unfulfilled plans, with verbs like *hope*, *plan* etc.:
  *I **was hoping** to find a new jacket.* (= but I didn't find one)

⚠ State verbs are used in the past simple, not the past continuous (≻ see p.3):
*I **didn't know** him.* (**not** ~~I wasn't knowing him.~~)

3 Used to (do) and would (do)

+	used to + verb	He **used to read** a lot.
−	did not use to + verb	We **didn't use to read** a lot.
?	did ... use to + verb?	**Did** you **use to read** a lot?

+	would + verb	He **would read** a lot.
−	would not + verb	We **wouldn't read** a lot.
?	would ... + verb?	**Would** you **read** a lot?

We use *used to* and *would* to talk about past habits when we are emphasising that they are no longer true:
*I **used to collect** all the autographs of film stars when I was a teenager.* (= she doesn't do this now)
*I **would go** up to town on my own.* (= she doesn't do this now)

Used to can describe actions and states, but *would* can only describe actions:
*All the teenagers **used to** / **would scream** at pop concerts.*
*They **used to be** crazy about the Beatles.*
(**not** ~~They would be crazy about the Beatles.~~)

⚠ *Used to* is much more common than *would*.

⚠ Do not confuse *used to* and *be / get used to*. *Be / Get used to* means 'be / become accustomed to doing' and can be past, present or future, but *used to* is a past tense.
Compare:

*I **used to work** at weekends.* (= in the past I worked at weekends, but I don't now)

*I'm **used to working** at weekends.* (= I often work at weekends, it doesn't worry me)

The question form is:
*Are you **used to working** at weekends?*

Be / Get used to can be followed by a noun:
*He **wasn't used to criticism** and found it hard to accept.* (= people hadn't criticised him before so he didn't like it)

C Grammar exercises

1 Fill in the gaps with the past simple of the verbs in the box.

be	~~begin~~	come	drink	eat	explain	feed
find	find	get	give	go	have	know	learn
meet	read	seem	speak	spread	tie	write

The mystery of **Caspar Hauser**

The mystery of Caspar Hauser ....began........ (1) in Nuremberg, Germany, about 200 years ago. One morning, the people of the town .... (2) a young man standing alone in the square. He was holding a piece of paper in his hand. The paper .... (3) only that he .... (4) the son of a soldier. Caspar .... (5) how to say a few words and when given a paper and pencil he .... (6) his name, but he .... (7) completely ignorant about everyday life. At first he .... (8) only bread and .... (9) only water, but he gradually .... (10) used to ordinary meals. He also .... (11) to talk properly.

No one ever .... (12) out the real truth about his birth, but it is probable that his father kept him in one small room for the whole of his early life. He .... (13) him on bread and .... (14) him water to drink. He .... (15) Caspar up and Caspar never .... (16) out, he never .... (17) to anyone or .... (18) other children. In spite of this extraordinary childhood, Caspar was not stupid. He .... (19) books and .... (20) discussions with teachers and philosophers. News about Caspar .... (21) through Europe and visitors .... (22) from abroad to meet him. Unfortunately, he lived only a few years, but his strange life story still fascinates many people.

2 Fill in the gaps with the past simple or past continuous of the verbs in brackets.

1 My parents ....*got*............... (*get*) to know each other when they
......*were studying*...... (*study*) at university.

2 Doctor Fisher .... (*travel*) widely as a young man and
.... (*always keep*) a diary.

3 I .... (*see*) my brother and his girlfriend when I ....
(*wait*) for the bus, but they .... (*not see*) me.

4 Lily .... (*fill*) in the application form and .... (*give*)
it to the receptionist.

5 While I .... (*work*) in Rome, I .... (*meet*) a girl who
.... (*look*) just like your sister.

6 Simon .... (*finish*) with his girlfriend because she ....
(*always cancel*) dates at the last moment.

7 Anna's feeling depressed because she .... (*hope*) for a pay rise
last week, but she .... (*not get*) one.

3 Underline the correct form of the verbs.

MAKING CHANGES

<u>*Ada Atkins, 93, explains why she has come to live in town*</u>

Years ago, nobody in my village <u>*would lock*</u> / *was locking* (1) their front doors. We *used to feel* / *would feel* (2) safe in those days. Last month, I *met* / *was meeting* (3) my neighbour in the street when I *was walking* / *would walk* (4) home from the shops and she *told* / *was telling* (5) me some bad news. Thieves *were breaking* / *used to break* (6) into people's houses while they *were sitting* / *would sit* (7) in their back gardens.

I *realised* / *was realising* (8) that I *wasn't wanting* / *didn't want* (9) to live there any more. So last week I *was moving* / *moved* (10) to this little flat. I *am not used* / *didn't use* (11) to being in the town yet, but people are more friendly than I *was thinking* / *thought* (12) they might be, and I feel much happier and safer.

Past tenses

4 Fill in the gaps with a suitable form of *be / get used to*.

1 Rita's very tired this morning. She ....*isn't used to*................ (*not*) going to bed late.

2 Don't worry about the children, they .... going to school by bus.

3 My new boss .... giving orders, not receiving them.

4 She .... (*not*) drinking wine and it made her ill.

5 .... (*you*) our climate or do you miss the sunshine?

6 I had never stayed in such an expensive hotel before, but I soon .... it.

5 Write four sentences about things which you used to do when you were a small child. Remember they must be things you don't do now!

1 *I used to drink milk with my meals.*

2 *My brother and I used to tease our sister.*

3 ....

4 ....

5 ....

6 ....

6 Complete these sentences using your own ideas.

1 When our neighbours went to Italy, they *saw some wonderful paintings.*

2 I was hoping to finish my homework by eight o'clock last night, but ....

3 The film star shouted at the director, then she ....

4 As a small child, I would sometimes ....

5 We were coming out of the café when ....

6 A hundred years ago people .... but now they go by car.

7 While you were lying on a beach, I ....

8 When my father was young, he was always ....

13

2

D Exam practice

Use of English Part 1

For questions **1–12**, read the text below and decide which answer (**A**, **B**, **C** or **D**) best fits each gap. There is an example at the beginning (**0**).

Example:

0 (A) spent   **B** made   **C** held   **D** went

A MUSICIAN IS DISCOVERED

When William was a small boy, the family **(0)** A... their holidays on his grandfather's farm in a valley **(1)** ...... by mountains. On their arrival, the children would race around the yard and orchard, overjoyed to be free from the strictly correct **(2)** ...... expected of them in the city. As the days passed, their parents also **(3)** ...... increasingly relaxed, and the house rang with the laughter of old friends. It was during one of these visits that William's **(4)** ...... to remember a tune led to the suggestion that the boy should **(5)** ...... up a musical instrument. One evening everyone was gathered in the living room, and a discussion **(6)** ...... about the differences between a piece of music which was popular at the time and a well-known folk song. Various adults tried to prove the similarity of the two tunes to those who **(7)** ...... with them, but without success. Silence fell, and then William, who was about five, made his **(8)** ...... to the piano and played first one tune and then the other. His parents and their friends were astonished **(9)** ...... no one had even heard William **(10)** ...... to play before. 'That child must go to a music teacher,' **(11)** ...... one neighbour, and the others agreed. William's parents were persuaded to accept help with payment of the fees, and his musical **(12)** ...... began.

1 A surrounded	**B** closed	**C** held	**D** circled
2 A manner	**B** behaviour	**C** style	**D** attitude
3 A showed	**B** acted	**C** became	**D** found
4 A talent	**B** gift	**C** ability	**D** skill
5 A take	**B** start	**C** pick	**D** bring
6 A happened	**B** came	**C** entered	**D** arose
7 A refused	**B** varied	**C** disagreed	**D** resisted

8 **A** path	**B** way	**C** route	**D** direction
9 **A** so	**B** although	**C** when	**D** as
10 **A** want	**B** decide	**C** try	**D** go
11 **A** told	**B** stated	**C** confirmed	**D** expressed
12 **A** work	**B** living	**C** career	**D** study

Grammar focus task

In the exam task, there are some irregular past simple verbs. Without looking back at the text, write the past simple form of these verbs.

1 arise ....*arose*....   2 become ....   3 begin ....   4 come ....

5 fall ....   6 find ....   7 go ....   8 hold ....

9 lead ....   10 make ....   11 ring ....   12 spend ....

Writing Part 2

You have seen a short story competition in an English language magazine. Readers are asked to send in stories about a significant event in their early childhood. The story must **begin** with the following words:

When I was quite young, I did something silly one day.

Write your **story** in **120–180** words.

Writing hints

This task gives you a chance to practise:
using the past simple and past continuous for events in the past.
using *used to* and *would* for past habits.

Useful words and expressions
at the time, by chance, I clearly remember, I now realise, in those days, luckily, one day, there was/were, unfortunately, when I was X years old

Present perfect and past simple
present perfect simple and past simple; present perfect simple and continuous

A Context listening

1 You are going to hear two people called Mike and Lucy talking to each other. Before you listen, look at the picture. How do Mike and Lucy know each other? *Due to mike's playing*

What is Lucy's problem? *Mike making to much noise*

2 🎧 3 Listen and check if you were right.

3 🎧 3 Listen again and write Mike and Lucy's exact words. Stop the recording when you need to.

1 What does Mike say about finishing work? Mike says '*I finished at lunchtime today.*'
2 What does he say about this afternoon? He says '...'
3 What does Lucy say about finishing her essay? She says '...'
4 When does she say she started it? She says '...'
5 What does Mike say about studying history? He says '...'
6 How long has Lucy lived next door? She says '...'
7 How long has Mike lived there? He says '...'
8 Why is Mike surprised? He says '...'

4 Look at your answers to Exercise 3 and answer these questions.

1 Look at answers 1, 4 and 5. What tense are they? ....
2 Look at answers 2, 3, 6, 7 and 8. What tense are they? ....
3 Which sentences are about a period of time which is still continuing? ....
4 Which sentences are about a period of time which is finished? ....

B Grammar

1 Present perfect simple or past simple?

	Present perfect simple	
+	*has / have* + past participle	*I've finished.*
–	*has / have not* + past participle	*She **hasn't finished**.*
?	*has / have ...* + past participle?	***Have** you **finished**?*

Some verbs are irregular: *break → broken;*
go → gone ≻ See Appendix 2.
For past simple forms, see Unit 2, B1.

We use the **present perfect simple**:

- with *since* or *for*, about a period of time which is still continuing:
  *I've **lived** there **for** four years.* (= and I still live there)

  ⟵————— four years —————⟶ now
  ▼   ▼
  I moved there   I live there

  *I've **lived** next door **since** June.* (= and I still live next door now)

- with questions asking *how long*:
  ***How long have** you **lived** here?* (= I know you still live here)
  ⚠ Sometimes we can also use the present perfect continuous. (≻ See B2)

- for unfinished actions and events, often with *still* or *yet*:
  *I **still haven't finished** it.*
  *I **haven't finished** it **yet**.*
  ⚠ *Still* and *yet* are always used with a negative in the present perfect. (*Still* goes before the verb and *yet* goes after it.)

- for events repeated over a period of time until the present (they may continue):
  *You've **played** the saxophone every night.* (= until now, and you will probably continue to play every night)

- for events which happened in the past at a time which is unknown and / or irrelevant:
  *I've **started** my essay.* (= we don't know when)
  *I've **lost** my new camera.* (= it's not important when or where)

We use the **past simple**:

- with *for*, about a period of time which is finished:
  *I **lived** there **for** four years.* (= but I don't live there now)

  ⟵——four years——⟶   now
  ▼   ▼   ▼
  I moved there   I moved out   I don't live there

- with questions asking *when*:
  ***When did** you **move** here?* (= the move is in the past)

- for completed actions and events in the past, often with *ago*:
  *I **finished** it half an hour **ago**.*

- for events repeated over a period of time in the past (they are now finished):
  *You **played** the saxophone every night.* (= but you don't any more)

We use the **present perfect simple**:

- for events that happened in the recent past (often with *just*):
  *Flight 206 **has landed**.* (= in the last few minutes)
  *She's **just gone** to the cinema.* (= and she's there now)

- when the time stated is not finished:
  *I've **spent** this morning writing an essay.* (= it's still morning)

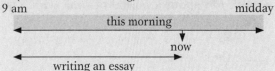

*The builders **have started** working on the kitchen this week.* (= it's still this week)

- when we talk about a period of time up to the present:
  *I've **been** to Los Angeles but not to New York.* (= in my life up to now)
  *The team **has won** several matches.* (= and may win more)

- when we talk about how many times something has happened:
  ***This is the first time** anyone **has complained**.*

- with adverbs like *already*, *before*, *ever* and *never*:
  *Nobody's **ever complained before**.* (= until now)
  *I've **never tried** Japanese food.* (= but I might one day)
  *She's **already gone** to the airport.*
  *I've **met** her **before** somewhere.*
  ⚠ *Never, ever* and *already* go between the auxiliary and the main verb. *Before* goes after the verb.

- after a superlative (> see Unit 7):
  *It's **the best** cup of coffee I've **had** here.*

We use the **past simple**:

- for events that happened at a particular time in the past:
  *Flight 206 **landed** at one o'clock.*
  or within a period of time in the past:
  *She **was** at the cinema between midday and two o'clock.* (= but she's not there now)

- when the time stated is finished:
  *I **spent** this morning writing an essay.* (= it's now afternoon so 'this morning' is in the past)

*I **started** my essay last week.* (= 'last week' is definitely in the past)
*I **lost** my new camera in London.* (= the place fixes it at a time in the past)

- when we talk about past events which are not connected to the present:
  *I **went** to Los Angeles but not to New York.* (= on a particular trip which is in the past)
  *The Chinese **invented** printing.*

2 Present perfect simple or continuous?

	Present perfect continuous	
+	*has / have been* + verb + *-ing*	*I've been working hard.*
–	*has / have not been* + verb + *-ing*	*She hasn't been working hard.*
?	*has / have* ... + *been* + verb + *-ing?*	*Have you been working hard?*

The present perfect and the present perfect continuous are both used to describe events or activities which started in the past and have continued up to the present, or activities which stopped recently. Some verbs can be used in either the present perfect simple or continuous with little difference in meaning. These are verbs which describe activities which normally happen over a period of time, e.g. *live, study, learn, wait, work*:
*Martin **has lived** / **has been living** in Australia for five years.*

We use the **present perfect continuous**:

- to talk about how long something has been happening:
  I've been driving since five o'clock this morning.
  *The children **have been playing** happily all morning.*
  We've been worrying about her all week.

  *How long **have** you **been watching** TV?*

- to focus on the activity or event itself (whether it is complete or not is unimportant):
  He's been reading the newspapers while he was waiting for her. (= we're interested in how he passed the time – not if he read every page)
  I've been mending the car. (= that's why I'm dirty)

We use the **present perfect simple**:

- to talk about how often or how many times something has happened:
  I've driven there several times before.

  *The children **have played** four games of tennis this morning.*
  I've worried about her every day since she set off.
  I've watched three programmes.

- to focus on the results of an activity or event which is complete:

  I've read the newspapers. (= I've finished reading them)

  I've mended the car. (= I've just finished so we can go out in it now)

⚠ We never use the present tense to talk about how long we have been doing something:
*I've been learning the piano **for a long time**.*
(**not** *I'm learning the piano for a long time.*)

State verbs are not usually used in the present perfect continuous (➤ see Unit 1):
I've known her since she was four years old. (**not** *I've been knowing her...*)

3

C Grammar exercises

1 Match these sentence halves.

1 He's talked to her on the phone ...j...
2 This summer the pool was only open ...h...
3 The whole team felt exhausted ....
4 The rent of my flat has gone up ....
5 She's had nothing to eat ....
6 I got very wet ....
7 I spent a month in Brazil ....
8 She's always enjoyed painting ....
9 I haven't had such a good time ....
10 The post arrived ....

a for years.
b on my way home from work yesterday.
c since nine o'clock this morning.
d when the match finished.
e ever since she was very young.
f by 20 per cent this year.
g a few minutes ago.
h from April till September.
i in 2002.
j every night this week.

2 Fill in the gaps with the present perfect or the past simple of the verbs in brackets.

1 This is only the second time I 've ever flown (ever fly) in an aeroplane.
2 The child .... (sleep) from seven till seven without waking once.
3 Gabriella .... (grow) five centimetres since last month.
4 I .... (send) Ed three emails last week but he .... (not reply) to any of them yet.
5 .... (you learn) to play chess when you were a child?
6 I .... (buy) this bicycle five years ago and I .... (use) it every day since then.
7 How long .... (you have) that bad cough?
8 The train .... (just arrive), so hurry and you might catch it.
9 I .... (never see) such a beautiful rainbow before.
10 I .... (dream) about a beautiful desert island last night.
11 On Sunday we .... (meet) outside the cinema as usual.
12 When .... (you get) that jacket? I .... (not notice) it before.

3 Fill in the gaps with a suitable verb in the present perfect or the past simple.

Photos	**Message board**	**Map**

Trip to Spain

I .ve been.............. **(1)** here in Spain for two weeks now and I'm having a really good time.
When I .... **(2)** at the airport
I .... **(3)** very lonely. But I
.... (already) **(4)** some friends and I'm staying with a really nice family. They
.... **(5)** me to the seaside last weekend and we .... **(6)** in the sea. I really
.... **(7)** it. I .... **(8)** some Spanish but I .... (not) **(9)**
to any language classes yet – they start next week. It's now midnight and I need to go to bed as
I .... **(10)** a very busy day. I .... **(11)** shopping this morning
and I .... **(12)** tennis this afternoon.
See you all in a month!
Richard

4 Read this conversation between two people in a sports club. Underline the most suitable form of the verb which fits best.

Anna: Excuse me. *We've waited / We've been waiting* (1) to play tennis since 10.30. It must be our turn now. How long *have you played / have you been playing* (2)?

Tim: Since about 9.30. *We've played / We've been playing* (3) two matches so far this morning and *we haven't finished / we haven't been finishing* (4) the third yet. You'll have to wait or do something else.

Anna: But *you've played / you've been playing* (5) for more than two hours and it's our turn now.

Tim: I said you'll have to wait.

Anna: We're tired of waiting and we haven't got anything to do. *We've read / We've been reading* (6) the magazines we brought with us.

Tim: Why don't you do something else? *Have you tried / Have you been trying* (7) the swimming pool?

Anna: We don't want to swim, we want to play tennis.

Tim: Well, I always play on a Saturday morning. Anyway, *we've already started / we've already been starting* (8) the third match.

Anna: Oh well, it looks like we've got no choice, but *we've booked / we've been booking* (9) for next Saturday so you'll be unlucky then.

3

Reading Part 3

You are going to read a magazine article about people who like clothes. For questions **1–15**, choose from the people (**A–D**). The people may be chosen more than once.

Which person

thinks people don't give enough importance to one kind of clothing?	1
learnt something after an experience with some clothing?	2
made a decision to buy something they had always wanted?	3
no longer does something which they now consider foolish?	4
prefers preparing to go out rather than the event itself?	5
did something out of character?	6
prefers not to draw attention to themselves?	7
wears a piece of clothing which makes people look at them?	8
never expected to go into their present line of business?	9
has found several opportunities to wear a special piece of clothing?	10
thinks it is important to keep a sense of humour?	11
is not good at self-promotion?	12
says when you're in your teens and twenties you can look good on a tight budget?	13
found a piece of clothing which serves two purposes?	14
is happy with the social requirements of their job?	15

Me and my clothes

A

Paula, a clothes designer

When you're young you can get away with cheap clothes though I think I had expensive tastes even then. In fact I've always spent a lot on clothes and I've always loved what they can do for you but I never intended to make money from them. At one point when I didn't have a job my husband said, 'Surely you must be able to make something'. That was the kick I needed to get me started.

I'm mad on swimsuits. Because I make my own clothes I'm always thinking about changing a collar on something or changing a fabric, but because I don't make swimsuits they're free from all that. I have several. People take one on holiday and think that's enough, yet they wouldn't dream of wearing the same trousers day after day. I don't understand that.

B

Len, a businessman

I've enjoyed motorbikes since I was 16. But for a long time I didn't own one; I rode my brother's instead. Then about two years ago I bought one. I thought if I don't get one now, I never will. I always walked to work every morning until I got the motorbike, but now I ride there most days. I bought a leather coat as a solution to the problem of needing to wear a suit to work and wanting to come in by bike. It would be impossible to be changing all the time. It's quite an amazing garment: it looks good, it feels good and although it's got a practical use, I am aware it does have an impact. It turns heads as I walk through the building. When I was younger I rode a bike several times without a helmet. That was in parts of the United States where it's not compulsory but it's madness. There's enough risk on a bike without adding more.

C

Marion, a singer

When I was in a musical I wore wonderful skirts made by a designer but they were incredibly heavy, and during the first performance I fell over twice on stage dancing in them. That hasn't happened to me again because I know now that you need much lighter clothes to dance in.

A little while after that, I was singing at a friend's wedding so I asked the same designer to make a really stunning dress for me. I absolutely love it but I wondered if I'd be able to wear it again. It's not an everyday kind of garment. In fact I've worn the dress several times since then – to awards ceremonies and dinners. I'm not actually a big one for those kinds of occasions though. I really like the process of getting ready but I'm not a big mixer.

My career's never been structured. Perhaps it should have been but I'm hopeless at pushing myself. I went to the States when a film I was in, *Enchanted April*, was really big but I never dreamed of hiring a publicist or anything. I suppose one measure of success was when I did my first TV advert and I went into the sort of shop I'd always been scared to go into before and bought something without looking at the price. That just wasn't like me.

D

Tom, chief executive of a charity

I worked as a lawyer until I was in my forties but I've been director of this charity for 10 years now. I'm out two or three nights a week at dinners to raise money. It goes with a job like this and it's fun too. I wear a suit and tie to most events. They're a kind of uniform, which is helpful because I'm not naturally a stylish dresser. I like to feel comfortable and fit in, and this way I'm not conscious of my appearance. If I was, I'd probably be horrendously shy. One of my big mistakes in my early days was to make a speech that was too serious. People said afterwards that it was very powerful but that wasn't what I'd intended. If you're too serious in my kind of business it puts people off.

Read these extracts from the texts. Without looking back, fill in the gaps with the present perfect simple or the past simple of the verbs in the box.

be   be   buy   enjoy   fall   happen   intend   own   spend   walk   wear   work

In fact I (*always*) .... (**1**) a lot on clothes but I never
.... (**2**) to make money from them.

I .... (**3**) motorbikes since I was 16. But for a long time I
.... (*not*) (**4**) one. Then about two years ago I .... (**5**)
one.

I always .... (**6**) to work every morning until I got the motorbike, but
now I ride there most days.

During the first performance, I .... (**7**) over twice on stage dancing in
them. That .... (*not*) (**8**) to me again.

In fact I .... (**9**) the dress several times since then.

I .... (**10**) as a lawyer until I .... (**11**) in my forties but
I .... (**12**) director of this charity for 10 years now.

Writing Part 1

You have seen an advertisement for a summer job. Read the advertisement and the notes you have made. Then write a letter of application using **all** your notes.

Mulberry Activity Centres

We provide holidays for 5 to 14-year-olds and we need enthusiastic young people to work with us.

Earn money and have a good time!

What can you offer – sports, cooking, drama, music, anything else?

Give information about my experience

Is your English good?

Yes! Give details

Are you free in July or August?

No, because ...

Send us a letter of application and tell us if you prefer to work in a city camp or a camp by the sea.

Say which and why

Visit our website at www.mulberryactivities.com for our address and more information.

Write a **letter** of **120–150** words in a style appropriate for the situation.

Writing hints

This task gives you a chance to practise:
using the present perfect to describe your experience.
using the past simple to say when you did something.

Useful words and expressions
to be keen on, to look after, to take part in, would prefer, available, fluent, unfortunately

A Context listening

1 You are going to hear a teenage boy called Richard talking to his mother. Before you listen, look at the picture. How has Richard spent the weekend? ....

....

How does his mother feel? ....

....

Why? ....

....

....

2 (🎧 4) Listen and check if you were right.

3 (🎧 4) Listen again and fill in the gaps. Stop the recording when you need to.

Richard: I _'d done_ .... (1) the ceiling, and I .... (2) one wall, when I .... (3) paint ...

Richard: And yesterday afternoon I .... (4) bored. I .... (5) to town for a few hours – you know round the centre. I .... (6) the shopping – everything on your list – and I .... (7) all my homework ...

Mother: I .... (8) for only an hour when the car .... (9) ...

4 Look at your answers to Exercise 3 and answer these questions.

1 Look at answers 1, 2 and 3. Did 3 happen before or after 1 and 2? ....
What tenses does Richard use? ....

2 Look at answers 4, 5, 6 and 7. Did 4 happen before or after 5, 6 and 7? ....
What tenses does Richard use? ....

3 Look at answers 8 and 9. Which happened first? ....
What tenses does Richard's mother use? ....

B Grammar

1 Past perfect simple

+	had + past participle	He'd painted the ceiling.
–	had not + past participle	He hadn't painted the ceiling.
?	had ... + past participle?	Had he painted the ceiling?

We use the **past perfect simple**:

● when we are already talking about the past and want to make it clear that we are referring back to an even earlier time:
*Yesterday afternoon I **was** bored. **I'd been** to town, **I'd done** the shopping and **I'd finished** all my homework so I **decided** to paint my room.*

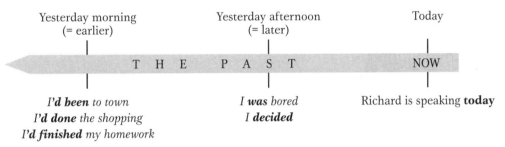

Yesterday morning (= earlier)	Yesterday afternoon (= later)	Today
THE PAST		NOW
I'd been to town *I'd done* the shopping *I'd finished* my homework	*I was* bored *I decided*	Richard is speaking **today**

● in some sentences with time expressions (*when, after, by the time, as soon as*) when one event happened before the other:
***By the time** Richard's mother **got** home, he**'d finished** painting the room.*
***I'd painted** one wall **when I ran out** of paint.*

● with the adverbs *just, already, ever* and *never*. They go between the auxiliary and the main verb (≻ see also Unit 8):
*He**'d just finished** painting when his mother came in.*
*When she got home he**'d already finished** painting the room.*
*Until last weekend he**'d never painted** a room.*

We don't use the past perfect:

● if one action happens at the same time as another:
*When Richard's mother **saw** the room, she **was** horrified.*
(**not** ~~When Richard's mother had seen~~ ...)

● if one action comes immediately after the other and is connected to it:
*When Jill **heard** the baby cry, she **ran** to pick him up.* (**not** ~~When Jill had heard~~ ...)
In sentences like these, the first action is often the cause of the second.

4

▲ Notice the difference in meaning between these two sentences:
*When Richard's mother came into the room, he **stopped** painting.*
(= she came in, so he stopped)

Richard's mother came into the room.

Richard stopped painting.

*When Richard's mother came into the room, he**'d stopped** painting.*
(= he stopped, then she came in)

Richard's mother came into the room.

Richard stopped painting.

2 Past perfect continuous

+	had been + verb + -ing	*I'd been working hard.*
−	had not been + verb + -ing	*She hadn't been working hard.*
?	had ... been + verb + -ing?	***Had** you **been working** hard?*

We use the **past perfect continuous**:

- to focus on the earlier activity itself or on how long it continued:
  *He had a headache because he**'d been playing** computer games for hours.*

- when we talk about how long something happened up to a point in the past:
  *How long **had** you **been driving** when the car broke down?*
  *By the time she arrived I**'d been waiting** for two hours.*

We use the **past perfect simple**:

- when we do not need to emphasise the activity or the period of time:
  *He**'d played** all of the computer games and wanted to do something different.*

- when we talk about how many or how often up to a point in the past:
  *I**'d driven** six kilometres when the car broke down.*
  *By the time I was 18 I**'d visited** Australia six times.*

State verbs (≻ see Unit 1) are not usually used in the past perfect continuous:
*I**'d known** her since she was four years old. (**not** ~~I'd been knowing her~~ ...)*

C Grammar exercises

1 Fill in the gaps with suitable verbs in the past perfect continuous.

1 The phone ...._had been ringing_......... for several minutes before I heard it.

2 Katya .... (*not*) German with Mr Fauser for very long when he retired.

3 Liz didn't know about the surprise party which her parents .... for weeks.

4 I was very pleased when the bus finally arrived because I .... that I would be late for work.

5 When the doctor eventually called my name I .... for 40 minutes.

6 My brother lost his job because he .... jokes to everyone in the office by email.

7 The band .... (*not*) for long when the lights went out.

8 We .... our money to buy a car but we decided to go to Australia instead.

9 How long .... (*they*) for their keys when they found them in the boot of the car?

2 All these sentences have a verb in the past perfect simple. Is it possible to replace it with the past perfect continuous?

1 I'd worked for the engineering company for three months before I realised my neighbour also worked there. _Yes: I'd been working_...............

2 As soon as George had finished the race, he drank three glasses of water. ....

3 Everything was white because it had snowed all night. ....

4 My parents were delighted when I qualified because they had always wanted me to be a doctor. ....

5 She was exhausted when she got out of the pool because she'd swum three kilometres. ....

6 We'd only just sat down when the waitress came to take our order. ....

7 I could tell from their faces that they had argued about something. ....

8 Our dinner wasn't cooked because I'd forgotten to switch the oven on. ....

3 Fill in the gaps with the past simple, the past perfect or the past perfect continuous of the verb in brackets.

1 I 'd never ridden (*never ride*) a bike until I went (*go*) to live in Amsterdam.

2 When Martin .... (*come*) into the room, his mother nearly .... (*faint*) because she .... (*not see*) him for nearly 20 years.

3 We were held up in a traffic jam so the concert .... (*begin*) by the time we .... (*arrive*).

4 How long .... (*you applying*) for jobs when you .... (*get*) this one?

5 .... (*you ever do*) any carpentry before you .... (*build*) that cupboard?

6 I .... (*not see*) Lisa when I went round last night because she .... (*go*) to stay with her grandmother.

7 As soon as I .... (*sit*) down on the train, I realised that I .... (*leave*) my passport at home.

8 I .... (*drive*) for about four hours when I .... (*realise*) that I was completely lost.

9 When I .... (*go*) into the room, everyone .... (*stop*) talking and .... (*look*) at me.

10 After he .... (*wash*) his clothes, he .... (*hang*) them outside to dry.

11 The manager was shocked when he .... (*discover*) that Jane was a thief. Up until then, he .... (*believe*) that she was completely honest.

4 Fill in the gaps with the past simple, the past perfect or the past perfect continuous of the verbs in the box.

> ~~agree~~   arrange   arrive   bang   come   forget   go   have
> move   not answer   not hear   phone   play   practise

THE BAND PLAYED ON ...

I had a rather embarrassing experience last year. At that time I played in a band with some friends of mine and, rather nervously, we 'd agreed (1) to play at a friend's wedding. We .... (2) together for about three months and it was the first booking we .... (*ever*) (3) so we .... (4) really hard for weeks.

The wedding was on a Saturday. The day before the wedding I had moved to a new flat so I .... (5) furniture all day and .... (6) to bed exhausted. At nine o'clock on the Saturday morning the rest of the band met, as we .... (7), to practise. They kept phoning me but I .... (8). So in the end one of them .... (9) round and .... (10) on the door for fifteen minutes until I woke up. He told me that they .... (11) me all morning. I .... (12) anything and I nearly missed the wedding. When I finally .... (13) at the wedding, I realised that I .... (14) my guitar.

31

D **Exam practice**

Reading Part 1

You are going to read an article about a travel competition. For questions **1–8**, choose the answer (**A**, **B**, **C** or **D**) which you think fits best according to the text.

OBSERVER NEWSPAPER YOUNG TRAVEL WRITER COMPETITION

Max Wooldridge, our first winner in 1988, writes about the award's significance and the excitement of being flung into a new world.

THE greatest buzz I've felt during the past five years was one afternoon on the seventh floor of the car park at Hong Kong's old Kai Tak airport. It was a warm Friday a few weeks before the airport closed in 1998. I'd been writing a feature article about the new airport for the last few days and had just sent it off to a newspaper so I had a free afternoon. I couldn't afford to go shopping – when you're freelance you never have any money – and I'd heard about the locals who regularly gathered in the car park to watch the infamous landings as jumbo jets made a 90-degree turn before flying in, almost brushing the tops of the neighbouring flats.

The group of locals welcomed me into their world, warmly applauding some of the landings and being less complimentary about others who got into trouble with crosswinds or came in too fast. The only things missing were scorecards, ice-skating style. While today's increasingly superficial culture may unkindly label these people as dull, they were local heroes to me; animated, cheerful souls passionate about their beloved airport.

It was a ground-breaking trip from which I sold many stories. And it was about this time that my life finally started to come together, too. Once again, Hong Kong had worked its magic. My life always changes there, turns a corner as

steep as the turn made by the pilots approaching Kai Tak. Ten years earlier, as a result of my first visit, I'd won the *Observer*'s first Young Travel Writer award. There are few better places to send budding travel writers. If you have nothing to say about Hong Kong, you should consider a career in soft furnishings instead.

I would probably have gone into writing anyway, sneaking in through the back door, but much, much later. Winning the *Observer* award threw me through the reception window. It was an official recommendation saying, 'you've got a talent, use it'. I was 21 when I won, a cheeky young man falling in and out of love and jobs every five minutes. Suddenly I'd won this great award, but was too young to know what to do with it. I realised I could write but knew nothing about the travel business or writing markets. Instead I retreated into a lonely existence, working through the night on bad novels that couldn't possibly sell. I had a lot of growing up to do.

For many years that followed I was a piece of driftwood, floating on an ocean of uncertainty, writing occasional travel pieces here and there, but still playing at writing, not really focused. It didn't help having a father who is a well-known sports writer, and the BBC's South Asia correspondent as a cousin. With such giants lurking in the

background, it's hard to ignore the pressure to succeed.

It wasn't an easy decade. I had a brief but enjoyable spell on a local newspaper and then too many years on company newspapers. My low-flying career ended just as my dad embarked on a round-the-world assignment for the *Daily Mail*. Each article he wrote was headlined: 'Where's Wooldridge Now?' I mention **this** only because a similar question was asked most mornings concerning my whereabouts in the office. The money was good, the people were nice, the chair just got too comfortable.

It was ten years after the award before I felt like a proper writer, eventually cashing in on my success. Regular commissions arrived and editors phoned me. Writing is a pain, but there's nothing as enjoyable. The desire to write is a bug you can't shake. It's scary, precarious, and a nervous existence. You may get two commissions the same day, then never work again. And while it's never easy, it's hugely rewarding. You never know what's around the next corner, but that's life.

1 Max spent the afternoon at the old Kai Tak airport because he
   A wanted to write a report about it for a newspaper.
   B wanted to visit it before it finally closed.
   C was looking for a way of passing the time.
   D had always wanted to watch the jumbo jets landing there.

	1

2 What did Max think of the people he met at the airport?
   A He admired their enthusiasm.
   B He found them boring.
   C He thought they were brave.
   D He thought they were wasting their time.

	2

3 What does Max say about Hong Kong in paragraph 3?
   A He enjoys reading the many things written about it.
   B He always finds it an inspiring place to visit.
   C He found it hard to get used to being there at first.
   D It is difficult for him to find anything new to write about it.

	3

4 Why does Max say he would have 'sneaked in through the back door' in paragraph 4?
   A Writing was a career he would have decided against.
   B It is unlikely he would have chosen to work for *The Observer*.
   C It would have been much harder for him to become a writer.
   D He may have taken a different type of job on a newspaper.

	4

5 How did Max react when he realised he had won an award?
   A He didn't know how to take advantage of the opportunity.
   B He was unsure whether he really deserved it.
   C He became more determined to succeed as a travel writer.
   D He found out as much as he could about the travel business.

	5

6 What does 'this' refer to in paragraph 6?
   A his low-flying career
   B his father's trip
   C the office where he worked
   D the headline of his father's articles

	6

7 What does Max say about journalism as a career?
   A It gets easier the longer you do it.
   B It can make you unwell if you accept too many commissions.
   C It is advisable to think carefully before agreeing to a job.
   D It is difficult to earn a regular income.

	7

8 What do we find out about Max in this text?
   A He was very ambitious.
   B He lacked self-confidence.
   C He was jealous of his father.
   D He preferred to stay in one place.

	8

4

This is an extract from the text. Without looking back at the text, fill in the gaps with the correct form of the verbs in the box.

~~be~~   be   gather   have   hear   send   write

The greatest buzz I've felt during the past five years ....was............ (1) one afternoon on the seventh floor of the car park at Hong Kong's old Kai Tak airport. It .... (2) a warm Friday a few weeks before the airport closed in 1998. I .... (3) a feature article about the new airport for the last few days and .... (4) (*just*) it off to a newspaper so I .... (5) a free afternoon. I couldn't afford to go shopping – when you're freelance you never have any money – and I .... (6) about the locals who regularly .... (7) in the car park to watch the infamous landings as jumbo jets made a 90-degree turn before flying in, almost brushing the tops of the neighbouring flats.

Writing Part 2

Your teacher has asked you to write a story for an international magazine. The story must **begin** with the following words:

The house was empty but I could see that someone had been there and had only just left.

Write your **story** in **120–180** words.

This task gives you a chance to practise:
using the past perfect (simple and continuous) when writing stories.

Study the opening sentence of the story carefully before you begin.

Useful words and expressions
to hold one's breath, to look round, to tiptoe, nervously, suddenly, to my surprise

A   Context listening

1   You are going to hear a man called Tom having four different conversations.
Before you listen, look at the pictures. What do you think Tom's job is? ....

2   **5a** Listen and check if you were right. As you listen, match the conversations
to the pictures. 1 ....   2 ....   3 ....   4 ....

3 (🎧 **5a**) **Listen to conversation 1 again and fill in the gaps.**

1 Tom's plane ....*leaves*.... at 11.05.

2 The conference .... on Wednesday at 9.30.

3 The main speaker .... on Tuesday afternoon.

Listen to conversation 2 again and fill in the gaps.

4 Steve says: I .... badminton in a few minutes with Paul.

5 Tom says: I .... to a conference in Amsterdam tomorrow morning.

6 Tom says: I .... my eyes tested on Saturday afternoon.

Listen to conversation 3 again and fill in the gaps.

Tom says:

7 I probably .... back in time.

8 I think I .... a meal in town.

9 I .... breakfast in my room.

Listen to conversation 4 again and fill in the gaps.

Tom says:

10 ... in a hundred years' time, the world .... a very different place.

11 ... there .... much oil available for energy.

12 ... people .... much longer.

4 **Look at your answers to Exercise 3 and answer these questions.**

1 Which sentences are about events fixed by a timetable? ....
What tense is used? ....

2 Which sentences are about actions being decided or still not certain? ....
What tense is used? ....

3 Which sentences are about arrangements people have made? ....
What tense is used? ....

4 Which sentences are about general predictions about the future? ....
What tense is used? ....

B Grammar

In English, several different tenses are used to talk about the future: the present simple (▸ see Unit 1), the present continuous (▸ see Unit 1), *will / shall*, the future continuous and *going to* (▸ see Unit 6 for *going to*).

1 Present simple

We use the **present simple** for scheduled events with a future meaning:

- for timetables (planes, buses etc. leaving and arriving):
  *My plane **leaves** Edinburgh on Tuesday at 11.05.*
  *My plane **arrives** at Amsterdam airport at 13.40.*

- for programmes (when a conference, a course, a football match, a film etc. begins and ends):
  *The conference **starts** on Wednesday at 9.30.*

- for people if their plans are fixed by a timetable:
  *The main speaker **arrives** on Tuesday afternoon.*

2 Present continuous

We use the **present continuous**:

- for plans which have already been arranged:
  *People **are travelling** from all over the world.*
  *What **are** you **doing** tomorrow evening? I'**m flying** to a conference in Amsterdam.* (= already arranged)
  *I'**m having** my eyes tested on Saturday afternoon.* (= I have an appointment)

3 *Will*-future

+	will + verb	*They'**ll arrive** soon.*
−	will *not* + verb	*They **won't arrive** today.*
?	will ... + verb?	***Will** they **arrive** soon?*

In formal English, *shall* is occasionally used with *I / we* instead of *will*.
▸ For the use of *shall* with offers and suggestions, see Unit 13, B3–4.

We use **will**:

- for decisions made at the moment of speaking:
  *I'**ll have** breakfast in my room.*
  *I'**ll ring** them now.*

37

- for anything which is uncertain, especially with *probably, maybe, I think, I expect* and *I hope*:
  I **probably won't be** back in time.
  I think I'll get a meal in town.

- for situations that we predict will happen but which are not definitely decided or arranged:
  *In 100 years the world **will be** a very different place. There**'ll be** millions more people but there **won't be** as much oil available for energy.*
  (= nobody knows definitely what the world will be like in 100 years)

  ⚠ Compare:
  *I'm **taking** my History exam again tomorrow.* (arranged)
  *I'**ll get** higher marks this time.* (not something which is arranged or decided in advance – a hopeful prediction)

- for something in the future which doesn't depend on a decision by the speaker:
  *I'**ll be** 23 on my next birthday.* (= I can't change this, it will just happen)
  *There'**ll be** a full moon tomorrow.*

4 Future continuous

+	will be + verb + -ing	She'**ll be working** at 7.30.
–	will not be + verb + -ing	She **won't be working** at 7.30.
?	will ... be + verb + -ing?	Will she **be working** at 7.30?

We use the **future continuous** for an event which is going on at a particular time or over a period of time in the future:
*I'**ll be working** at seven o'clock.* (= I will start before seven and I will continue after seven)

*By the time you read this postcard, I'**ll be walking** in the mountains.*

⚠ Compare:
*I'**ll be interviewing** him at 6.30.* (= the interview begins before 6.30 and continues afterwards)

*I'm **interviewing** him at 6.30.* (= the interview is arranged to begin at 6.30)

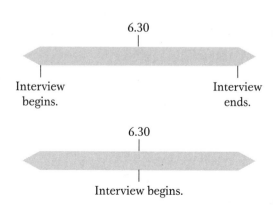

7 pm

◄——————— I'll be working. ———————►

6.30

Interview begins.   Interview ends.

6.30

Interview begins.

C Grammar exercises

1 Underline the most suitable form of the verbs.

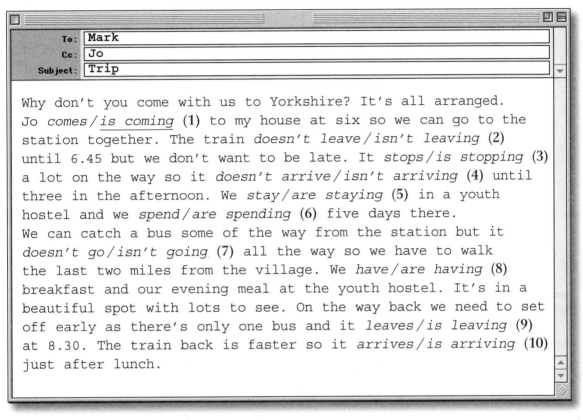

To: `Mark`
Cc: `Jo`
Subject: `Trip`

Why don't you come with us to Yorkshire? It's all arranged.
Jo *comes / is coming* (1) to my house at six so we can go to the
station together. The train *doesn't leave / isn't leaving* (2)
until 6.45 but we don't want to be late. It *stops / is stopping* (3)
a lot on the way so it *doesn't arrive / isn't arriving* (4) until
three in the afternoon. We *stay / are staying* (5) in a youth
hostel and we *spend / are spending* (6) five days there.
We can catch a bus some of the way from the station but it
doesn't go / isn't going (7) all the way so we have to walk
the last two miles from the village. We *have / are having* (8)
breakfast and our evening meal at the youth hostel. It's in a
beautiful spot with lots to see. On the way back we need to set
off early as there's only one bus and it *leaves / is leaving* (9)
at 8.30. The train back is faster so it *arrives / is arriving* (10)
just after lunch.

2 Fill in the gaps with the present continuous or the *will*-future of the verb in brackets.

1 Tim: Where are you going?
   Julie: To the cinema.
   Tim: Wait for me. I think I 'll come .... (*come*) with you.

2 From next week all enquiries should be sent to Mary because Frances
   .... (*leave*) on Friday.

3 Rachel: I .... (*give*) Sophie a CD for her birthday. What
   .... (*you give*) her?

   Fiona: I .... (*probably get*) her a new purse. She keeps losing
   money from her old one.

4 John: I need to finish packing today because we .... (*move*) tomorrow
   and there's still lots to do.

   Peter: Don't worry. I .... (*come*) round tonight and help you.

5 The government hopes that the national strike .... (*not continue*) after next week's meeting, otherwise the economy .... (*not recover*) for years.

6 James: Never walk under a ladder or you .... (*have*) ten years' bad luck.

  Kay: Rubbish!

7 Details of the president's visit are now confirmed. He .... (*stay*) at the Castle Hotel for two days.

8 Assistant: We have milk chocolate, plain chocolate, with nuts, with fruit.

  Man: Er ... what a lot of choice. I .... (*have*) a bar of milk chocolate, please.

9 Sarah: .... (*you do*) anything special next Saturday?

  Lee: Yes, I am. My cousin .... (*arrive*) from Italy so I .... (*drive*) to the airport in the afternoon to meet him.

10 Carol: Have you finished that book I lent you?

  Sam: Oh sorry. I forgot all about it. I .... (*get*) it now.

3 **Read the following situations. Write about what you think will happen.**

1 Anna has two cousins called Rebecca Smith and Rebecca Jones. Anna gets on very well with Rebecca Smith but she doesn't like Rebecca Jones. She has received letters from her cousins asking her if they can visit. She replies to them both. She wants to see Rebecca Smith but not Rebecca Jones. Unfortunately she puts the letters in the wrong envelopes.

How will her cousins feel when they receive her letters? ....

What will happen? ....

....

How will Anna feel when she finds out? ....

Example: Rebecca Smith won't understand why Anna doesn't want her to visit.

2 A tour guide has just arrived in a foreign city with a group of 30 teenagers and their teachers at the end of a long journey. They don't know it yet but when they get to the hotel where they have booked rooms they will find that their rooms have been given to a group of elderly tourists who are already asleep in the rooms.

What will happen? ....

What will the hotel manager do? ....

....

How will the teenagers and their teachers feel? ....

4 Look at the pictures and fill in the gaps with suitable verbs in the present continuous, the *will*-future, the present simple or the future continuous.

1 I expect my parents
   will give me books again for
   my birthday.

2 Sam .... tomorrow
   morning at ten o'clock.

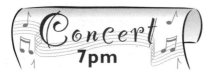

3 My grandfather ....
   on his next birthday.

4 The concert .... at
   seven pm.

5 I think I .... when I
   grow up.

6 At midday tomorrow I
   .... over
   the Atlantic.

7 The sale ....
   on Friday.

8 This time next week we
   .... in Austria.

9 We .... to Ireland by
   ferry this summer.

10 Maybe my father ....
    the money I need.

D Exam practice

Listening Part 2

(🎧 **5b**) You will hear a tour guide talking to a group of tourists about a day out. For questions **1–10**, complete the sentences.

HOTEL

Breakfast will be available in the [_____ **1** _____] from 6.45 to 9.15.

Tourists should [_____ **2** _____] their lunch from reception.

Everyone will meet for dinner at [_____ **3** _____]

If there are any difficulties with the hotel, see the [_____ **4** _____]

TOUR OF SOUTH WALES VALLEYS

Morning

The tour will visit a beautiful [_____ **5** _____]

There will be a chance to see the remains of a [_____ **6** _____]

The tour will visit a museum on the site of a [_____ **7** _____]

The souvenir shop sells special [_____ **8** _____]

Afternoon

There will be an opportunity to go for a walk or try [_____ **9** _____]

Everyone should bring a coat, wear [_____ **10** _____] and remember a camera.

Grammar focus task

1 **⊕ 5c** Listen to conversation 1 again and fill in the gaps.

1 ... the coach ......*is picking*...... us up ...

2 ... we .... back there today to have a better look ...

3 ... then we .... a bit further up the valley ...

4 ... we .... our lunch up there ...

5 ... then we .... our way back south ...

6 ... there .... time for a walk ...

7 ... we .... do those today ...

8 ... we .... at a café ...

9 ... you .... a coat ...

2 Which verbs are in the present continuous and why? ....
....

43

Writing Part 1

You have received an email from your English-speaking friend, Alison, who is coming to spend a day with you in your town. Read Alison's email and the notes you have made. Then write an email to Alison using **all** your notes.

From: Alison
Sent: 1st February
Subject: My visit

Hi,

I'm looking forward to visiting your town next week. I'm sorry we only have one day together. I know you've already made some plans so can you tell me what they are?

I can arrive as early as you want. Where shall we meet? —— Say where and when

What about lunch? Shall I bring some food? —— No, because ...

What are we doing in the afternoon? I don't mind what we do as long as you enjoy it too. —— Describe plans

I want to stay as long as possible. What's the latest time I can leave by public transport? —— Give information

See you soon.
Love, Alison

Write your **email** of **120–150** words in a style appropriate for the situation.

Writing hints

This task gives you a chance to practise:
using the present continuous for definite arrangements.
using the present simple for when things begin and end.
using the *will*-future.

Useful words and expressions
sightseeing, to wander, typical, opening hours, timetable, afterwards

A Context listening

1 You are going to hear a man called Simon Trite talking to a group of people on the remote and uninhabited island of Wildrock in the North Atlantic earlier this year. They went there as an experiment in survival. Simon has just come to the island.
Before you listen to the recording, look at the picture. Why has Simon come to the island? ....
....

What do you think it is like to live on the island? ....
....

2 [🎧 6] Listen and check if you were right.

3 [🎧 6] Listen again and answer these questions. Stop the recording when you need to.

1 How long were they going to stay on Wildrock? *For at least a year.*................

2 Why are the people going to leave Wildrock? ....
....

3 When are they going to leave? ....

4 By the end of this week, what will they have achieved? ....
....

5 By the end of this week, how long will they have been living on Wildrock? ....

6 When are they going to eat a big hot meal? ....

7 Who is going to stay on the island? Why? ....

4 Look at Exercise 3 and answer these questions.

1 Which questions are about plans for the future? ....

2 Which question is about old plans which have been changed? ....

3 Which questions are about actions which are not complete yet? ....

B Grammar

1 *Going to*

+	*am / is / are going to* + verb	*I'm going to leave.*
−	*am / is / are not going to* + verb	*They're not going to leave.*
?	*am / is / are ... going to* + verb?	*Are you going to leave?*

Pronunciation note: *going to* is often pronounced *gonna*. You may see it spelt this way in comic books and pop songs.

It is often possible to use *going to* to express the future instead of the present continuous or *will* (➢ see Unit 5). *Going to* is used extremely often in everyday speech. In formal and written English *will* and the present tenses are used more often than *going to*.

We use ***going to***:

* for future actions which we have already decided about.
  Compare:
  *We're **going to pack** up our stuff, we're **going to send** a message to the mainland and we're **going to leave**.* (= they already have a clear plan)
  *We'll **pack** up our stuff ...* etc. (= a decision as she speaks or a statement of fact, not a plan) (➢ see Unit 5).

* to predict something, when we already see evidence for our prediction:
  *It's **going to rain** soon.* (= the speaker knows it's going to rain because he can see the clouds)

There are many situations when either *going to* or *will* can be used with no real difference in meaning.

2 Present tenses after time conjunctions

In clauses referring to future time and beginning with *when, until, before, after, as soon as*, we use:

* a present tense (for actions at the same time as the other verb):
  *Everyone's going to be very surprised **when** you **arrive**.*

* the present perfect (for actions completed before the other verb):
  *And we're not going to talk to any reporters **until** we've **had** a long sleep.*

Sometimes we can use either a present or present perfect tense with the same meaning:
*We're going to eat a big hot meal **as soon as** we **find** a restaurant.*
*We're going to eat a big hot meal **as soon as** we've **found** a restaurant.*

3 Future in the past (*was / were going to*)

We use *was / were going to*:

● to talk about something which was planned but did not or will not happen:
*You **were going to stay** here for at least a year.* (= but now you have changed your mind)

● to show that we don't mind changing our plans:
Boy: *Are you busy this evening?*
Girl: *Well, I **was going to write** some letters.* (= she may forget about the letters if he has a more interesting idea)

4 Future perfect simple and future perfect continuous

+	*will have* + past participle	*I'll **have finished** by six o'clock.*
−	*will not have* + past participle	*He **won't have finished** by six o'clock.*
?	*will ... have* + past participle?	***Will** you **have finished** by six o'clock?*

We use the **future perfect simple** to say that an action will be complete before a point of time in the future. It is usual to mention the point in time:
*By the end of this week we'**ll have survived** longer than anyone else.*

+	*will have been* + verb + *-ing*	*By one o'clock, I'**ll have been waiting** for three hours.*
−	*will not have been* + verb + *-ing*	*She **won't have been waiting** for long.*
?	*will ... have been* + verb + *-ing?*	***Will** they **have been waiting** for a long time?*

We use the **future perfect continuous** to emphasise how long an action will have lasted at a point in the future. It is usually necessary to mention the point of time and the length of time:
*By the end of this week, we'**ll have been living** here for six months.*

State verbs (➢ see Unit 1) are not used in the future perfect continuous.

5 *To be about to*

+	*am / is / are about to* + verb	*I'**m about to go** out.*
−	*am / is / are not about to* + verb	*He **isn't about to go** out.*
?	*am / is / are ... about to* + verb?	*Are you **about to go** out?*

We use *to be about to* to talk about something which is going to happen very soon and for which we are already preparing:
*Actually, we'**re about to leave**.*

⚠ In the negative, *to be about to* often means 'do not intend to' do something:
*We **aren't about to change** the rules just because you don't like them.*
(= we refuse to change the rules just because you don't like them)

6

1 Look at these pictures and predict what is going to happen. First complete the sentences using *going to*, then complete them using *about to*.

1 She 's going to fall asleep.
   She 's about to fall asleep.

2 They ....
   They ....

3 He ....
   He ....

4 It ....
   It ....

5 It ....
   It ....

6 She ....
   She ....

2 These are a researcher's notes, with her predictions about how the world will have changed by the year 2100. Use the notes to write sentences in the future perfect simple.

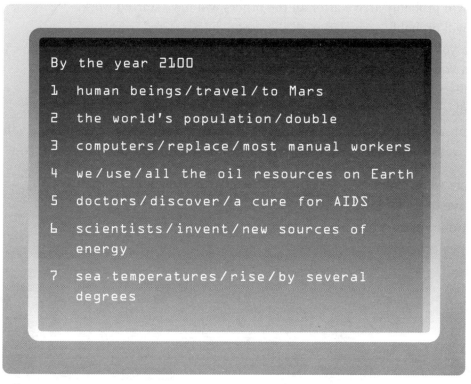

```
By the year 2100

1   human beings/travel/to Mars

2   the world's population/double

3   computers/replace/most manual workers

4   we/use/all the oil resources on Earth

5   doctors/discover/a cure for AIDS

6   scientists/invent/new sources of
    energy

7   sea temperatures/rise/by several
    degrees
```

1 Human beings will have travelled to Mars. ....
2 ....
3 ....
4 ....
5 ....
6 ....
7 ....

Write three predictions of your own, using the future perfect simple.

8 ....
9 ....
10 ....

6

3 Choose the correct sentence from each pair.

1 a I'm not going to pay you until you have cleaned up all this mess! ✓
  b I'm not going to pay you until you'll have cleaned up all this mess!
2 a Paul will probably arrive after all the others will have started work.
  b Paul will probably arrive after all the others have started work.
3 a When you'll see David, will you ask him if he wants to come to the cinema?
  b When you see David, will you ask him if he wants to come to the cinema?
4 a I'll collect your things from the cleaners when I go to the shops tomorrow.
  b I'll collect your things from the cleaners when I'll go to the shops tomorrow.
5 a Margaret's going to phone as soon as she'll have found out what the tickets will cost.
  b Margaret's going to phone as soon as she's found out what the tickets will cost.

4 These people work in a hotel. It's now twelve o'clock. How long will they have been working by two o'clock? Write a sentence about each person, using the future perfect continuous.

1 chef / cook meals (started work at eight o'clock)
  The chef will have been cooking meals for six hours.

2 secretary / type letters (started work at ten o'clock)

3 manager / interview new staff (started work at eight-thirty)

4 waitress / stand in the dining room (started work at eleven o'clock)

5 cleaner / vacuum floors (started work at seven o'clock)

5 Fill in the gaps with the correct form of the verbs in brackets. Use *going to*, future in the past, the present simple, *about to* or the future perfect.

a John: What are your plans for the weekend?

Sue: Well, we've just changed our plans, actually. ......We were going to have......
(*have*) **(1)** a barbecue on Sunday. But the weather forecast says
it .... (*be*) **(2)** cold and windy, so we
.... (*stay*) **(3)** indoors and watch a film.

b Beth: Is it all right for you to use the boss's office while he's on holiday?

Nick: Oh, I'm sure he won't mind when he ....
(*find out*) **(4)** how many cars I've sold this week.

c Terry: Are you very busy this afternoon?

Eddy: Well, that depends on why you're asking. I ....
(*wash*) **(5)** the car. Do you have a better idea?

Terry: Yes. I .... (*look round*) **(6)** the new sports club.
Do you want to come? You can wash the car tomorrow.

Eddy: Sure. Let's go.

d Ben: Hurry up! We .... (*miss*) **(7)** the beginning
of the concert.

Mary: Don't be silly. We've got plenty of time.

Ben: But it starts at nine. I want to arrive before the hall
.... (*get*) **(8)** full, otherwise other people
.... (*take*) **(9)** all the good seats by the time
we're there.

e Chloe: By next Friday I .... (*work*) **(10)** in this office
for three years. Nobody has ever thanked me for anything I've done, so
I .... (*start*) **(11)** looking for another job!

D Exam practice

Reading Part 3

You are going to read a magazine article about what people do during the time between school and university. For questions **1–15**, choose from the people (**A–E**). Some of the people may be chosen more than once. When more than one answer is required, these may be given in any order.

Of which person or people are the following stated?

She is confident that she will be able to find work after her holiday. | **1** |

She is about to start a job. | **2** | **3** |

She intends to find a job as soon as she can. | **4** |

She plans to spend time preparing for her course after a holiday. | **5** |

Her parents are very happy about her academic success. | **6** | **7** |

She has no holiday plans for this summer. | **8** |

Her parents do not want her to spend her money on a holiday. | **9** |

She believes it will be hard for her to earn money over the summer. | **10** |

She wants to spend time with her friends at home before going to university. | **11** |

She intends to have a good time at university. | **12** |

She thinks earning money will make a good change from studying. | **13** |

She does not know where she will be at the start of the summer. | **14** |

She will have a job similar to one she's done before. | **15** |

SCHOOL'S OUT

You've finished school, passed those vital exams and got a place waiting for you at university in the autumn. What are you going to do for the next ten weeks? *Prize* magazine asked five girls who've just finished school about their plans for the summer.

A Angie Hook has got it all sorted. 'I'm going to be pretty busy. First I've got to get some money, because I know I won't have enough when I'm a student, and the course I'm going to follow is really demanding, so I won't be able to take a part-time job in term time. So I've signed up with a company as a temporary secretary for most of the summer. Luckily, I'm good on a word processor and I did the same sort of thing in previous years, so I've got a bit of experience behind me, which is a big help. I am going to have a break though. Just before the university term starts I'm going to have a fortnight in Spain with some of the people who've just left school with me. My mum and dad are giving me the money for that as a reward for doing well in my exams, so I won't have to use up my savings, which is really nice of them, because I know it means they'll have less to spend on their own holiday.'

B Sally Price is less certain about her plans. 'I'm definitely going to have to work before I do anything else, because I'm so short of cash. I want to go away for a holiday somewhere by the sea, and I'll have to earn enough for that, so I've got to look for a temporary job first. I think I'll find something fairly quickly. After that, it'll be too late to find any more work I expect, because other people will have taken all the jobs by then, so I'll just have a month hanging about at home, messing around with my friends and things, spending time with my parents. That'll be good really, because I'm going to be a long way from home when I'm at university and I won't see them much.

C Tracy Chadwick says she has little choice about what to do. 'I have to spend the last month of the summer break getting ready for my course. I've got a job in a shop for the first month until I go on my holiday. That will give my brain a rest and pay for the holiday. But I've already had this enormous reading list from the university, so as soon as I've had a couple of weeks' holiday, I'm going to settle down and get on with studying, because I don't want to be behind at the beginning of term.'

D Polly Targett would like to work. 'But the thing is, we live such a long way from town and I don't have my own car yet – I'm going to get one next year, for my birthday, but it's rather difficult to get anywhere at the moment. Well, there's a bus, early in the morning and I think there's one in the evening, but to be honest it's much easier to stay at home. I doubt whether I'll go away, because I've already been on holiday with my parents earlier in the year and anyway I'll have to do some studying before the term starts, because otherwise I'll just have to work so hard when I get to university there won't be time to enjoy myself with my friends.'

E Hilary Lee is going to start with a break. 'I'm really exhausted after all our school exams and stuff and so I'm going to have a fortnight with my parents, just relaxing completely. We're going somewhere abroad, but I don't know where, it's a surprise, a sort of present, because I've done well. I know it'll be lovely. Then I'll find a job, it doesn't matter what, just so that I can have some pocket money for the rest of the year. It won't be hard to get something, in a hotel or whatever, summer's the high season for businesses in this area. Then I'll spend a couple of weeks doing nothing much, I hope, perhaps I'll paint my bedroom or something. And that'll be it – summer'll be over. I'll be a university student.'

Grammar focus task

This is an extract from the text. Without looking back, fill in the gaps with the correct form of the verbs in brackets.

1 I've got to get some money, because I won't have enough when I ....*am*................ (*be*) a student.

2 Just before the university term .... (*start*) I'm going to have a fortnight in Spain.

3 I'm definitely going to have to work before I .... (*do*) anything else.

4 It'll be too late to find any more work because other people .... (*take*) all the jobs by then.

5 I'm going to be a long way from home when I .... (*be*) at university.

6 I've got a job in a shop for the first month until I .... (*go*) on my holiday.

7 As soon as I .... (*have*) a couple of weeks' holiday, I'm going to settle down.

8 Otherwise I'll just have to work so hard when I .... (*get*) to university there won't be time to enjoy myself.

Writing Part 1

Your class has received this email from a class of students in England who are going to visit your school. Read it carefully and write a reply, giving the information they ask for.

Email
_____

Hi there!

We're looking forward to our visit. Can you tell us a bit
about what is going to happen each day? ———— normal lessons

We all enjoy sport. Do we need to bring sports
equipment? ———— yes, say what

Have you planned any evening activities? ———— say which and what

Please write soon and tell us about your plans. ———— give details

Regards,

Class 10B

Write your **email** to the class in **120–150** words in a style appropriate for the situation.

Writing hints

This task gives you a chance to practise:
using *going to* for talking about plans you have made.

Useful words and expressions
in groups/pairs, to have a great time, altogether, essential, to provide, to accompany, in the morning / afternoon / evening, alternatively

7 Adjectives

**comparative and superlative adjectives; position; order;
adjectives ending in *-ing* and *-ed***

A Context listening

1 You are going to hear some advertisements. Before you listen, look at the
pictures and guess what will be advertised.

1 ....   2 ....   3 ....   4 ....

2 ⏏ 7 Listen and check if you were right.

3 ⏏ 7 Listen to the advertisements again and write the words which describe these
people and things. Stop the recording when you need to.

1 The sort of person you can become: ....

2 The lions and monkeys: ....

3 The way you feel when you decide to phone Sparklers: ....

4 The variety of CDs: ....

4 ⏏ 7 Listen again and fill in the gaps with the words that describe these people and
things. Stop the recording when you need to.

1 professional advisers   .... route   .... welcome   .... facilities

2 .... day out   .... wildlife park   .... brochure   .... offers

3 .... carpets   .... sinks and surfaces   .... finger marks
.... prices

4 .... bargains   .... rock and pop   .... jazz
.... classical music

B Grammar

Adjectives are words which describe nouns (things and people).
➤ Compare with adverbs in Unit 8.

1 Comparative and superlative adjectives

We make comparative and superlative forms of adjectives in the following ways:

Adjective	Comparative	Superlative
one syllable *strong* *great*	add *-er* *stronger*	add *-est* *the strongest*
	*You can become **stronger** at Transformers Fitness Centre.* *The Music Store's got **the greatest** variety of CDs ever!*	
two syllables, ending in *-y* *tidy* *funny*	drop *-y* and add *-ier* *tidier*	drop *-y* and add *-iest* *the tidiest*
	*Their flat is **tidier** than ours.* *They're **the funniest** monkeys you've ever seen.*	
two/three/four syllables *famous* *beautiful* *self-confident*	*more ...* *more beautiful*	*the most ...* *the most beautiful*
	*You can become a **more self-confident** person.* *He is **the most famous** actor in the film.*	

A few two-syllable adjectives (e.g. *quiet, pleasant, common, polite*) sometimes also use *-er* or *-est*:
*It's **quieter** than any garden I've visited before.*

Two-syllable adjectives ending in *-ow*, *-er* and *-le* can usually add *-er* or *-est*:
cleverer; the narrowest

Most adjectives ending in a vowel and *-b*, *-d*, *-g*, *-n*, *-p* or *-t* double the last letter before adding *-er* or *-est*:
bigger; the saddest

A few adjectives have irregular comparative and superlative forms:
good → better → best
bad → worse → worst
far → farther → farthest

2 Comparative structures

We can use comparative structures to say that:

- things are **more**:
  *Our prices are **better than** any of our rivals.*
  *We have a **more interesting** range of music **than** you'll see anywhere else.*

- things are **less**:
  *Cassettes usually aren't **as/so expensive as** CDs.*
  *The CDs in the sale are much **less expensive than** usual.*

- or things are **equal**:
  *Classical music is **as popular as** rock music with our customers.*

3 Adjectives ending in *-ing* and *-ed*

Some common adjectives are formed from verbs and have both *-ing* and *-ed* forms.

We use the ***-ed* form** to describe our feelings:

*I'm **tired**.* (= a description of how I feel: I've used up all my energy so I need a rest)

We use the ***-ing* form** to describe the things which make us feel like this:

*This work is **tiring**.* (= a description of the work: it takes a lot of energy to do it)

Compare these sentences:

*It's a **boring** film.* (= there's no action in it)	*The visitors are **bored**.* (= they have nothing to do)
*We had a **relaxing** holiday.* (= the atmosphere was restful)	*Good driving instructors always have a **relaxed** manner.* (= they don't seem nervous)
*That was a very **satisfying** meal.* (= there was plenty to eat)	*The airline has many **satisfied** customers.* (= the customers feel happy)

4 Adjective position

Adjectives in English usually go in front of the word they describe:

*We visited an **old** house.*
*We saw some **beautiful** paintings and some **elegant** furniture.*

Adjectives can also follow some verbs (such as *be, get, become, look, seem, appear, sound, taste, smell, feel*):

*Everything **seemed pleasant** when we started.*
*The flowers **smelt beautiful** and the gardens **looked wonderful**.*
*But the weather **got very hot** and we all **felt exhausted** by the end of the day.*

⚠ There are many nouns in English which are used as adjectives:

*a **diamond** ring; a **library** book; a **seaside** hotel; **folk** music; **strawberry** jam*

5 Adjective order

When we use more than one adjective, we usually put them in a certain order. We say:

*a **strange old wooden** chair* (**not** *a ~~wooden old strange~~ chair*)

We usually begin with adjectives which give an opinion or general impression:

*a **dangerous** old car; a **delicate** oval tray; a **valuable** silver spoon*

Adjectives which give factual information usually follow the opinion / impression adjective. They go in this order:

	Size	Age	Shape	Colour	Origin	Material	Purpose	
an	enormous	old		red				car
a	small		oval		French			mirror
an		antique				silver	soup	spoon

Two colour adjectives are separated by *and*:

*a **black and white** photograph*

When we put more than one adjective after a verb, we use *and* to separate the last one:

*The day was **hot and tiring**.*
*Lord Byron was described as **mad, bad and dangerous** to know.*

C Grammar exercises

1 Complete this email with comparative or superlative forms of the adjectives given and any other words (e.g. *more*, *the*, *as*) that are needed.

Hi Lily,

Well, we've moved at last! When we got here, the house seemed ....larger............ (large) (**1**) than we remembered, because it was empty, but now it's got our furniture in it, it doesn't feel .... (spacious) (**2**) before. We've got to do some decorating, and that will be .... (expensive) (**3**) we expected because the walls are in a .... (bad) (**4**) condition than we thought. But we'll manage somehow, and soon we'll have .... (smart) (**5**) house in the town. And if your Uncle Bob has his way, we'll have .... (lovely) (**6**) garden as well. We'll also be .... (poor) (**7**) and .... (exhausted) (**8**) householders in the country, but never mind. We still think moving here is .... (good) (**9**) thing we've done for years. We can't imagine now why we didn't do it when we were .... (young) (**10**). Come and see us soon. Catch a train if you can, because it's almost .... (cheap) (**11**) the bus, and the railway station is .... (near) (**12**) our end of town.

Love from us both,

Auntie Rosie

2 Underline the correct adjectives.

1 James told us some *fascinating* / *fascinated* stories about the music business.

2 Why are you looking so *depressing* / *depressed*? What's wrong?

3 Sarah's got an *amazing* / *amazed* collection of rock CDs.

4 Felix has this really *annoying* / *annoyed* habit of reading my letters.

5 The *boring* / *bored* students started causing trouble in class.

6 I watched the show for a while, but it wasn't really *interesting* / *interested*, so I left.

7 As the football team came out onto the pitch, their *exciting* / *excited* fans went wild.

8 The food in this canteen is absolutely *disgusting* / *disgusted*.

9 The astronaut gave a *relaxing* / *relaxed* wave and entered the space capsule.

3 Look at this designer's sketch of a costume for a film and complete the notes. Fill in the gaps with adjectives for each part of the costume.

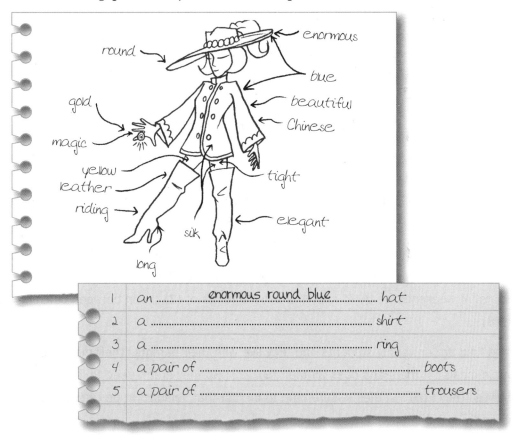

1	an	*enormous round blue*	hat
2	a		*shirt*
3	a		*ring*
4	a pair of		*boots*
5	a pair of		*trousers*

4 Choose the correct sentence from each pair.

1 a That was the worse film I've ever seen!
   b That was the worst film I've ever seen! ✓

2 a Michael's got a fantastic new leather jacket.
   b Michael's got a leather new fantastic jacket.

3 a I didn't eat any bread because I thought it stale looked.
   b I didn't eat any bread because I thought it looked stale.

4 a Our last holiday wasn't so enjoyable than this one.
   b Our last holiday wasn't so enjoyable as this one.

5 a My boyfriend is tall dark handsome.
   b My boyfriend is tall dark and handsome.

6 a Lucia should catch an earlier train if she wants to get to London by five.
   b Lucia should catch a more earlier train if she wants to get to London by five.

7

D Exam practice

Use of English Part 1

For questions **1–12**, read the text below and decide which answer (**A, B, C or D**) best fits each gap. There is an example at the beginning (**0**).

0 **A** repairing **Ⓑ** recovering **C** revising **D** retiring

WELCOME GUESTS?

My flatmate Penny and I are (**0**) ͫB̎... from weekend visitors. Don't misunderstand me – we enjoy company and love to (**1**) .... our friends and relatives. But not this time. Fred and Kate are old friends from our school (**2**) .... So you would think we would have a fairly (**3**) .... idea what sort of people they were, even though we hadn't seen them for (**4**) .... years.

Over the weekend we discovered that our lives had (**5**) .... very different directions. Penny and I have both worked since leaving school. We like our jobs but they are very (**6**) .... and we work long hours. At weekends we try to snatch a few moments of (**7**) .... in between catching up with all the (**8**) ....

Kate and Fred are university students and they live with their parents. Their mother still cooks their main meals for them and does all their (**9**) .... So they aren't used to looking after themselves. They (**10**) .... their leisure time to be just that, leisure. To be (**11**) .... , Kate isn't as bad as Fred. But she isn't much better.

By the time they left, Penny and I were exhausted. We didn't know whether to laugh or cry. Luckily, we (**12**) .... to laugh.

1 **A** entertain	**B** visit	**C** receive	**D** host
2 **A** terms	**B** days	**C** times	**D** ages
3 **A** fine	**B** strong	**C** good	**D** right
4 **A** numerous	**B** plenty	**C** passing	**D** several
5 **A** taken	**B** left	**C** chosen	**D** had
6 **A** tired	**B** tiring	**C** excited	**D** exciting
7 **A** extension	**B** relaxation	**C** expression	**D** reflection
8 **A** homework	**B** housekeeping	**C** household	**D** housework
9 **A** wash	**B** clothes	**C** washing	**D** clothing
10 **A** intend	**B** expect	**C** insist	**D** rely
11 **A** fair	**B** true	**C** real	**D** straight
12 **A** achieved	**B** succeeded	**C** reached	**D** managed

The adjectives in the box are from the text. Without looking back,
fill each gap with the adjective which describes each noun in the text.

different	few	good	leisure	long
main	old	school	university	~~weekend~~

1 *weekend* .... visitors
2 .... friends
3 .... days

4 .... idea
5 .... directions
6 .... hours

7 .... moments
8 .... students
9 .... meals

10 .... time

Writing Part 2

You see this competition in an international design magazine.

My bedroom

Write an article describing your bedroom. Say what's good
about it and how it could be improved.

The best article will be published next month and the writer
will win a laptop computer.

Write your **article** in **120–180** words.

This task gives you a chance to practise:
using adjectives.

Useful words and expressions
to display, to keep, to share
carpet, cupboard, noticeboard, poster, shelf, space
boring, exciting, expensive, favourite, giant, (im)possible, tiny
in one corner, near the door, under the window
the best improvement would be ..., what I like best is ..., what I'd really like to change is ...

A Context listening

1 You are going to hear the beginning of a radio commentary on a football
match. Before you listen, think about what you can see and hear at a match.
Tick the words you think you might hear.

☐ ball   ☐ chair   ☐ goal   ☐ ground   ☐ helmet   ☐ loudly   ☐ peacefully
☐ quickly   ☐ racket   ☐ scored   ☐ shyly   ☐ stadium   ☐ spectators   ☐ whistle

2 (🔊 8) Listen and check if you were right. Number the words in the order you
hear them and cross out the ones you don't hear.

3 (🔊 8) Listen again and fill in the gaps. Stop the recording when you need to.

1 And ....*finally*.... the players are coming onto the pitch.

2 There were such terrible traffic jams ....
that the match is starting ....

3 ... the spectators have been waiting .... since two o'clock ...

4 ... they're cheering ....

5 Rossi ... is running .... down the pitch ...

6 ... he's fallen ....

7 He's so experienced in these kinds of conditions that
he .... falls.

8 Now Parker is running .... towards the goal ...

9 Parker is playing incredibly ....

10 .... he scored the winning goal ...

11 It's .... Parker who shoots that important goal.

4 All the words you have filled in are adverbs or adverb phrases.
They tell us about when, where, how or how often something happened.
Put each of your answers to Exercise 3 in the correct column below.

When?	Where?	How?	How often?
finally	in the city	patiently	rarely

B Grammar

1 Formation of adverbs

Adjectives (*happy, beautiful*) tell us about a noun. Adverbs (*happily, beautifully*) tell us about a verb, an adjective or another adverb. They give us information about time (when?), place (where?), manner (how?) and frequency (how often?):

*Today I feel **happy** because the weather is **beautiful**. Some children are playing **happily** in the street and a blackbird is singing **beautifully** in a tree outside.*

Some adverbs are phrases:

*He's arriving **on Tuesday**, so we're meeting him **at the station**.*

Most adverbs are formed by adding *-ly* to an adjective:

sad → sadly; clear → clearly

This table shows spelling rules for these adverbs:

Adjective		Adverb	
ending in a vowel and -*l*	*beautiful*	add -*ly*	*beautifully*
ending in -*y*	*angry*	drop -*y* and add -*ily*	*angrily*
ending in -*le*	*miserable*	drop -*e* and add -*y*	*miserably*
ending in -*e*	*extreme*	keep -*e* and add -*ly*	*extremely*

An adjective ending in -*ly* (e.g. *friendly, likely, lively, lonely, lovely, silly, ugly*) cannot be made into an adverb. We have to use a phrase instead:

*She started the interview **in a friendly manner**.*
*He laughed **in a silly way**.*

2 Adverbs and adjectives easily confused

Some adjectives and adverbs have the same form. Some common ones are: *fast, early, hard, late, daily, weekly, monthly*:

Adjectives

*He caught the **fast** train.*

*He caught the **early** train.*

*She's a **hard** worker.*

*The bus is always **late**.*

*My **daily** newspaper costs 90p.*

Adverbs

*He ran **fast** to catch the train.*

*He always arrives **early**.*

*She works **hard**.*

*I arrived home **late**.*

*I swim **daily**.*

Hard and *hardly* are both adverbs but they have different meanings. *Hardly* means 'almost not'. It can go in various positions in the sentence:

*She **hardly** noticed when he came into the room.* (= she almost didn't notice)
*I had **hardly** finished my breakfast when they arrived.* (= only just)
*Rachel is **hardly** ever absent.* (= almost never)

Hardly is often used with *any*:

*There was **hardly** anyone in the cinema.* (= almost nobody)
***Hardly** any of the children could read.* (= almost none of them)

Late and *lately* are both adverbs but they have different meanings.
Lately means 'recently':
*I haven't read any good books **lately**.*

The adverb for *good* is *well*:
*It was a **good** concert. The musicians played **well**.*

But *well* is also an adjective which means the opposite of *ill*:
*I had a bad headache yesterday but I'm **well** today.*

⚠ Some verbs are followed by adjectives, not adverbs (⊱ see Unit 7, B4).

3 Comparative and superlative adverbs

Most adverbs use *more* or *less* to make comparatives and *the most* or *the least* to make superlatives:

*My brother speaks Italian **more fluently than** I do.*
*I speak Italian **less fluently than** my brother does.*
*Out of all the students, Maria speaks English **the most fluently**.*

Adverbs without *-ly* make comparatives and superlatives in the same way as short adjectives (⊱ see Unit 7, B1):

hard → harder → hardest	high → higher → highest	late → later → latest

*I work **hard**, my sister works **harder** than I do but Alex works **the hardest**.*

⚠ Note also: *early → earlier → earliest* (**not** ~~more early/the most early~~)
Some comparative and superlative adverbs are irregular:

well → better → best	badly → worse → worst	far → farther → farthest

*I did **better** than him in the test.*
*None of the students lives very near the school, but Darren lives **farthest** away.*

Adverbs use the same comparative structures as adjectives:

*He shouted **as loudly as** she did.*
*I can't add up **as quickly as** you can.*
*They arrived **later than** we did.*

4 Modifying adverbs and adjectives

Some adverbs are used to change the strength of adjectives or adverbs.
Here are some common ones:

incredibly   extremely   really   very   rather   fairly   quite   slightly

←————————————————————————————————————→
stronger   weaker

*He dances **extremely** well.*
*The weather was **very** hot.*
*He spoke to her **rather** fiercely.*
*The house was **quite** old.*

Some adjectives (e.g. *perfect, impossible, excellent*) can only be strengthened with adverbs like *completely, absolutely, totally, entirely*. We can say:
*This crossword puzzle is **completely** impossible.* (**not** ... ~~is very impossible~~.)

5 Adverb position

Adverbs which tell us:

- **how, where** and **when** something happens usually go at the end ('**end-position**'):
  *The meeting took place **suddenly**. (how?)*
  *The meeting took place **in the Town Hall**. (where?)*
  *The meeting took place **last Tuesday**. (when?)*

  If there are several end-position adverbs, we put them in this order:

	how?	where?	when?
The meeting took place	**suddenly**	**in the Town Hall**	**last Tuesday**.

Adverbs which tell us:

- **how often** something happens usually go in the middle ('**mid-position**') before a single word verb:
  *I **usually** travel by train.*

  but after *am/is/are/was/were*:
  *I am **often** late.*

  If the verb has two or more parts, the adverb usually goes after the first part:
  *I have **never** been to this part of town before.*

- **when** something happens can go at the beginning for emphasis ('**front-position**'):
  ***Yesterday** he painted the kitchen.*

  We can put other adverbs in front-position for emphasis:
  ***Angrily**, she stormed out of the room.*
  ***Suddenly**, she burst into tears.*

- **how** something happens can sometimes go in all three positions:
  ***Carefully**, he packed his suitcase.*
  *He **carefully** packed his suitcase.*
  *He packed his suitcase **carefully**.*

An adverb does not usually go between a verb and its object:
*She held his hand **tightly**. (**not** ~~She held tightly his hand.~~)*

67

C Grammar exercises

1 Use the adjectives in brackets to make adverbs and fill in the gaps.

1 Franca picked up the sleeping baby ....._gently_..... . (_gentle_)

2 When she handed him his lost wallet, he smiled at her .... (_grateful_)

3 Irma couldn't see her son anywhere and called his name .... (_anxious_)

4 They followed the directions to the hotel .... (_easy_)

5 Tomo admitted his mistake and apologised .... (_sincere_)

2 Underline the correct words.

1 Eleni stepped _confident_ / _confidently_ onto the stage to begin her talk.

2 The meeting at lunchtime was a _complete_ / _completely_ waste of time.

3 Marushka did _good_ / _well_ in the exam and she won a prize.

4 Mark tried _hard_ / _hardly_ to make the hotel receptionist understand him, but his Spanish wasn't _fluent_ / _fluently_ enough.

5 After looking at the computer screen all day I had an _awful_ / _awfully_ headache.

6 Even though Deborah did the job _efficient_ / _efficiently_, they sacked her after two months.

7 The doctor couldn't understand why Carol felt so hot because her temperature was _normal_ / _normally_.

8 The boy behaved _bad_ / _badly_ on a school trip so the school refused to take him on any more.

3 Rewrite each sentence with the adverbs in brackets in suitable positions.

1 Katja plays the guitar well for her age. (_incredibly_)
   Katja plays the guitar incredibly well for her age.

2 They eat steak because it is so expensive. (_rarely, nowadays_)
   ....

3 My grandfather used to take us swimming. (_in the summer holidays, in the lake_)
   ....

4 There is a good film on TV. (_usually, on Sunday evenings_)
   ....

5 My mother insisted that good manners are important. (_terribly, always_)
   ....

4 Use one word from the box to fill each gap.

> always   earlier   hardly   now   rather
> ~~silently~~   skilfully   stiffly   very   warmly

> She shut the door ...*silently*... (1) after her. Her father wasn't
> expecting her — she had arrived .... (2) than she had
> said. He was sitting where he .... (3) sat, in his favourite
> armchair by the window. It was .... (4) old but had been
> repaired .... (5) so that he could continue using it. The
> room had been redecorated since her last visit and was looking
> .... (6) elegant. On the shelves were all the books which
> her father .... (7) ever looked at any more. She called
> her father's name. He stood up and she noticed that he moved
> very .... (8). He smiled and held out his arms to her. She
> hadn't been in touch with him for five years but .... (9)
> he welcomed her as .... (10) as he always had.

5 Choose the correct sentence from each pair.

1 a The child spread the jam thickly on the piece of bread. ✓
   b The child spread thickly the jam on the piece of bread.

2 a My grandmother drives more careful since she got older.
   b My grandmother drives more carefully since she got older.

3 a I never have bought anything from that expensive shop over there.
   b I have never bought anything from that expensive shop over there.

4 a I always have my car repaired at Tony's garage.
   b At Tony's garage I always have my car repaired.

5 a My uncle speaks Spanish very well because he lived in Peru for a while.
   b My uncle speaks very well Spanish because he lived in Peru for a while.

6 a My sister doesn't make friends as easily than I do.
   b My sister doesn't make friends as easily as I do.

8

D Exam practice

Use of English Part 3

For questions **1–10**, read the text below. Use the word given in capitals at the end of some of the lines to form a word that fits in the gap **in the same line**. There is an example at the beginning (**0**).

ASTRONAUTS

There are two types of astronaut – (**0**) .....*commanders*.... who   **COMMAND**
fly the spacecraft and carefully trained specialists who
conduct (**1**) .... experiments and carry out   **SCIENCE**
spacewalks to repair damaged (**2**) ....   **EQUIP**

   Astronauts have to pass a medical and have a
(**3**) .... in a relevant subject. They have to be   **QUALIFY**
willing to live in an (**4**) .... small space and   **EXTREME**
work well with other people. Experiments can go
(**5**) .... wrong, risking the lives of astronauts.   **DANGER**
They have to be able to react (**6**) .... in a   **CALM**
difficult situation as well as be prepared to work hard.

   The first British astronaut was, (**7**) .... , a   **USUAL**
woman – most astronauts are male. Helen Sharman
got the job after hearing an (**8**) .... on the radio. **ANNOUNCE**
There were 18,000 applicants and, (**9**) .... for   **LUCK**
Helen, she was chosen. She said that the most
(**10**) .... thing for her was seeing the earth   **AMAZE**
from 120 miles into space.

Find eight adverbs in the text (including the gaps). Write the adverb and the adjective which it comes from.

1 *carefully* , *careful*   2 .... , ...   3 .... , ...

4 .... , ...   5 .... , ...   6 .... , ...

7 .... , ...   8 .... , ...

Writing Part 2

You recently saw this advertisement in an English language magazine.

REVIEWS WANTED

What's the best film you've seen recently? What's the worst?
Write a review comparing them and explaining your opinion.
The best reviews will be published next month.

Write your **review** in **120–180** words.

This task gives you a chance to practise:
using comparative adverbs.

Useful words and expressions
to act, to impress, performance, skilfully, interestingly, beautifully, extremely well, plot

9 Questions

yes / no questions; short answers; question words; question tags; agreeing

A Context listening

1 You are going to hear a telephone conversation between Peter and his girlfriend Mina. Before you listen, look at the picture. Why do you think Peter is unhappy?

....

....

2 ⓟ 9a Listen and check if you were right.

3 ⓟ 9a Listen again and answer these questions.

1 Who went out? _Mina_ ....
2 How many times did Peter phone Mina and get no answer? ....
3 Who had a change of plan? ....
4 Who is sorry? ....
5 Where are they meeting tomorrow? ....

4 ⓟ 9a Listen again for these replies. Write down the question when you hear each reply.

1 _Are you home at last?_ .... Yes, I <u>am</u>.
2 .... No, I haven't.
3 .... Yes, I did.
4 .... Of course I do.
5 .... You know I do.
6 .... Of course I will.
7 .... Yes, let's.

Underline the verbs in the replies and in the questions which they refer to.

B Grammar

1 Making *yes*/*no* questions

To make questions:

- which can be answered with *yes* or *no*, we put the auxiliary verb before its subject:
  You're going on holiday soon. → **Are you going** on holiday soon?
  He's packed his case.   → **Has he packed** his case?

- in the present simple or past simple (▷ see Units 1 and 2), we use the auxiliary verb *do(es)* or *did* to make the question:
  I like Italy.   → **Do you like** Italy?
  She prefers Greece.   → **Does she prefer** Greece?
                               (**not** ~~Does she prefers Greece?~~)
  They went to Corsica.   → **Did they go** to Corsica?

- with the verb *to be*, we put *to be* before the subject:
  They're in Madrid today.   → **Are they** in Madrid today?

- with modal verbs, we put the modal verb before the subject:
  We can stay here.   → **Can we stay** here?

We make negative questions in the same way:
They like big cities.   → **Don't they like** big cities?
She can't stay here.   → **Can't she stay** here?

These questions often express surprise:
Don't they like big cities? (= I thought they liked big cities. Am I wrong?)
Can't she stay here? (= I thought she could stay here. Is that impossible?)

2 Short answers

We answer a *yes*/*no* question using the same auxiliary or modal verb as in the question.
If we agree with a positive question, the answer is *yes*:

Are you going to Greece?	**Yes, I am.**
Did you like the hotel?	**Yes, I did.**

If we agree with a negative question, the answer is *no*:

Aren't you going to Greece?	**No, I'm not.**
Didn't you like the hotel?	**No, I didn't.**

If we disagree with a positive question, the answer is *no*:

Are you going to Greece?	**No, I'm not.**
Did you like the hotel?	**No, I didn't.**

If we disagree with a negative question, the answer is *yes*:

Aren't you going to Greece?	**Yes, I am.**
Didn't you like the hotel?	**Yes, I did.**

3 Making questions with question words (*who, what, where, why, how, which*)

When we use *what*, *which* or *who* to make questions about the **subject** of the verb we do not change the word order (unlike *yes / no* questions):

The pool looks too small. → ***What** looks too small?*
(Answer: *The pool.*)

This hotel offers the best view. → ***Which hotel** offers the best view?*
(Answer: *This hotel.*)

We make questions about all other parts of the sentence in the same way as *yes / no* questions:

*They'll be in Madrid **tomorrow**.* → ***When will they be** in Madrid?*
(Answer: *Tomorrow.*)

*We can't stay here **because it's full**.* → ***Why can't we stay** here?*
(Answer: *Because it's full.*)

*She prefers to travel **by train**.* → ***How does she prefer** to travel?*
(Answer: *By train.*)

Compare these **subject** and object questions:

Molly's visiting Shirin. → ***Who's** visiting Shirin? **Molly**.* (= subject)
Who's Molly visiting? Shirin. (= object)

⚠ In a subject question, *who* is always followed by a singular verb:
***Who is** coming to your party?* (**not** *Who are coming?*)
unless two or more people are actually mentioned in the question:
***Who are** your favourite **singers**?*

⚠ Remember the difference between these questions with *like*:
*What **does** Molly **like**?* (= what does she enjoy?) *She likes dancing.*

*What **does** Molly **look like**?* (= tell me about her appearance) *She's pretty.*

*What's Molly **like**?* (= tell me about her character and / or appearance)
She's intelligent and pretty.

4 Question tags

We often make a statement into a question by adding a question tag at the end. The verb in the tag must match the form of the auxiliary verb in the statement.

If the statement is positive, the tag is negative:

\+   –
*They're going to Greece, **aren't** they?* (speaker expects the answer *yes*)

If the statement is negative, the tag is positive:

–   \+
*You **aren't** going to Greece, **are** you?* (speaker expects the answer *no*)

74

We make question tags:

- in the present simple or past simple with *do(es)* or *did* for all verbs except *to be*:
  You like the seaside, **don't you**?
  Molly prefers Greece, **doesn't she**?
  Your friends aren't in Madrid now, **are they**?

- with the same auxiliary or modal as in the statement:
  We can stay here, **can't we**?
  They haven't arrived yet, **have they**?

⚠ The question tag for *let's* is *shall we?*
  Let's go to France, **shall we**?

⚠ The question tag for *I am* is *aren't I?*
  I am doing the right exercise, **aren't I**?

The question tag for *I'm not* is *am I?*
  I'm not in the right place, **am I**?

We use question tags:

- to check that something we have just said is true. This is not a real question so our voice does not rise at the end:

  They're going to Greece, **aren't they**?

- to ask a question. Our voice rises at the end:

  They're going to Greece, **aren't they**?

5 Agreeing with statements

To agree with statements we use *so* (for positive statements) and *neither* or *nor* (for negative statements) and put the verb before its subject. We can do this:

- with the verb *to be*:
  We're lost.
  So am I.

- with an auxiliary verb:
  I went to Spain last year.
  So did they.

  I don't want to quarrel.
  Neither do I.

- with a modal:
  He can't speak French.
  Nor can I.

9

C Grammar exercises

1 Choose the correct sentence from each pair.

1 a Who made the cake for the wedding? ✓
  b Who did make the cake for the wedding?

2 a We haven't got to do the washing-up, do we?
  b We haven't got to do the washing-up, have we?

3 a Does your sister live with your parents or she has got a flat of her own?
  b Does your sister live with your parents or has she got a flat of her own?

4 a Why can't you walk faster?
  b Why can't walk you faster?

5 a You went to school in Paris, haven't you?
  b You went to school in Paris, didn't you?

6 a What does Julie's brother look like?
  b What is Julie's brother look like?

2 Write suitable questions for these answers, using the words in brackets and your own ideas.

1 Where would you like to go on holiday? .... (go)
  The Caribbean.

2 Did you finish all the ice cream? .... (finish)
  No, I didn't. There's some in the fridge.

3 .... (spend)
  About an hour, usually.

4 .... (try)
  No, I haven't. But I'd love to.

5 .... (do)
  Sometimes I watch a film and other times I read.

6 .... (see)
  About once a week. It depends how busy I am.

7 .... (enjoy)
  Not really. The music wasn't good, and the people weren't very interesting.

8 .... (be)
  Because I overslept.

3 Read this article and write questions to match the answers given below.

LAST NIGHT BRIAN BAINES was celebrating his appointment as manager of Farley City Football Club. He says he is particularly happy to be going back to Farley, where he was born in 1968, after playing for a number of European teams. Baines telephoned his wife Shirley as soon as he had signed the contract. He said that she is really pleased that their three children will be able to settle at schools in the city. Their many old friends are looking forward to welcoming them back to Farley.

1   What was Brian Baines celebrating last night? ....

His appointment as manager of Farley City F.C.

2   ....

In Farley.

3   ....

His wife Shirley.

4   ....

As soon as he had signed the contract.

5   ....

Three.

6   ....

Because their children will be able to settle at schools in Farley.

7   ....

Their many old friends.

9

4 Add the correct question tags to these questions.

1 He always forgets his homework, ...doesn't he...... ?
2 The teachers didn't see me, ... ?
3 You would like to come with us, ... ?
4 I've got plenty of time, ... ?
5 Let's have another coffee, ... ?
6 It couldn't possibly rain, ... ?
7 Those men played really well, ... ?
8 Molly will have to tell the truth, ... ?
9 We can't stop here, ... ?
10 You promise you'll never tell anyone, ... ?

5 Match the statements and short answers.

1 (I started learning English when I was ten.) d....   a (So am I.)

2 (I didn't find it very easy.) ....   b (Neither will I.)

3 (I was always trying to sing English songs.) ....   c (Neither did I.)

4 (But I couldn't understand the words at first.) ....   d (So did I.)

5 (I'm quite good at English now.) ....   e (So must I.)

6 (I've read a couple of novels in English.) ....   f (So have I.)

7 (I won't have many problems in England, I guess.) ....   g (Neither could I.)

8 (And I must do my homework now.) ....   h (So was I.)

78

D Exam practice

Listening Part 1

(🎧 9b) You will hear people talking in eight different situations. For questions **1–8**, choose the best answer (**A**, **B** or **C**).

---

1 You hear a man talking to some tourists. Who is he?
A a café owner
B a tourist guide
C a street trader

B **1**

2 You hear a woman and her friend in an airport. What has the woman lost?
A her handbag
B her passport
C her boarding pass

2

3 You hear a man talking about his holiday. Which place did he enjoy most?
A the seaside
B Bangkok
C the north

3

4 You hear a girl talking about choosing a coat. Whose advice did she follow?
A her mother's
B her sister's
C the shop assistant's

4

5 In an office, you hear a man talking on the telephone. Where is Mr Richardson?
A in a hotel
B in America
C at home

5

6 You overhear a man telling a friend about a trip to a gym. How does the man feel?
A ashamed
B determined
C angry

6

7 You hear a woman talking to a doctor's receptionist. Why does she want an early appointment?
A because she mustn't eat before she comes in
B because she's having problems eating
C because she wants to see the doctor without taking time off work

7

8 You hear a man talking about selling his bicycle. How did he do it?

    A He paid for an advertisement in the newspaper.

    B He told all his friends about it.

    C He advertised it at work.

8

Grammar focus task

These sentences are from the recording. Complete the missing question tags.

1 Let's order some drinks, ...*shall we*......... ?

2 I didn't give it to you to hold, ... ?

3 You know the sort of thing I mean, ... ?

4 It looks OK, ... ?

5 It was unlucky, ... ?

6 You can do that, ... ?

7 I am right, ... ?

Writing Part 2

You have just received the first letter from your new English penfriend.
Read the letter and write your reply, giving him the information he asks for.

> ... so that's some information about me. Can you tell me about yourself, your family and your interests? What else would you like to know about me?
>
> Write soon.
>
> Best wishes,
>
> Michael

Write your **letter** in **120–180** words.

Writing hints

This task gives you a chance to practise:
asking questions.
giving information about yourself.

Useful topics
age, appearance, occupation, hobbies, sport, pets, music, future plans

Countable and uncountable nouns; articles

countable and uncountable nouns; *a(n)*, *the* and no article;
special uses of articles

1 You are going to hear four people talk about their jobs. Look at the pictures and guess what jobs they do.

1 ....

2 ....

3 ....

4 ....

2 🎧10 Listen and check if you were right.

3 (🔊10) **Listen again and answer these questions.**

Angela

1 What does Angela's company make? Furniture. ....

2 What important part of her work does she mention? ....

3 What does she care about? ....

4 What is not always available? ....

Ken

5 When does Ken get calls from drivers who don't think ahead? ....

6 Who calls Ken after an accident? ....

7 What does he say that motorists should have? ....

Charlie

8 Why does Charlie deliver pizzas? ....

9 What subject is he studying? ....

Hazel

10 What is terrible? ....

11 What does she have to pay for? ....

12 Why does she say she mustn't grumble? ....

4 (🔊10) **Listen again and answer these questions.**

1 What does Angela avoid eating? ....

2 Where does Ken work? ....

3 What does Charlie deliver? ....

4 What does Charlie usually avoid? ....

5 What sort of job does he want when he graduates? ....

6 How long has Hazel been driving a taxi? ....

7 What does Hazel say about her family? ....

5 Look at the nouns in your answers to Exercise 3 and compare them with the nouns in your answers to Exercise 4. Can you say how they are different?

....

B Grammar

1 Countable and uncountable nouns

Countable nouns:

- can be singular:
  a company, a job, a biscuit

- or plural:
  many companies, few jobs, some biscuits

Uncountable nouns:

- cannot be plural:
  health, advice, luggage, scenery
  (**not** ~~healths, advices, luggages, sceneries~~)

- take a singular verb:
  Petrol is *expensive.* ***Exercise is*** *good for you.*

- use expressions like *a piece of* to refer to quantity:
  *a **piece** of furniture, a **sum** of money, a **litre** of petrol* (**not** ~~a furniture, a money, a petrol~~)

⚠ Many nouns can be countable and uncountable, but with different meanings:

*These grammar **exercises** are easy!* (= tasks for practising grammar)	***Exercise** is good for you.* (= taking exercise in general)
*The gallery was showing **works** by several artists.* (= paintings, sculptures, etc.)	*I don't enjoy hard **work**.* (= tasks and activities)
*The French produce some wonderful **cheeses**.* (= different types of cheese)	*Do we have any **cheese** in the fridge?*

2 *A(n)*, *the* and no article

	Means:	Introduces:	Use it with:
A(n)	one of many	a new item of information	singular countable nouns
The	the only one(s) **or** the particular one(s)	items we have mentioned before **or** when the speaker and listener know which items we are talking about	countable **and** uncountable nouns
No article	all **or** that quantity is uncertain or unimportant	things in a general sense	uncountable nouns **and** plural countable nouns

Compare the use of articles in these sentences:

*There's **a supermarket** in most towns nowadays.* (= one of many that exist)
*We buy most of our food from **the local supermarket**.* (= one particular
supermarket near our house)

*Have you got **a pen**?* (= one of many that exist)
***The pen** is by the phone.* (= the only pen here)

*I don't like **the music** my brother plays.* (= that particular music)
***Music** helps me to concentrate when I'm working.* (= any music)

*We planted **the trees** in our garden five years ago.* (= the particular trees in our
garden)
***Trees** are easily damaged by **pollution**.* (= all trees; any pollution)

***The cheese** is in **the fridge**.* (= the cheese you need; the only fridge here)
*Help yourself to **cheese** and **biscuits**.* (= as much cheese and as many biscuits as
you want)

***People** used to believe **the moon** was **a goddess**.* (= people in general; the moon
that goes round this planet; one of many goddesses)

3 Special uses of articles

Look out for special uses of articles. Here are some common examples:

Places

We use *the* with:

- oceans, seas and rivers:
  the Black Sea,
  the Danube

- regions: *the Far East,*
  the Midlands

- groups of islands:
  the Philippines

- names of countries that include a word
  such as *Republic, Kingdom, States*
  or *Emirates: the United States, the People's
  Republic of China*

- deserts and mountain ranges: *the
  Kalahari, the Alps*

We say:
*the sea, the coast, the seaside, the country, the
mountains, the hills.*
*My parents spend their holidays by **the coast**,
but I prefer walking in **the mountains**.*

We do not use *the* with:

- lakes: *Lake Garda*

- continents, most
  countries, states, cities,
  towns and villages:
  *Europe, France,
  Florida, Rome*
  ⚠ but we say: *the Netherlands, The Hague*

- buildings and locations that use the
  name of their town in the name:
  *Manchester Airport, Birmingham City Art
  Gallery, Cardiff station, Edinburgh Castle,
  Durham University, Chelmsford High
  School*

Fixed expressions

Some fixed expressions use *the* and some use no article:
*We travel **by train / bus**. (**not** ~~by the train / bus~~)*
*We **have lunch / dinner** at one. (**not** ~~the lunch / dinner~~)*
*We listen to **the radio**. but We watch **television**.*
*We play **the guitar**. (a musical instrument) but We play **tennis**. (a sport)*
*We go to **the cinema**, **the theatre** etc.*

We say:
*My mother is **at work.***
but:
*My mother is **at the office**. (= the office where she works)*

⚠ We use *the* or no article before some places, with a difference in meaning:
*The children are **at school** now. (= they are students there)*
*My father is **at the school** now. (= he is visiting it)*

*Peter spent a lot of time **in hospital** as a child. (= he was a patient)*

*Dr Dibble has an office **in the hospital** and another at home. (= she works there)*

This rule also applies to *at church, in prison, at college* and *at university*.

Jobs

We use *a(n)* to say what job someone does:
*I'm **a doctor**. (**not** ~~I'm doctor.~~)*

Definitions

We use *a(n)* to give a definition of something:
*A **department store** is a shop which sells a wide range of goods.*
*(**not** ~~Department store~~ is a shop which sells a wide range of goods.)*

Exclamations

We use *a(n)* with exclamations:
*What **an exciting film**! (**not** ~~What exciting film!~~)*

C Grammar exercises

1 a Complete each phrase with a noun from the uncountable or the countable box. Use your dictionary if necessary. Can any of the phrases be used with more than one of the nouns?

Uncountable:	glass	~~luggage~~	meat	paper	rice

Countable:	books	cards	clothes	shoppers	tools

1 an item of ..luggage.......... 2 a pack of .... 3 a sheet of ....
4 a crowd of .... 5 a pane of .... 6 a slice of ....
7 a set of .... 8 a bundle of .... 9 a grain of ....
10 a pile of ....

b Use your dictionary to find words to use with these uncountables. There may be more than one possible answer for each.

1 a .... of bread   2 a .... of ice   3 a .... of oil
4 a .... of wood   5 a .... of dust
Remember to make a note of other words like these when you meet them.

2 Complete the diagram with the words that belong in each group. Use your dictionary if necessary.

accommodation	advice	cheese	coffee	experience
experiment	glass	~~hair~~	hobby	homework
information	journey	leisure	luck	~~luggage~~
meat	scenery	time	traffic	~~vegetable~~

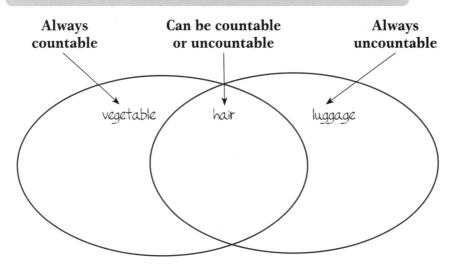

Always countable   **Can be countable or uncountable**   **Always uncountable**

vegetable   hair   luggage

3 Fill in the gaps with *a*, *an*, *the*, or – (for no article).

Pancake recipe

You need 100 grams of flour, ...*an*........ (1)
egg, a little milk, and 25 grams of butter.
Beat .... (2) egg with .... (3)
flour. Add .... (4) milk until the
mixture is runny. Heat .... (5)
butter in .... (6) frying pan. Pour
.... (7) 25 grams of .... (8)
mixture into .... (9) pan. Cook for
one minute. Turn .... (10) pancake
over and cook a little longer.
Serve hot, with .... (11) sugar
and .... (12) lemon juice.

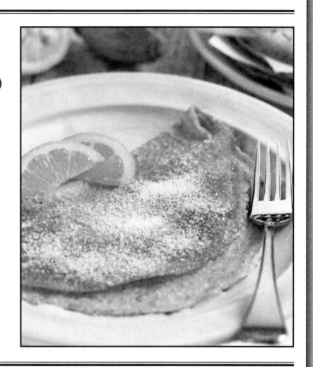

4 Fill in the gaps with the words in brackets. Add *a* or *the* if necessary.

1 We've got some important visitors flying in from ...*the West Indies*... next week.
Can you meet them at ....? *(West Indies, Birmingham Airport)*

2 Ferdinand spent his holiday sailing across .... from ....
to .... *(Mediterranean, Naples, Corsica)*

3 My brother's idea of a holiday is trekking across .... or exploring
.... Personally, I'd rather explore .... and do some
shopping! *(Sahara, Andes, Paris)*

4 Have you met Cora's new boyfriend? He's .... from ....
(ski instructor, Switzerland)

5 What ....! Our train broke down near Ely and we had to get a
bus from there to .... and then wait hours for the next train.
(terrible journey, Peterborough station)

5 Correct the mistakes in this email.

Dear Monique,

We had ⟨a⟩ great trip to the France last weekend. We went to little hotel that you recommended and it was very pleasant. Foods at the hotel weren't so good, as you warned us, but we strolled down to city centre on Saturday evening and had lovely meal there. In fact, we ate so much for the dinner that we didn't want a breakfast on Sunday!

Thanks again for the advice and informations. Now I must unpack and do the washings.

Here is photo of the hotel to remind you.

See you soon.

Love, Freda

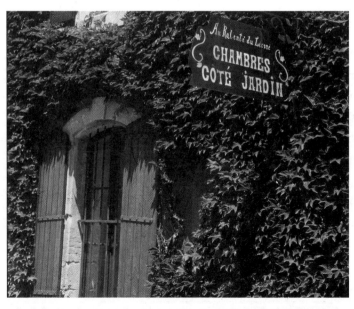

D Exam practice

Use of English Part 4

For questions **1–8**, complete the second sentence so that it has a similar meaning to the first sentence, using the word given. **Do not change the word given**. You must use between **two** and **five** words, including the word given. Here is an example (**0**).

Example:

0 Ethan gets top score even in the hardest computer games.

    WINS

    Ethan ....*wins even the most*.............. difficult computer games.

---

1 The hotel staff had permission to use the tennis courts on Mondays.

    PLAY

    The hotel staff were .... on Mondays.

2 Alison loves to buy presents for her grandchildren.

    PLEASURE

    Alison .... presents for her grandchildren.

3 My boss advised me which computer I should buy.

    GAVE

    My boss .... choosing a computer.

4 Can you tell me precisely how much money was stolen?

    EXACT

    Can you tell me .... that was stolen?

5 The customs officer checked every garment in my luggage.

    ITEM

    The customs officer checked every .... in my luggage.

6 I can't talk for long because I have to be at school very soon.

    ABOUT

    I can't talk for long because I .... school.

7 We've been standing in this queue for an hour and we still have another hour to wait.

    WAITING

    By the time we get to the front of the queue we .... two hours.

8 Although Toby keeps his room tidy he seldom cleans it.

    EVER

    Toby keeps his room tidy .... cleans it.

Which of these nouns from the exam task are countable (*C*) and which are uncountable (*U*)? Can any of them be both (*B*)? Use your dictionary if you want to.

1 permission ..U..   2 pleasure ....   3 advice ....   4 money ....
5 garment ....   6 clothing ....   7 queue ....   8 room ....

Writing Part 2

You see this competition in an international student newsletter.

EAT WELL, STAY HEALTHY.

◆ ◆

Write an article describing a diet which is both healthy and enjoyable. Say why you recommend it to other students.

The winning article will be printed next month.

Write your **article** for the magazine in **120–180** words.

This task gives you a chance to practise:
writing about food and diet.

Useful words and expressions
to cook, to go on a diet, to prepare, to put on/lose weight, to serve
delicious, fresh, frozen, good for you, instant, tinned
a balanced diet, dish, fast food, healthy eating, meal

Pronouns and determiners

possessives; reflexive pronouns; *each other* etc.; *there* and *it*;
someone etc.; *all, most, some, none*; *each* and *every*; *both, neither* etc.

11

A Context listening

1 You are going to hear a female travel agent and a male customer having a conversation. Before you listen, look at the pictures below. Which place do you think the woman went on holiday to last year? ....
Which place do you think the man would prefer to go to?
....

a

b

c

d

2 [🎧 11] Listen and check if you were right.

3 [🎧 11] Listen again and fill in the gaps. Stop the recording when you need to.

1 Have you looked at any of our brochures? Do ......*help yourself*...... .

2 I went to this place .... last year with some friends ....

3 .... of those would suit me.

4 Are you going on your own?
   Yes, ...

5 That's better because you get to know .... really well.

6 All I want is .... quiet.

7 .... of the holidays look enjoyable at all.

B Grammar

1 Possessive 's and *of*

The position of the apostrophe is important:
my brother's friends (= one brother)
my brothers' friends (= more than one brother)

When we speak we sometimes omit the second noun:
*I stayed at **Simon's**.* (*house* is omitted)
*I went to the **dentist's**.* (*surgery* is omitted)
*I stopped at the **newsagent's**.* (*shop* is omitted)

We use 's with people, countries and animals:
The girl's clothes were very dirty. (**not** ~~the clothes of the girl~~)
Britain's roads get more crowded every year.
I tripped over the dog's tail.

and with time expressions:
*I want to go on a **week's** holiday.*
*That's last **year's** brochure.*

but we usually use *of* instead of 's with things:
*What's the price **of** that holiday?* (**not** ~~the holiday's price~~)

2 Reflexive pronouns

myself   yourself   himself   herself   itself   ourselves   themselves

We use a reflexive pronoun:
● to make it clear that we are talking about the subject of the verb:
  *Amy blamed **herself** for what had happened.* but *Amy blamed **her** for what had happened.* (= Amy blamed another person, not herself)

● for emphasis:
  *I went to this place **myself** to see what it was really like.*

● with a number of common expressions like *by (your)self, enjoy (your)self, behave (your)self, help (your)self, make (your)self at home*:
  ***Help yourself** to some brochures.*
  *It's got everything you need to **enjoy yourself**.*

▲ We don't usually use a reflexive pronoun after *wash, shave* and *dress* but we can for emphasis:
She dressed quickly. but *The little girl managed to dress **herself** quickly.*
(= it was difficult for her)

3 Possessive pronouns and adjectives

Possessive pronouns:	mine	yours	his	hers	ours	theirs
Possessive adjectives:	my	your	his	her	its	our	their

Possessive adjectives are used before a noun:
*I went with **my** friends.*

We always use them with parts of the body and clothes:
*My father broke **his** leg.*
*They washed **their** clothes in the river.*

We can say:
my friends or *some friends **of mine** / **yours** / **Tim's*** etc. (**not** ~~friends of me~~)

We use a possessive adjective + *own* to emphasise possession:
*I'd rather have **my own** apartment.* (= just for me) or *I'd rather have an apartment **of my own**.*

On (your) own means 'alone' and can be used instead of *by (your)self*:
*I went diving **on my own**.* or *I went diving **by myself**.*

Own can be used for emphasis in the same way as *myself*:
*I prefer to make my **own** meals.* or *I make my meals **myself**.*

4 *Each other*, *one another* and *someone else*

There is a difference between the reflexive pronouns and *each other* / *one another*:
*The two boys hurt **themselves**.* (= each boy was hurt)
*The two boys hurt **each other** / **one another**.* (= when they had a fight)
*The two boys hurt **someone else**.* (= together they hurt a third person)

There is also a possessive form of *each other* / *one another*:
*They borrow **each other's** / **one another's** shoes because they take the same size.*

5 *There* and *it* + the verb *to be*

We use *there* + the verb *to be*:
- to say that somebody / something exists (or not) especially when we refer to somebody / something for the first time:
  ***There are** some lovely apartments.*
  ***There's** a tour guide.*
  ⚠ Note that the verb after *there* agrees with the noun which follows.

We use *it* + the verb *to be*:
- to refer to a particular thing, action, situation or place already mentioned:
  ***There's** a hotel by the sea. **It's** quite old.*

- to introduce information about time, weather and distance:
  *It's twenty past five and **it's sunny** here in New York.*
  It's only a few metres from the beach.

- to avoid using a phrase with *-ing* or *to* infinitive as the subject:
  It's surprising to see you here. (= *To see you here is surprising.*)
  It's a waste of time coming here. (= *Coming here is a waste of time.*)

6 *Someone, anywhere, everybody* etc.

Words like *someone, anywhere* etc. follow the same rules as *some* and *any*:
Some is used in positive sentences:
*I want to go **somewhere** sunny.*

Some is also used in questions when we expect the answer 'yes':
*Have you had **something** to eat?*

Any is used in questions and negative sentences:
*Are you interested in **anywhere** in particular?*
*I haven't got **anything** as cheap as that this year.*

Any is also used in positive statements to show 'it doesn't matter which':
***Anywhere** quiet will be fine.*

⚠ Words like *someone, everybody* etc. are followed by a singular verb:
***Everyone's** going there this year. **Nobody wants** to go to that hotel.*

7 *All, most, some* and *none*

all	most	some	none

Things/people in general	Things/people in a particular group
All + noun: *All hotels have bedrooms.* (= hotels throughout the world)	*All (of)* + *the/my/this* etc. + noun: *All (of) the hotels (in this street) have a restaurant.*
Most/Some + noun: *Most hotels have a restaurant.* *Some hotels have a private beach.*	*Most/Some of* + *the/my/this* etc. + noun: *Most of the hotels (in this town) are expensive.* *Some of the hotels (in the brochure) have a swimming pool.* ⚠ Note that we can omit *of* after *all* but not after *some* or *most*.
No + noun without *the*: *No hotel is perfect.*	*None* = *not any* and is usually followed by a singular noun but a plural is also possible: *None of* + *the* + noun: *None of the apartments has/have a balcony.* *All/Most/Some/None* + *of* + pronoun: *All/Most/Some/None of them have a private beach.* (**not** *All them have ...*)

We use *all* for emphasis:
*They are **all** near the airport.*

All can also stand alone:
***All** I want is somewhere quiet.* (= the only thing)

Whole is used instead of *all* before a singular noun:
*The **whole trip** was spoilt by the weather.*
but we use *all* with a plural noun:
***All the hotels** were booked.*

8 *Each* and *every*

Each and *every* can be used with the same meaning:
***Every / Each** apartment has a balcony.*

but sometimes they have different meanings:
- *Each* is used for individual things or people in a group:
  ***Each** child drew a picture of her own parents.*
  *The customs officer checked **each** passport in turn.*

- *Every* emphasises that all the people or things in a group are included:
  ***Every** brochure you've shown me ...*

Each (but not *every*) can be followed by *of* + a plural noun or pronoun:
***Each** apartment / **Each of** the apartments / **Each of them** has a balcony.*
(**not** *Every of the apartments / every of them*)

⚠ Notice the difference between *every* and *all*:
*He sat by the river **every** morning.* (= regularly)
*He sat by the river **all** morning.* (= one complete morning)

9 *Both*, *neither* and *either*

We use *both*, *neither* and *either* when we refer to two items:
***Both** places are too noisy.* or ***Both (of)** the places ...* or ***Both of** them ...*
***Either / Neither** place suits me.* or ***Either / Neither of** the places ...* or
***Either / Neither of** them ...*
⚠ Note that with plurals we can omit *of* after *both* but not after *either* or *neither*.

We can use *both / neither / either* alone:
*Which holiday would you prefer? **Either. / Neither.***
*Which holiday did you enjoy? **Both.***

and with a verb:
*They **both** agreed the hotel was excellent.*

We use *both ... and / neither ... nor / either ... or* to connect two things or actions:
***Both** the Hotel Flora **and** the Hotel Princess **have** a good restaurant.*
***Neither** the Hotel Flora **nor** the Hotel Princess **has** a restaurant.*
*I'd like to stay at **either** the Hotel Flora **or** the Hotel Princess.*

C Grammar exercises

1 Fill in the gaps with *it is*, *there is* or *there are*.

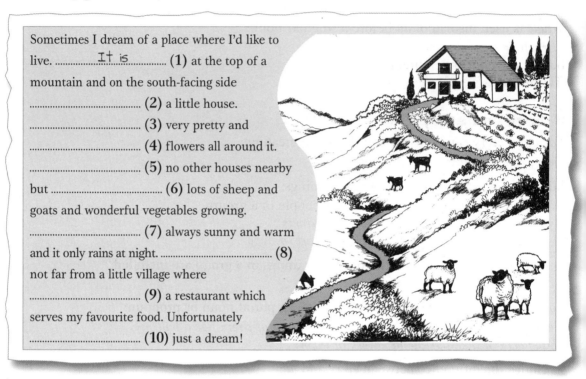

Sometimes I dream of a place where I'd like to live. ....It is............ **(1)** at the top of a mountain and on the south-facing side .... **(2)** a little house. .... **(3)** very pretty and .... **(4)** flowers all around it. .... **(5)** no other houses nearby but .... **(6)** lots of sheep and goats and wonderful vegetables growing. .... **(7)** always sunny and warm and it only rains at night. .... **(8)** not far from a little village where .... **(9)** a restaurant which serves my favourite food. Unfortunately .... **(10)** just a dream!

2 Choose the correct sentence from each pair.

1 **a** I saw your advertisement in yesterdays' newspaper.
   b I saw your advertisement in yesterday's newspaper. ✓

2 **a** I always enjoy when I visit my friends in Madrid.
   b I always enjoy myself when I visit my friends in Madrid.

3 **a** A friend of mine recommended this film.
   b A friend of me recommended this film.

4 **a** The college decided to publish the students' results in the newspaper because they had done so well.
   b The college decided to publish the student's results in the newspaper because they had done so well.

5 **a** Nobody wanted to come to the cinema with me so I went on myself.
   b Nobody wanted to come to the cinema with me so I went by myself.

3 Underline the correct words.

I'm going to tell you about a party game you might want to play. It's a game
<u>most</u> / most of (1) people would enjoy and it's a good way for people to get
to know *each other* / *themselves* (2) when they first arrive. There is a pile of cards
and *all* / *every* (3) card has the name of a famous person on it. *Every* / *Each* (4)
of the famous people has a partner, for example, Romeo's partner is Juliet. It's
important that they're people that *all* / *everyone* (5) has heard of. *Everyone* /
Someone (6) has one of these cards pinned to their back and they have to find
out who they are by questioning *every* / *all the* (7) other people in the room. The
first pair to find *one another* / *the other* (8) gets a prize. *The whole* / *All the* (9)
game takes about twenty minutes and by the end *nobody* / *anybody* (10)
is feeling shy any longer.

4 Complete these sentences describing the three brothers, Pete, John and Rob.
Use the words in the box.

| bald   beard   earring   ~~fair hair~~   glasses   moustache   short hair |

Pete   John   Rob

1 Both ....John........ and ..Rob have fair hair...
2 Both .... and ....
3 Neither .... nor ....
4 All of them ....
5 They all ....
6 None of them ....

Write sentences about your own family or three of your friends.

7 Both .... and ....
8 Neither my .... nor my ....
9 All of my family / friends ....
10 None ....

97

D Exam practice

Use of English Part 2

For questions **1–12**, read the text below and think of the word which best fits each gap. Use only **one** word in each gap. There is an example at the beginning (**0**).

NAMES

If, like me, you are called John Smith and you live in England, you have the same name (**0**) ....*as*........ thousands of other people. When I was a child, I thought that (**1**) .... in the world had a different name and I had a name of my (**2**) .... , but when I went to school I realised that I was wrong because I found (**3**) .... were two other boys with my name. In fact, one of them became a close friend of (**4**) ....

When I meet someone for (**5**) .... first time, they often think that they have met me before somewhere, but then they realise that in fact they are thinking of somebody (**6**) .... – another John Smith. If I say my name in a hotel or a bank, the receptionist often looks at me suspiciously as (**7**) .... is a name which people use (**8**) .... they have to invent one quickly.

Having met people with all kinds of names, I have decided it is better to have a common name rather (**9**) .... a very unusual one.
(**10**) .... parent chooses a name they like but when I recently met two people called Honey Moon and Holly Bush I wondered what their parents were thinking of. (**11**) .... of them appeared to mind having unusual names although they (**12**) .... agreed that people sometimes did not take them seriously.

Grammar focus task

Look at these phrases and find expressions in the text and answers which mean the same.

1 all the people = ... *everyone/everybody* ....

2 My name was unique to me = ...

3 one of my best friends = ...

4 a different person = ...

5 every sort of = ...

6 both of them seemed happy = ...

7 two people said the same thing = ...

Writing Part 2

Your class has recently been discussing the advantages and disadvantages of the growth of international travel both for travellers and for the countries they visit. Your teacher has now asked you to write an essay, giving your own views on the following statement:

International travel is becoming easier, faster and cheaper for many people. Is this good?

Write your **essay** in **120–180** words.

Writing hints

This task gives you a chance to practise:
using *all*, *most* and *some*, *anywhere* etc., *both*, *each* and *every*, *neither* and *none*, *someone*, *there* and *it*.

Useful words and expressions
to benefit, to damage, to get to know, to improve, to increase, to spoil
abroad, economy, environment, sustainable tourism, trade
for example, on the one hand, on the other hand, in my opinion

12

Modals 1
use of modals; obligation; necessity

A Context listening

1 You are going to hear a conversation between Chris and a girl called Alice. Look at the picture of Chris. Can you think of some of the things he does every day? ....
....
....
....
....

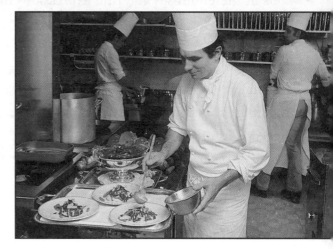

2 ⏵12 Listen and check if you were right.

3 ⏵12 Listen again and answer these questions.

1 Why isn't Alice at school? <u>She's left school.</u> ....

2 How many rich and famous people does Chris meet? ....

3 Why isn't Chris at work today? ....

4 How is this job different from Chris's last job? ....

5 What does Chris offer to do? ....

4 ⏵12 Listen again and match the beginnings and endings of these phrases. Stop the recording when you need to.

1 ... you need ..<u>c</u>..	a think about the hotel kitchen today.
2 Chefs have	b to work every day except Monday.
3 I needn't	c to spend their time in the kitchen.
4 You don't have	d come to the hotel one day.
5 I need	e to talk to me ...
6 I have	f to work longer hours.
7 I had	g to work all day ...
8 I'll have	h go now.
9 I must	i to get up early.
10 You must	j to stay until all the food is cooked and served ...

5 Look at your answers to Exercise 4. Which verbs aren't followed by *to*? ....

B Grammar

1 Use of modals

The modal verbs *can, could, may, might, must, ought to, shall, should, will* and *would*:

- are always used before another verb:
  *He **can** swim.*

- never change – they do not add *-s* or *-ed* or *-ing*.

- are followed by a verb in its infinitive form without *to*:
  *You **should** get up earlier.* (**not** ~~You should to get up earlier.~~)
  but notice that we say:
  *You **ought to** get up earlier.*

- are immediately followed by *not* in the negative:
  *You **should not** (or **shouldn't**) be late for college.*
  but notice that we say:
  *You **ought not to** be late for college.*

- go immediately before the subject in a question:
  ***Could you** wake me up?*

Need can be a modal verb as well as a main verb (⋗ see B3).

2 Obligation

Must and *have to*

+	must + verb	We **must leave** now.
?	must ... + verb?	**Must** we **leave** now?

+	have to / has to + verb	He **has to leave** now.
?	do / does ... + have to + verb?	**Do** we **have to leave** now?

For obligation, we can often use *must* or *have to*:
*I **must** go now or I'll miss the bus.* or *I **have to** go now or I'll miss the bus.*

We use *must* to give orders or strong advice, including to ourselves:
*You **must** tell me everything.* (= I feel strongly about this)
*Lucia **must** be home by midnight.* (= these are my instructions)
*You **must** come to the hotel one day.* (= I strongly advise you to)
*I **must** go now.* (= I have decided to do this)

When there is a rule or where the obligation does not come from the speaker, *must* is possible but *have to* is more usual:
*You **have to** pay to park your car here.* (= this is a rule)
*I **have to** stay until the food is cooked.* (= this is part of my job)

We usually use *have to* for habits:
*I **have to** get up early to cook breakfast.*
*Franco **has to** practise the piano for twenty minutes a day.*

We only use *must* in the present tense. In all other tenses, we use *have to*:
*I **had to** work every day.* (past simple)
*I'll **(will) have to** work longer hours.* (future)
*I avoided **having to** speak to him by crossing the street.* (verb + -ing)
*If I got the job, I'd **(would) have to** buy a car.* (conditional)

Mustn't and *don't have to*

must not + verb	We ***mustn't be** late.*
do / does not have to + verb	We ***don't have to be** early.*

Although *must* and *have to* both express obligation, *mustn't* and *don't have to* have different meanings. *Mustn't* means 'don't do it' and *don't have to* means 'it's not necessary to do it':
*We **mustn't** make a lot of noise.* (= it is wrong to do this, it isn't allowed)
*You **don't have to** stay at school until you're 18.* (= you are not obliged to but you can if you want)

Should

When we are talking about the right thing to do, we use *should*:
*Saurav **should** take more care when he's cycling.* (= it's a good idea but he doesn't)
*I **shouldn't** spend so much time watching TV.* (= it's a bad idea but I still do)

To talk about the past, we use *should have* + past participle:
*I **should have** told the truth.* (= it was a good idea but I didn't)
*We **shouldn't have** lent her that money.* (= it was a bad idea but we still did)

It is also possible to use *ought to* in these sentences, but it is less common.
(▷ See also Unit 13, B5)

3 Necessity

We can use *need* like a normal main verb in all the tenses, but it can also be a modal verb in questions and in the negative:
***Need I** come with you?* (= ***Do I need to** come with you?*)
*I **needn't** come.* (if I don't want to) (= *I **don't need to** come. / I **don't have to** come.*)

In positive statements, we say:
*I **need to** come.* (**not** ~~I need come.~~)

To talk about the past, we say:
*Oliver **needed** to buy a computer.* (= it was necessary because he didn't have one)
*Oliver **didn't need to** buy a computer.* (= it wasn't necessary because he already had one)

⚠ *Needn't have* has a different meaning:
*Oliver **needn't have** bought a computer.* (= he bought a computer but his parents gave him one so now he has two!)

C Grammar exercises

1 Fill in the gaps with the correct form of *have to* or *must*.

1 Most students in Britain ....*have to*.......... pay at least part of their university fees.
2 Joe .... get up early on Fridays as he has no lectures in the morning.
3 You .... talk during the film because other people will get annoyed.
4 These library books are overdue so I .... pay a fine when I return them.
5 Luke .... drive to work because the bus gets there too late.
6 Because Sanja could already play the piano, she .... practise much when she learnt to play the organ.
7 You .... borrow this DVD – you'll enjoy watching it.
8 .... (*you*) work every Saturday in your new job?
9 Non-swimmers .... go into the deep end of the pool.
10 You .... come to the rehearsal tomorrow if you want to be in the play.
11 When I was a child, I .... change schools seven times because my parents moved house a lot.
12 I .... share a room with my sisters because our flat is small.
13 I .... stop eating so much chocolate or none of my clothes will fit.
14 They've promised to lend me a tennis racket so I .... take mine.

2 Match the beginnings and endings of these sentences.

1 I shouldn't ..*g*..
2 Need I ....
3 We don't need ....
4 They needn't ....
5 Konrad should ....
6 Should you ....
7 Lewis needs ....
8 Do they need ....

a wear a helmet when he's cycling on a busy road.
b to take any money or is it free?
c to ask his boss before he leaves the office.
d take sandwiches with them because Jenny's cooking lunch.
e to send them our new address because they already have it.
f fill in my application form now? I'm busy at the moment.
g spend so much time playing computer games.
h carry that suitcase with your bad back?

3   Read this article about a pop star.

The diary column

Popstar Lee Divine travelled from London to New York yesterday by plane. Lee had visited his hairdresser before he went to the airport and wore his latest designer clothes, as he likes to look his best in photos. Press photographers usually follow him wherever he goes but the weather was very bad yesterday and, to Lee's obvious disappointment, there were no photographers at the airport. Because he is famous, he didn't stand in the queue and his bodyguard carried his luggage for him. Although most people have to walk from the car park, Lee has a driver who drove him right to the door. Even this did not seem to make him happy. Lee got angry with his driver on the way because he said she wasn't driving fast enough. Of course, they arrived at the airport in plenty of time.

Write six sentences about Lee Divine.

1   He needn't have <u>visited his hairdresser.</u> ....

2   He needn't have ....

3   He didn't need to ....

4   He didn't need to ....

5   He didn't need to ....

6   He needn't have ....

4 **Rewrite these sentences using the correct form of *must, need, should* or *have to*.**

1 It's her fault that she's lost her watch because she didn't look after it.
   She *should have looked after her watch.*

2 I don't expect you to phone me before you come.
   You ....

3 It is essential for students to buy a good dictionary.
   Students ....

4 It was wrong of you to take money from my purse without asking.
   You ....

5 I was getting ready to drive to the station to pick up my sister when she arrived in a taxi.
   I ....

6 It's not fair that I do the washing-up on my own.
   You ....

7 Students aren't allowed to smoke in the canteen.
   Students ....

8 She turned the music down to avoid disturbing her neighbours but they'd gone out.
   She ....

9 I think she's wrong to make promises which she doesn't keep.
   She ....

10 You can give the tour guide a tip but it is not necessary.
   You ....

D Exam practice

Reading Part 2

You are going to read a magazine article about offices. Seven sentences have been removed from the article. Choose from the sentences **A–H** the one which fits each gap (**1–7**). There is one extra sentence which you do not need to use.

Find your energy again

Even the best designed of today's offices represent an artificial environment where it can be difficult to stay positive and bursting with energy. Complaints about feeling tired, having no energy or no interest in food, headaches and backaches are commonplace.

Office workers often say that health problems are the inevitable consequences of working in an office. **1** [   ] While there may be little you can do about the ever-ringing phones or the tempers of your colleagues, you needn't feel unwell. There is plenty you can do to restore those energy levels and feelings of well-being.

The first thing you must address is tiredness. If at the weekend you stay up all night dancing or going to dinner parties and sleep all the following morning, you can't expect your body to adjust on a Monday morning to a completely different routine. **2** [   ] For most of us, however, it's a very bad idea.

Our diets are another way we mistreat ourselves. Many office workers say they don't have breakfast – but you really should eat something, however small, before you leave home. And if you're busy over lunch or have to go shopping, it's possible to forget to eat then, too. So you get to the evening and suddenly realise how hungry you are. **3** [   ] The sooner you do, the better because nothing is more important than eating and drinking regularly.

You should also do a session of exercise once or twice a week in the evenings. **4** [   ] Recent

American research has established that regular, vigorous exercise is a good way of improving your mood and that the effects last far longer than the session itself. It does have to be vigorous though – walking or tennis have to be kept up for at least an hour to have a positive effect.

All the advice on exercise says that you should choose something which you like doing. To this, many people reply: but I don't like doing any form of exercise! Most people start off with the intention of exercising but soon lose interest. **5** [   ] Then you will miss it when you don't do it. In order to motivate yourself, you need to keep reminding yourself of the advantages.

If you're working in an office with no natural light, you should go out for a walk for at least half an hour a day, even when the weather is dull and rainy. The importance of spending some time in daylight is often ignored. We now know that lack of sunlight can cause depression. **6** [   ] Time spent out of doors, even if it's only a few minutes, is never wasted.

You may be bothered by some of your colleagues' bad temper or lateness. Take a few moments to think about how they influence your own state of mind. **7** [   ] You are much more likely to enjoy your evening if you leave work feeling positive and it's the same for your colleagues. Take steps to make sure work is a place where you look forward to going. You will spend many hours of your life there!

A The answer here is you must keep doing it until you get really used to it.

B This is, of course, a disastrous way for anyone to run their life and you need to realise that.

C Always remember that you don't need to behave in the same way.

D That solution to the problem may not work for everyone.

E However, this is not the case.

F This can be avoided, however, by careful planning of the working day.

G This will help you to get to sleep and wake up refreshed.

H Some people seem to be able to keep this up without any negative effects on their health.

Grammar focus task

Look at these sentences and find expressions in the text or sentences A–H which mean the same.

1 It is not necessary for you to feel ill. *You needn't feel unwell.*

2 It is essential first of all for you to deal with tiredness. ....

3 It is important that you exercise at least once a week after work. ....

4 It is essential to walk or play tennis for at least an hour. ....

5 It is important that you do a form of exercise that you enjoy. ....

6 It is essential that you continue until it is a habit. ....

7 It is necessary that you don't forget the positive things. ....

8 It is not necessary for you to behave like them. ....

Writing Part 2

You have received this email from your British penfriend. Read it carefully and write your reply, giving her the information she asks for.

... and I'm really looking forward to my stay with you and coming to your school. Does your school have any rules? Do you have to wear uniform? What do I need to bring with me?

Please answer soon.

Megan

Write your **email** in **120–180** words.

Writing hints

This task gives you a chance to practise:
using modal verbs to talk about obligation (rules) and necessity (what you need).

Useful words and expressions
although, because, locker, canteen, otherwise, so, sports ground, writing materials

A Context listening

1 You are going to hear a teenage girl called Sophie asking her mother to do five things for her. What do you think Sophie might ask? ....
....
....
....

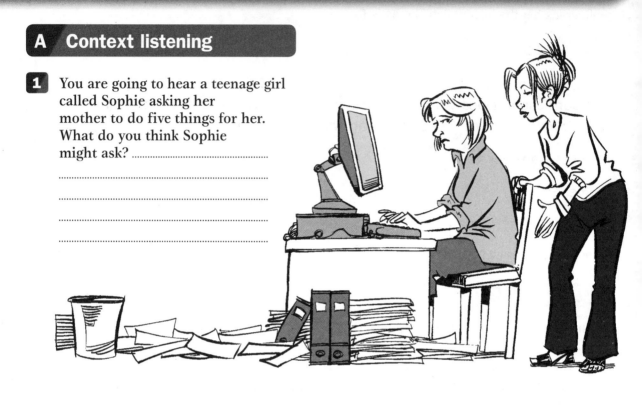

2 🎧 **13a** Listen and write Sophie's questions. Were any of your guesses right?

Sophie says:

Her mother agrees (✓) or doesn't agree (✗):

1 <u>Will you lend me ten pounds?</u>   ✓

2 ....

3 ....

4 ....

5 ....

3 🎧 **13a** Listen again and put a tick (✓) in Exercise 2 if Sophie's mother agrees to do something and a cross (✗) if she doesn't agree.

4 🎧 **13a** Listen again. Sophie asks her mother two things for a second time at the end of the conversation. What does she say? Why does she ask differently the second time?

....
....

B Grammar

1 Asking for and giving permission

We can ask for permission by saying: *Can I? Could I?* or *May I?*
Can I *leave my bag here while I look round the museum?* (= a simple request which expects the answer *yes*)
Could I *borrow your car for a few days?* (= more polite or a request which is less sure of the answer being *yes*)
May I *sit here?* (= a more formal request, particularly to a stranger)

We usually answer by saying:
Of course (you can). / OK. / Certainly.
I'm afraid not. (= polite) / *No, you can't.* (= not very polite)

May is often used in written notices to say what is or is not allowed:
*You **may** borrow six books from the library.*
*You **may not** keep any book for longer than three weeks.*

2 Making requests

We use *Can you?* and *Will you?* to ask someone else to do something:
Can you *pass me the bread?*
Will you *get me some stamps from the post office?*

To be more polite, we use *Could you?* and *Would you?*:
Could you *tell me where the station is?*
Would you *lend me your camera?*

We usually answer by saying:
*Of course (I **can** / **will**).* or *OK.*
*I'm sorry I **can't**.* (**not** ~~No, I won't~~, which sounds rude)

⚠ We never use *May you?* to ask someone to do something.
(**not** ~~May you give me a lift?~~)

3 Making offers

There are several ways of offering help to someone else:
Can I / **we** *help you to cook dinner?*
Shall I / **we** *clean the car for you?*
I can / **I could** / **I'll** *lend you some money.*
Why don't I *carry that bag for you?*

4 Making suggestions

To make a suggestion, we can use all the following expressions:

Shall I / we **Why don't I / we**	**go** *by bicycle today?*
Let's	**go** *by bicycle today.*
How about **What about**	**going** *by bicycle today?*

If we are less sure of what we are suggesting, we can say:
We could go *by bicycle today.*

5 Giving orders and advice

To give orders and advice, we use:

must	*had better*	*ought to/should*	*could*

strong ←――――――――――――――――――――――→ less strong

You really **must** *start looking for a job.* (= an order – I am telling you to do this, or this is my opinion which I feel very strongly about)
You' **d better** *start looking for a job.* (= advice – otherwise you may regret it)
You **should / ought to** *start looking for a job.* (= advice)
You **could** *start looking for a job.* (= this is only a suggestion)

In the negative we use *had better not* and *oughtn't to / shouldn't*:
You' **d better not** *forget to post that application form.*
You **shouldn't / ought not to** *wear those clothes for the interview.*

▲ We don't use *mustn't* or *couldn't* when giving advice.

To talk about the past we say:
You **should have / ought to have** *accepted that job.* (= it was a good idea to accept but you didn't)

In the negative we say:
You **shouldn't have / ought not to have** *worn those clothes.* (= you wore them but it wasn't a good idea)

We can use all these verbs to talk about the right thing to do:
I **must** *try harder not to be late.*
She **should / ought to** *be more thoughtful.*
He' **d better** *go and say sorry.*
I' **d better not** *upset her today.*
They **shouldn't / ought not to** *talk so much.*

To talk about the right thing to do in the past we say:
They **shouldn't have / ought not to have** *talked so much.*

(⮞ See also Unit 12, B2)

C Grammar exercises

1 Fill in the gaps in these sentences.

1 ....*Can*........ I change traveller's cheques here?

2 I'm sorry to bother you. .... I look at your timetable, please?

3 .... cycling to town today for a change? It will be good for us.

4 We .... ask Paula if she'd like to come riding with us. What do you think? I know she'll enjoy it.

5 .... you get that tin down from the shelf for me, Dad? I can't quite reach.

6 I .... post your parcel on my way to work if you want.

7 We haven't got any plans this weekend so .... we go sailing? The weather's going to be fine.

8 Excuse me, ... you tell me where the nearest tube station is?

9 A: '..................... I take this bag onto the plane?'

B: 'No, I'm afraid not.'

10 .... you turn that television down? I need to use the phone.

2 Daniel runs his own business. He isn't very tidy. Tomorrow an important client is coming to visit him in his office. Give him some advice, using at least four different structures and the words in the box.

| coat   cups   ~~desk~~   filing cabinet |
| lampshade   telephone |
| wastepaper bin   window |

1 *You'd better tidy the desk.*...............

2 ....

3 ....

4 ....

5 ....

6 ....

7 ....

8 ....

3 Fill in the gaps with the phrases in the box.

> Can I do   ~~Can I help~~   Could I see   I'm afraid
> Shall I ask   Would you exchange   You can't have
> You could give   You'd better not   You should ask
> You shouldn't have done

Assistant: ....Can I help....... **(1)** you?

Laura: I'd like to have a refund on a CD which I was given as a present. .... **(2)** that here?

Assistant: Yes you can. I'll do it for you. .... **(3)** the receipt, please?

Laura: .... **(4)** not. I haven't got one, you see, because it was a present.

Assistant: .... **(5)** a refund without the receipt. Those are the rules, I'm afraid.

Laura: .... **(6)** it for something else then?

Assistant: What CD is it? Oh, but you've taken it out of its wrapping. .... **(7)** that if you wanted to return it.

Laura: Christabel did it before she gave it to me.

Assistant: Did you say Christabel? Does she work here at weekends?

Laura: I don't know. She's got dark hair and glasses.

Assistant: .... **(8)** her where she got this. She was probably given it free because it has no wrapping. .... **(9)** the manager what he thinks?

Laura: .... **(10)** do that. I don't want to get her into trouble.

Assistant: .... **(11)** it to someone else for their birthday, I suppose.

4 **What would you say in the following situations? Write sentences.**

1 You have just started work in a new office and you want to know how the coffee machine works. Ask someone.
Excuse me, could you tell me how the coffee machine works, please?

2 Your sister has just moved into a new flat and you offer to help her clean it.

3 Your friend is trying to decide what to buy her mother for her birthday. Give her some suggestions.

4 Your brother puts lots of salt onto his food. You don't think this is a good idea because too much salt is bad for you. What do you say?

5 You want a book which you can't find in the bookshop. Ask the assistant to order it.

6 You are buying something in a shop and you want to pay by credit card. Ask the assistant if this is possible.

7 Your friend is always late because he doesn't have a watch although he can afford to buy one. What advice do you give him?

8 You have been at a party at a friend's house and the kitchen is in a terrible mess. Offer to help clear up.

9 Your sister is going shopping. You need a new battery for your camera. Ask her to get one for you.

10 You need a lift home. Your friend has a car but lives in the other direction. Ask him politely for a lift.

D Exam practice

Listening Part 3

13b You will hear five different people giving advice. For Speakers **1–5**, choose from the list (**A–F**) who is speaking. Use the letters only once. There is one extra letter which you do not need to use.

A a neighbour

                              Speaker 1   **1**

B a teacher

                              Speaker 2   **2**

C a parent

                              Speaker 3   **3**

D a tour guide

                              Speaker 4   **4**

E a colleague

                              Speaker 5   **5**

F a shop assistant

These extracts are from the recording. Which ones make offers? Which ones give advice? Which ones give orders or strong advice? Write *F* for offers, *A* for advice, and *O* for orders or strong opinion.

1 Shall I leave you to think about it ... ?   *F*

2 You must bring something warm ... .

3 ... you'd better all go and get a pullover ... .

4 ... I could lend it to you ... .

5 Why don't I pop across the road and get it? ....

6 ... you must bring one of those wonderful shirts back. ....

7 You ought to take things for the daytime ... .

8 ... you'd better not spend all your money in the airport shop ... .

Writing Part 2

Every term your class goes on a day trip to a place of interest. Your English teacher has asked you to write a report on a recent trip, giving suggestions and advice for the person who will organise the next one. Write your **report** in **120–180** words.

This task gives you a chance to practise:
using modal verbs to make suggestions and give advice.

Useful words and expressions
to check, to make sure, to remind
castle, museum, gallery, traffic, delay, disaster, problem
luckily, interesting

A Context listening

1 You are going to hear two college students called Clare and Fiona talking about a boy called Danny. Before you listen, look at the picture. Do you think Danny is sitting with his sister, his girlfriend or his mother? ....

....

2 🎧14 Listen and check if you were right.

3 🎧14 Listen again and answer these questions.

1 Who does Clare think Danny is with at first? ....

2 Fiona doesn't agree. Why not? ....

3 What do the two girls decide to do? ....

4 Why doesn't Fiona want to say hello? ....

5 What do you think Fiona really feels about Danny? ....

4 🎧14 Listen again and fill in the gaps.

1 Clare: It ....*might be*.......... Danny.

2 Clare: She .... his mother.

3 Fiona: She .... his mother.

4 Fiona: He .... me.

5 Fiona: She .... his new girlfriend.

5 Look at the sentences in Exercise 4. In which sentences does the speaker:

1 seem sure that something is true? ....

2 think something is possible, but isn't sure? ....

B Grammar

1 Ability

Can and *be able to* – present

+	can + verb	I **can** swim.
−	can't + verb	She **can't** swim.
?	can ... + verb?	**Can** you swim?

+	am/is/are able to + verb	I**'m able to** swim.
−	am/is/are not able to + verb	He**'s not able to** swim.
?	am/is/are ... able to + verb?	**Are** you **able to** swim?

We use *can* or *be able to* to say that someone has an ability:
*James **can** / **is able to** play chess but he **can't** / **isn't able to** ride a bicycle.*

Can and *be able to* – past

+	could + verb	I **could** swim.
−	couldn't + verb	She **couldn't** swim.
?	could ... + verb?	**Could** you swim?

+	was/were able to + verb	I **was able to** swim.
−	was/were not able to + verb	I **wasn't able to** swim.
?	was/were ... able to + verb?	**Were** you **able to** swim?

We use *could* or *was able to* to say that someone had an ability in the past:
*He **could** / **was able to** read when he was three but he **couldn't** / **wasn't able to** catch a ball when he started school.*

⚠ We do not use *could* to talk about one occasion in the past, but we can use *couldn't*:
*She **was able to** (**not** ~~could~~) come to the meeting but she **couldn't** / **wasn't able to** stay for lunch.*
*They **were able to** (**not** ~~could~~) see the match because they had a day off.*

Be able to – other tenses

For ability, *can* is only used in the present tense and *could* is only used in the past.
In all other tenses we use *be able to*:
*I **will be able to** give you a lift on my way to college.* (future)
*They **haven't been able to** contact Mary because of the storms.* (present perfect)
*If you saved enough money, you **would be able to** visit me in New Zealand.* (conditional)
*They hope **to be able to** visit me next year.* (infinitive)

2 Deduction: certainty and possibility

Talking about the present

Certainty

We use:

- *must* when we are sure something is true:
  It **must be** *from Steven because he's in Australia.*
  (= I am certain it is from Steven ...)

- *can't / couldn't* when we are sure something
  is not true:
  It **can't be / couldn't be** *from Steven because that's
  not his writing.* (= I am certain it's not from Steven ...)

Possibility

We use:

- *might / may / could* when we think something is possibly true:
  The parcel **might be** / **may be** / **could be** *from Dad's friend, Tony, because he
  moved to Australia recently.* (= I know Tony lives there and it is possible,
  not certain, that the parcel is from him)

- *might not / may not* when we think something is possibly not true:
  It **may not be** / **might not be** *from anyone that we know.* (= it is possible
  that it is not)

Present	True	Not true
Certainty	*must* + infinitive without *to*	*can't/couldn't* + infinitive without *to*
Possibility	*might/may/could* + infinitive without *to*	*might not/may not* + infinitive without *to*

⚠ Notice that *could* means the same as *might* and *may*,
but *couldn't* is different from *might not* and *may not*.
All the verbs in the box above can also be followed by
be + verb + *-ing*:
Steven **might be travelling** *home at this moment.*

Talking about the past

Certainty

We use:

- *must have* when we are sure something is true:
  Steven **must have arrived** *in Perth by now.*
  (= I am certain he has arrived ...)

- *can't / couldn't have* when we are sure something is
  not true:
  He **can't / couldn't have got** *there yet because it will
  take at least two weeks.* (= I am certain he hasn't
  got there ...)

Possibility

We use:

- *might have / may have / could have* when we think something is possibly true:
  He **might / may / could have stopped** for a few days on the way.
  (= it is possible)

- *might not have / may not have* when we think something is possibly not true:
  He **might / may not have had** time to do everything he wanted. (= it is possible he didn't)

Past	True	Not true
Certainty	*must have* + past participle	*can't have/couldn't have* + past participle
Possibility	*might have/may have/could have* + past participle	*might not have/may not have* + past participle

Notice that *could have* means the same as *might have* and *may have*, but *couldn't have* is different from *might not have* and *may not have*.

Talking about the future

We also use *might (not)*, *may (not)* and *could* when we are not certain about the future:

*James **might** go out to see Steven in Australia next month.*

3 Expectations

When we expect something will happen, we use *should (not)* + infinitive without *to*:

*Steven **should email** us soon.* (= I expect he will email ...)
*It **shouldn't be** too long before we hear from Steven.* (= I expect it will not be too long ...)

We also use *should* when we discover that a situation is not as we expected:

*This postcard is from Melbourne. Steven **should be** in Sydney.* (= he is in Melbourne but I'm surprised because I expected him to be in Sydney)

When we talk about a past situation, we use *should (not) have* + past participle:

*He **should have left** Alice Springs several days ago.* (= I expect he left Alice Springs ...)
*He **shouldn't have had** any trouble finding places to stay.* (= I expect he didn't have any trouble ...)

C Grammar exercises

1 Fill in the gaps with *can('t)*, *could(n't)*, or the correct form of *be able to*. Sometimes there are two possible answers.

The maths genius
Ryan Kennedy speaks to Nick Evans about his amazing talent.

'One day when I was four years old, my father was telling my mother how much money he'd spent and while he was talking I added it all up. They didn't believe that I <u>could / was able to</u> (1) do that because I .... (2) read or write. I'm now at university and I .... (3) still add up complicated sums in my head. I did a maths exam once which I finished so quickly I .... (4) eat a meal in the canteen before the others had finished. Next year we have to write essays and I'm not sure whether I .... (5) do that because I .... (*never*) (6) spell very well. I would like .... (7) use my mathematical skill in a job but I haven't decided what yet. I .... (8) be a maths teacher – I'd enjoy the maths but I'm not sure about the children! I entered a maths quiz show on TV once but when they asked me the questions I .... (9) think of the answers because I was just too nervous. So I .... (10) imagine myself as a TV star. I .... (11) always get work in the supermarket when the tills break down, I suppose!'

2 Complete each sentence about the man in the picture by choosing one of the modal verbs in the box.

can't	could	couldn't	~~may~~	might
must	must			

1 He .... *may* .... be famous.

2 He .... be fit.

3 He .... be married.

4 He .... be disappointed.

5 He .... be Spanish.

6 He .... be an excellent tennis player.

7 He .... be a grandfather.

3 Read about what has happened on a camping trip.

> Two boys are camping with their families near a lake. One day they find an old boat and decide to row out to an uninhabited island. They explore the island until suddenly they realise it's getting dark. They run to find the boat, but it's gone.

Here are some of the things their families say when they don't come back.

1 There can't be much to eat on the island.
2 Someone may have noticed them rowing across the lake.
3 They could be stuck there for days.
4 A fishing boat might see them.
5 They must have forgotten how late it was.
6 They must be getting scared.
7 There may be a cave or hut they can shelter in.
8 The boat could have sunk.
9 Someone may have taken the boat.
10 They can't have tied the boat up properly.

Write the number of the sentences with their meanings, a or b.

a I feel certain about this. 1..
b I think this is possible. ....

4 Fill in the gaps with a modal verb and the correct form of the verb in brackets.

1 Jenny's brother ...._can't be_........ (be) a doctor because he's only 18.
2 Samantha said she'd go for a swim as soon as she reached the seaside so she .... (swim) in the sea right now.
3 I don't seem to have my wallet. I .... (leave) it at home because I paid for my train ticket.
4 A: I left Camilla a message on her answerphone but she hasn't rung yet.
   B: She .... (not listen) to it yet. She usually has a shower as soon as she gets home from work.
5 A: I found this watch in the changing rooms.
   B: It .... (be) Peter's. I think he's got one like that.
6 I can't make the video recorder work. I .... (do) something wrong. Where are the instructions?
7 I can't think what's happened to Annie. She left home hours ago so she .... (be) here by now.
8 These football boots don't fit me any more. My feet .... (grow).

123

9 He remembers when there were fields here instead of houses so he
.... (be) very old.

10 A: I don't really like James. Why did you invite him?

B: Don't worry. He .... (not come) anyway. He said he wasn't
sure what his plans were.

5 **Read this police report about a stolen painting.**

A very small but valuable painting has been stolen from Sidcombe art gallery.
We know it was stolen between 6.00 and 7.30 on Friday evening.
There are several suspects. They all have keys to the art gallery:

The caretaker, Sam Willis
Sam, who has worked at the gallery for 32 years, locked up at 6.30 as usual after the cleaners had left.

A student, Daniel Foreman
When the gallery shut at 5.30 Daniel begged the caretaker to let him stay a bit longer to finish his work. The caretaker saw him coming out of the toilets at 6.30 and told him to leave. He bought an expensive car on Saturday.

A cleaner, Sandra Thompson
Sandra cleaned the offices and the galleries with two other cleaners. They finished at 6.00 and had a chat in the cloakroom before leaving together at 6.15. She says the picture was still there at 6.00.

The shop manager, Sophie Christie
Sophie closed the museum shop at 5.30 but had to stay and wait for a delivery. The driver got delayed in the traffic and arrived at 6.05. He left straight away and Sophie said she left at about 6.15 but nobody saw her leave the building.

The director, William Rees
William was on the phone in his office between 6.00 and 7.00. He says he left the gallery at 7.15 but nobody saw him leave.

The cloakroom attendant, Josie McCartney
The cloakroom closed at 5.30 and Josie tidied up. She was just leaving when the cleaners arrived and she stopped to have a chat with them. They all left together at 6.15.

**Who had the opportunity to steal the painting? Complete these sentences
using *must have*, *can't have*, *couldn't have*, *might have*, *may have* and *could
have*. Use each structure once.**

1 Sam Willis ....*might have stolen*........ the painting because *he was there until 6.30.*

2 Sandra Thompson .... the painting because ....

3 William Rees .... the painting because ....

4 Daniel Foreman .... the painting because ....

5 Sophie Christie .... the painting because ....

6 Josie McCartney .... the painting because ....

D Exam practice

Use of English Part 3

For questions **1–10**, read the text below. Use the word given in capitals at the end of some of the lines to form a word that fits in the gap **in the same line**. There is an example at the beginning (**0**).

THE WOMAN ON THE HILL

A woman has lived in complete (**0**) ...isolation... in a large house **ISOLATE**

on a hill in north Yorkshire for the last fifty years. She (**1**) .... **OCCASION**

visits the nearby village to order food. She walks (**2**) .... **CONFIDENCE**

down the main street but she only speaks to the different shop

(**3**) .... in order to ask for something. Apart from that, she **ASSIST**

doesn't speak to anyone at all. She receives a (**4**) .... of **DELIVER**

wood once a year for her fire but the van driver has (**5**) .... **INSTRUCT**

to leave it on the doorstep and go away. She must have been very

(**6**) .... when she was young and her clothes were probably **ATTRACT**

(**7**) .... 50 years ago. She must be about 70 years old now. **FASHION**

She gives the (**8**) .... from the way she behaves that she **IMPRESS**

might have been an (**9**) .... once. But nobody in the village **ACT**

knows who she is and they are (**10**) .... to find out unless **LIKE**

she tells them.

Grammar focus task

What do you think the villagers say about the woman on the hill? Complete the sentences using *must, might (not), may (not), could(n't)* or *can't*.

1 *She might be* shy.   4 .... any family nearby.

2 .... happy.   5 .... rich.

3 .... lonely.   6 .... an interesting background.

Writing Part 2

You have decided to enter a short story competition organised by an international magazine. The competition rules say that the story must **begin** with the following words:

We found the car with its doors open and a briefcase full of money on the back seat.

Write your **story** in **120–180** words.

Writing hints

This task gives you a chance to practise:
using modal verbs e.g. *can't be, couldn't have, may be, might have, must be.*

Useful words and expressions
to hide, to be in danger, nearby, rich, mysterious, detective, to run away

A Context listening

1 You are going to hear a radio news bulletin. Before you listen, look at the pictures and decide what happened. Put the pictures in order.

1 .... 2 .... 3 .... 4 ....

2 🎧15 Listen and check if you were right.

3 Read this newspaper article.

BURGLARS' 'LUCK' WAS WELL PLANNED

FOUR BURGLARS have escaped from custody only hours after...........being............ **(1)** sentenced to ten years in prison. They .... **(2)** transferred from the law courts in Manchester to Strangeways Prison. They .... **(3)** found guilty of stealing electrical goods and money from shops in the Manchester area. It .... **(4)** thought that they were all members of the same gang. They escaped from the van in which they .... **(5)** transported, when the driver .... **(6)** forced to stop because of a tree across the road. It .... **(7)** believed that the tree .... **(8)** placed there by other members of the gang, who .... **(9)** informed of the route .... **(10)** taken by the van. A full investigation of the events leading to the escape .... **(11)** ordered and anyone with information .... **(12)** asked to contact the police to help with their enquiries.

🎧15 Listen again and fill the gaps. Stop the recording when you need to.

4 How many of the verbs you completed in Exercise 3 are in the passive? ....

B Grammar

1 The passive
How the passive is formed
We form the passive by using the verb *to be* followed by the past participle:

Active:	Passive:
The police officer **saw** the robber at the airport.	The robber **was seen** at the airport.
She's **following** him.	He's **being followed**.
She'**ll catch** him soon.	He'**ll be caught soon**.

Active		Passive
to catch	→	to be caught
to have caught	→	to have been caught
catching	→	being caught
having caught	→	having been caught
am / are / is catching	→	am / are / is being caught
catch(es)	→	am / are / is caught
will catch	→	will be caught
am / are / is going to catch	→	am / are / is going to be caught
has / have caught	→	has / have been caught
caught	→	was / were caught
was catching	→	was being caught
had caught	→	had been caught
would catch	→	would be caught
would have caught	→	would have been caught

2 When the passive is used

The passive is used quite often in English, both in speech and writing.
We use the passive when:

- we don't know who or what did something:
  *My mobile's **been stolen**. (= Someone has stolen my mobile.)*
  *The first tools **were made** in Africa two million years ago. (= People made the first tools ...)*

- the action is more important than who did it:
  *Income tax **was introduced** in England in 1798.*

- it is obvious who or what did something:
  *The thief's **been arrested**.*

We can use *by* + person / thing to show who does the action if this
information is important:
*The robber was seen **by the police officer**. (= **The police officer** saw the
robber.)*

Verbs with two objects

Sometimes an active verb (e.g. *give*) has two objects:
*A witness gave **the police some information**.*

or *A witness gave **some information** to **the police**.*

Either object can be the subject of a passive sentence:
***The police** were given **some information** by a witness.*
or ***Some information** was given to **the police** by a witness.*

3 *To have something done*

When we ask someone else to do something for us, we often use the
structure *to have something done*. It is not usually necessary to say who did
the action:
*The president **had** the car **taken** to the airport (by his driver).*
*(= The president's driver **took** the car to the airport.)*

*I **had** my hair **cut**. (= The hairdresser **cut** my hair.)*
*I'**m having** my kitchen **painted**. (= The decorator **is painting** my kitchen.)*
*They want **to have** their car **fixed**. (= They want the garage **to fix** their car.)*

In informal speech, we sometimes use *get* instead of *have*:
*I **got** my hair **cut**. (= I **had** my hair **cut**.)*

C Grammar exercises

1 Choose the correct sentence from each pair.

1 a The children wanted to be allowed to stay up late and see the fireworks. ✓
  b The children wanted to been allowed to stay up late and see the fireworks.

2 a Our flight was delaying by fog and we missed our connection.
  b Our flight was delayed by fog and we missed our connection.

3 a Lauren was sulking because she hadn't been invited to Ralph's party.
  b Lauren was sulking because she wasn't been invited to Ralph's party.

4 a By the time we arrived at the market, the best fruit had be sold.
  b By the time we arrived at the market, the best fruit had been sold.

5 a While the meal was being prepared we had a drink on the terrace.
  b While the meal was been prepared we had a drink on the terrace.

6 a The new library will be opened by the Mayor next Saturday.
  b The new library will be open by the Mayor next Saturday.

7 a The rock star was sent a chocolate cake by one of his fans.
  b The rock star was sent a chocolate cake to one of his fans.

2 Fill in the gaps with the correct passive form of the verb in brackets.

1 A government minister .... *was found* .... (*find*) guilty of fraud yesterday.

2 It was a lovely surprise to find all the washing-up .... (*do*) while I was asleep.

3 These souvenirs .... (*make*) by children from the local school.

4 I didn't come here in order .... (*make*) a fool of!

5 The votes .... (*count*) right now and we should know the result before midnight.

6 This parcel appears .... (*open*) before it .... (*delivered*).

7 As he .... (*sack*) from his previous job, he found it hard to get another.

8 The judges still have to decide which design .... (*award*) the top prize.

3 Read this report in the *Cybernian News*.

CYBERNIAN NEWS   22 October 3008

| Home | News | Entertainment | Sport | Business | Video Report | Weather | Going Out | TV Guide |

Victory for Cybernia

The victorious Cybernian Inter-galactic Forces report:

Yesterday we invaded Planet Upstart with a large force. We have completely crushed the year-old rebellion there. Our space ships have destroyed ninety per cent of the Upstart space fleet. A special Cybernian task force landed near the central communications building and captured it without difficulty. We immediately broadcast a message to the population announcing that we had liberated them from the illegal Upstart government and we called on them to cooperate with the new government of their planet. We have arrested the rebel leaders and we are taking them back to Cybernia where the government will put them on trial.

Fill in the gaps below with the passive form of the verbs in the *Cybernian News* above.

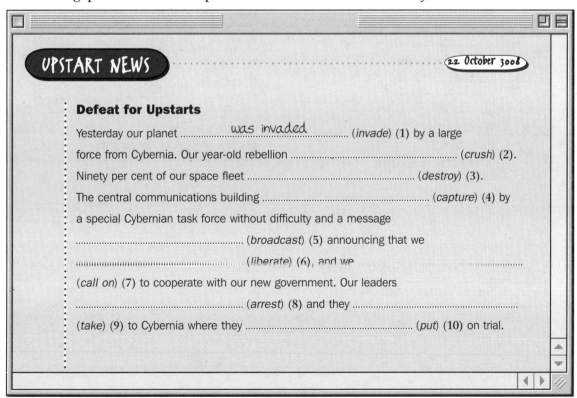

UPSTART NEWS .... *22 October 3008*

Defeat for Upstarts

Yesterday our planet .... *was invaded* .... (*invade*) (1) by a large

force from Cybernia. Our year-old rebellion .... (*crush*) (2).

Ninety per cent of our space fleet .... (*destroy*) (3).

The central communications building .... (*capture*) (4) by

a special Cybernian task force without difficulty and a message

.... (*broadcast*) (5) announcing that we

.... (*liberate*) (6), and we ....

(*call on*) (7) to cooperate with our new government. Our leaders

.... (*arrest*) (8) and they ....

(*take*) (9) to Cybernia where they .... (*put*) (10) on trial.

4 Match the two halves of the conversations and fill in the gaps with the correct form of the verbs in brackets.

1 (I thought those chairs were broken.) ...e...

a (I ....
(*have / colour*).

2 (Your bike's got a flat tyre!) ....

b (Yes, you need ....
(*have / take in*).

3 (This carpet's filthy.) ....

c (I can ....
(*have / fix*) at the cycle shop.

4 (What's happened to your hair?) ....

d (I agree – we should ....
(*have / redecorate*).

5 (I don't like this room. It's too dark.) ....

e (I've ...._had them mended_....
(*have / mend*).

6 (These jeans are much too loose.) ....

f (At the garage. We ....
(*have / service*) before we go away.

7 (What a beautiful garden!) ....

g (We must ....
(*have / clean*).

8 (Where's the car?) ....

h (Thank you. We ....
(*have / design*) by an expert.

D Exam practice

Use of English Part 4

For questions **1–8**, complete the second sentence so that it has a similar meaning to the first sentence, using the word given. **Do not change the word given.** You must use between **two** and **five** words, including the word given. Here is an example (**0**).

0 My grandfather hasn't spoken to me since Sunday.

   SPOKE

   My grandfather .... *last spoke to me on* .... Sunday.

---

1 The students gave a concert after their exams.

   WAS

   A concert .... students after their exams.

2 The children played football and also went swimming.

   ADDITION

   The children played football .... swimming.

3 Jane's neighbours looked after her flat while she was away.

   BY

   Jane's .... her neighbours while she was away.

4 The assistant forgot to pass my message to the shop manager.

   NOT

   My message .... to the shop manager.

5 The teacher said Simon had cheated.

   ACCUSED

   Simon .... his teacher.

6 As children we would often make fires in the garden.

   USED

   When we were children we .... fires in the garden.

7 He had said he'd help us so we were disappointed when he didn't come.

   PROMISED

   Having .... help, we were disappointed
   when he didn't come.

8 My computer needs to be repaired before the weekend.

   HAVE

   I need .... before the weekend.

15

Grammar focus task

Which of the sentences test the passive?

....

Writing Part 2

You have received the following email from a British friend. Read the email and write your reply.

> In your last email you mentioned a local celebration. Can you tell me about it? How are the streets or houses decorated? What do people do?
>
> I look forward to your answer.
>
> Robbie

Write your **email** in **120–180** words.

Writing hints

This task gives you a chance to practise:
using the passive (for example, you can say things like *the streets are decorated* but it is not always necessary to say who does it).

Useful words and expressions
to display, to march, to organise, to plan
atmosphere, balloons, band, costumes, flags, flowers, parade
bright, cheerful, colourful, loud, noisy

Reported speech
tense changes in reported speech; reporting in the same tense; verbs used for reporting; reporting questions

16

A Context listening

1 You are going to hear part of a radio programme. Rachel is a radio reporter in a studio in London. She is talking to a man called James Baker who is taking part in a round-the-world yacht race. What do you think she is asking him? ....

....

....

2 🎧16 Listen and check if you were right.

3 🎧16 Later, Rachel tells a colleague about the conversation. Read what Rachel says, then listen again and fill in the gaps with James's actual words.

1 Rachel: James told me he was about 100 kilometres off the coast of Australia.

James: 'I _'m about_ 100 kilometres off the coast of Australia.'

2 Rachel: He said he hadn't seen another boat for a few days.

James: 'I .... another boat for a few days.'

3 Rachel: He said he thought he might win.

James: 'I .... win.'

4 Rachel: He said there had been a terrible storm.

James: 'There .... a terrible storm.'

5 Rachel: He said he hadn't slept for three days.

James: 'I .... for three days.'

6 Rachel: He told me the sea was calm, the sun was shining.

James: 'The sea .... calm, the sun .... '

7 Rachel: He said that he could sometimes see sharks and dolphins swimming.

James: 'I .... sometimes see sharks and dolphins swimming.'

8 Rachel: He said he would spend two hours in a hot bath.

James: 'I .... two hours in a hot bath.'

9 Rachel: He said he had to get his hair cut.

James: 'I .... hair cut.'

4 🎧16 **Listen again and complete the questions Rachel asked.**

1 Rachel: I asked him where he was.

'Where ....?'

2 Rachel: I asked him if he thought he was going to win.

'Do you .... to win?'

3 Rachel: I asked him what the weather was like.

'What .... like?'

4 Rachel: I asked him if he could see dolphins there.

'.. dolphins there?'

5 **Can you see any pattern to the changes to the tenses in Exercises 3 and 4?**

....

B Grammar

1 Tense changes in reported speech

When we report what someone else said, we are usually reporting at a later time so we change the tenses used by the original speaker:

present simple	→	**past simple**
'I**'m** (**I am**) about 100 kilometres from Australia.'	→	He said (that) he **was** about 100 kilometres from Australia.
present continuous	→	**past continuous**
'The sun**'s** (**is**) shining.'	→	He said (that) the sun **was shining**.
past simple	→	**past perfect**
'There **was** a terrible storm.'	→	He said (that) there**'d** (**had**) **been** a terrible storm.
present perfect	→	**past perfect**
'I **haven't** (**have not**) **seen** another boat.'	→	He said (that) he **hadn't** (**had not**) **seen** another boat.
past perfect	→	**past perfect**
'I **hadn't** (**had not**) **expected** the storm.'	→	He said (that) he **hadn't** (**had not**) **expected** the storm.
am going to	→	**was going to**
'I**'m** (**I am**) **going to** win.'	→	He said (that) he **was going to** win.
will	→	**would**
'I**'ll** (**I will**) **spend** two hours in a bath.'	→	He said (that) he**'d** (he **would**) **spend** two hours in a bath.
can	→	**could**
'I **can** see sharks and dolphins.'	→	He said (that) he **could** see sharks and dolphins.
may	→	**might**
'I **may** win.'	→	He said (that) he **might** win.
might	→	**might**
'I **might** win.'	→	He said (that) he **might** win.
must	→	**had to**
'I **must** get my hair cut.'	→	He said (that) he **had to** get his hair cut.

⚠ These verbs do not change when they are reported at a later time:
could, would, should, might, ought to and *used to*, and verbs in the past perfect.

When we report *must*, we can use either *must* or *had to* in the reported speech but *had to* is more common:
Kate: 'I **must** buy some fruit.' → Kate said she **must** / **had to** buy some fruit.

⚠ We use *must*, not *had to*, when we report:
● a negative:
   Paul: 'You **mustn't** tell Sally our secret.' → Paul said we **mustn't** tell Sally our secret.
● or a deduction:
   Sarah: 'Jim **must** be tired after the flight.' → Sarah said Jim **must** be tired after the flight.

2 Reporting in the same tense

If the reporting verb (e.g. *says*) is in the present tense, we use the same tenses as the original speaker:

Amy: *'I've missed the bus so I'll be a bit late.'* → *Amy says she's missed the bus so she'll be a bit late.*

If the reporting verb (e.g. *said*) is in the past, we sometimes use the same tenses as the original speaker if the situation is still true:

Robert: *'I have three sisters.* → *Robert said he has three sisters.* or
Robert said he had three sisters.

Carlo: *'I'm getting married in June.'*
If we report what Carlo said before June we can say:
Carlo said he is getting married in June. or
Carlo said he was getting married in June.

3 Verbs used for reporting

We often use *say* to report what somebody said:
He said (that) he was going to win.

If there is an object (a noun or a pronoun), *say* must be followed by *to*:
He said to me (that) he was going to win. (**not** *He said me ...*)

When we use *tell* to report what someone said, it is always followed by an object without *to*:
He told them (that) he was going to win. (**not** *He told to them ...* ,
He told that ...)

We often use other reporting verbs instead of *say* and *tell*.
Some are nearly always followed by *that* and usually have no object:
He answered that ..., *He replied that ...*

Some behave like *tell*:
He reminded me (that) ..., *He persuaded me (that) ...*, *He informed me (that) ...*

Some are nearly always followed by *that* and sometimes have an object:
I suggested (to my uncle) that Nicholas joined us for a cup of coffee.
The advertisement mentioned that the pool would open on Saturday.

138

4 Reporting offers, advice and promises

After some reporting verbs the *to* infinitive is usually used:
'I'll be a good leader.' → He **promised to be** a good leader.
'You should vote for me.' → He **advised us to vote** for him.
'We could help you.' → They **offered to help** me.

The infinitive is sometimes used after *tell* and *ask* (➢ see Unit 17):
'Be careful.' → I **told him to be** careful.
'Please don't smoke.' → I **asked her not to smoke**.

5 Reporting questions

Questions are reported using the word order of a statement rather than a question.

Questions with question words (*who*, *what*, etc.) keep these words when they are reported:
'How do you *feel*?' → Rachel **asked** James how he **felt**. (**not** ~~Rachel asked James how did he feel.~~)

'*What's* the weather like?' → Rachel **asked** James what the weather **was** like. (**not** ~~Rachel asked James what was the weather like.~~)

Yes/no questions are reported with *if* or *whether*:
'*Can* you hear me?' → Rachel **asked** James **if** / **whether** he **could** hear her.

'*Is* the weather good?' → Rachel **wanted to know if** / **whether** the weather **was** good.

▲ We use the same structure when we ask politely for information:
Can you tell me what time the next train **leaves**?
I'd like to know if there's a flight to Australia next Thursday.

6 References to time, place etc.

Unless we are speaking on the same day, we have to change references to time when we report what someone said:

yesterday	→ *the day before*
today	→ *that day*
tomorrow	→ *the next / following day*
next week	→ *the following week*
now	→ *then*

Other changes include:

here	→ *there*
this	→ *that*

'I **saw** him **here yesterday**.' → She explained that she **had seen** him **there the day before**.

C Grammar exercises

1 You talk on the phone to a friend, Luke.
    This is what he says.

   1 'I've given up my job.'

   2 'I can easily find another one.'

   3 'I'm going to travel round Africa.'

   4 'I lived there as a child.'

   5 'I might get a part-time job there.'

   6 'I'm packing my bag.'

   7 'I'm really excited.'

   8 'I'll be away for a year.'

   9 'I may stay longer.'

  10 'You could come too.'

After Luke has left, you tell another friend what he said. Complete the sentences.

   1 He said he <u>had given up his job.</u>

   2 He said he ....

   3 He said he ....

   4 He said he ....

   5 He said he ....

   6 He said he ....

   7 He said he ....

   8 He said he ....

   9 He said he ....

  10 He said I ....

2 Match the beginnings and endings of these sentences.

   1 She told ..c..   a I could help my neighbour mend his car.

   2 My sister asked ....   b whether my sister could give me a lift.

   3 I said ....   c me she couldn't afford to come to the theatre.

   4 My parents said .... d to me, 'You shouldn't watch so much TV.'

   5 I wanted to know .... e if I wanted to go on holiday with her.

   6 I told ....   f the dentist that Thursday was the only day I was free.

3 You apply for a job at a children's holiday camp.
When you meet the organiser he asks the following questions:

1 Are you married?
2 How old are you?
3 Which university are you studying at?
4 Where do you come from?
5 Have you worked with children before?
6 What sports do you play?
7 Will you work for at least two months?
8 Can you start immediately?
9 Do you need accommodation?
10 Would you like any more information?

Work abroad
We are looking for enthusiastic and lively young people to work in a children's holiday camp over the summer.

A friend of yours called Miguel is also going to apply for a job at the same camp. Complete the email, telling him what questions you were asked.

Dear Miguel

Good luck with the job application! These are the things the organiser asked me about – he'll probably ask you the same sorts of questions.

He asked me .... if I was married .... (**1**).

He wanted to know .... (**2**),

which university .... (**3**) at

and where .... (**4**). Then he asked

.... (**5**) with children before

and what sports .... (**6**).

He wanted to know .... (**7**) for at least

two months and .... (**8**) immediately.

He asked .... (**9**) accommodation

and wondered .... (**10**) any more information.

Let me know how you get on.

4 A teacher is talking to Andy, a student.

> You need to work harder.

> You could do well.

> Do you study every evening?

> What time do you go to bed?

> You won't get good marks.

> You spend too much time with your friends.

> Have you decided on a career yet?

Later, Andy tells a friend what the teacher said. Complete his sentences.

1 He said *I needed to work harder.*

2 He told ....

3 He wanted to know ....

4 He wondered ....

5 He warned ....

6 He complained ....

7 He asked ....

5 Read what happened to Suzie the other day. Then write the conversation that she actually had.

I travel to college on the same bus every day. The other day when I got on the bus I realised that I had left my purse at home and didn't have the money for the bus fare. But the woman sitting behind me told me not to worry because she would lend me some money. She said the same thing had happened to her the day before. I asked her what she had done. She said someone had lent her the fare and she was going to give it back that day on the bus, so she was happy to do the same for me. She told me I could give the money back to her the following day. I thanked her very much and told her I was very glad she was there.

Woman: *Don't worry. I'll lend you some money.*

....

Suzie: ....

Woman: ....

....

....

Suzie: ....

D Exam practice

Use of English Part 4

For questions **1–8**, complete the second sentence so that it has a similar meaning to the first sentence, using the word given. **Do not change the word given.** You must use between **two** and **five** words, including the word given. Here is an example (**0**).

0 The tourist guide said to us: 'Take a map if you go walking in the hills.'
ADVISED
The tourist guide .... *advised us to take* .... a map if we went walking in the hills.

---

1 Laura didn't try to be friendly to us.
MADE
Laura .... be friendly to us.

2 The weatherman forecast that there would be sunshine all day.
SHINE
The weatherman said: 'The .... all day.'

3 'I haven't heard from Helen for a long time,' Paul said to me.
TOLD
Paul .... heard from Helen for a long time.

4 How about going to the top of the tower to look at the view?
WE
Why .... to the top of the tower to look at the view?

5 'Did you book a room with a balcony?' I asked my mother.
IF
I asked my mother .... a room with a balcony.

6 Jack wanted to know what time they would leave the next day to catch the train.
WE
Jack asked: 'What time .... to catch the train?'

7 The little boy said he could dress himself without any help.
I
The little boy said: '.. without any help.'

8 'Are we meeting David in the morning or the afternoon?' Karen asked.
WHETHER
Karen wondered .... in the morning or the afternoon.

16

Grammar focus task

Which of the sentences test reported speech? ....

In three of the reported sentences the verbs can be replaced with the following: *predict; insist; complain*. Write the reported sentences again using these verbs.

1 ....

2 ....

3 ....

Writing Part 2

Your school is thinking of starting a film club. You went to a meeting where the students talked about how the club would be organised and what it would do. Your English teacher couldn't attend the meeting and wants to know the students' different opinions. He has asked you to write a report explaining what was said. Write your **report** in **120–180** words.

Writing hints

This task gives you a chance to practise:
using reported speech to tell the teacher what the different students said.

Useful words and expressions
to agree, to check, to choose, to decide, to discuss, to suggest, committee, membership fee, review, variety, the best place, the best time

The *to* infinitive and *-ing*

verb + *to* infinitive; verb + infinitive without *to*; verb + *-ing*;
verb + object + *to* infinitive; verb + *that*; adjectives

17

A Context listening

1 You are going to hear a TV chef telling a group of people how to cook something. Look at the picture below which shows the things he uses. Can you guess what the man is going to make?

2 ⓐ17 Listen and check if you were right.

3 ⓐ17 Listen again and fill in the gaps. Stop the recording when you need to.

1 *Continue* ......*doing*...... this ...
2 *Avoid* .... the eggs all at the same time ...
3 ... *keep* .... all the time.
4 ... don't *forget* .... the baking powder ...
5 I *recommend* .... sultanas and apricots ...
6 ... if you *prefer* .... dates or raisins, that's fine.
7 Some people *like* .... some nuts too ...
8 If you *decide* .... nuts, chop them up small.
9 *Remember* .... if the fruit cake is ready ...
10 I *suggest* .... a little lemon juice ...
11 Don't *try* .... the cake ...
12 ... don't *expect* .... much fruit cake left ...

4 What do you notice about the forms of the verbs you have filled in? ....

....

B Grammar

When one verb follows another, the second verb can either be the *-ing* form or the *to* infinitive. It depends on the first verb.

⚠ All the verbs in this unit marked * can also normally be followed by a *that* clause with the same meaning (≻ see B8).

1 Verb + *to* infinitive

> *(can't) afford   *agree   aim   appear   *arrange   attempt choose   *decide   *demand   deserve   fail   *hope   learn manage   neglect   offer   omit   plan   prepare   *pretend *promise   refuse   seem   tend   *threaten   (can't) wait   wish*

*If you **decide to add** nuts ...*
*Don't **expect to have** much cake left.*

Notice how the negative is formed:
*If you decide **not to ice** it ...*

The following verbs + *to* infinitive **always** have an object:

> *dare   encourage   force   invite   order persuade   remind   teach   tell   warn*

*Her father **taught** her **to play** tennis.*
*The teacher **reminded** the children **to bring** their swimming things.*

The following verbs + *to* infinitive **sometimes** have an object:

> *want   ask   *expect   beg   help   *intend*

*We **expected to be late**. or We **expected** Tom **to be** late.*
*We **wanted to stay** longer. or We **wanted** them **to stay** longer.*

⚠ *Would like, would love, would prefer* etc. are also followed by the *to* infinitive (≻ see B4).

2 Verb + infinitive without *to*

Modal verbs (*can, could, may, might, must, needn't, shall, should, will, would*), *had better* and *would rather* are followed by the infinitive without *to* (≻ see also Units 12–14):
*You **should add** them slowly.*
*You **needn't include** nuts.*

Help can be followed by the infinitive with or without *to*:
*We **helped** them **(to) start** their car.*

Make and *let* (always with an object) are followed by the infinitive without *to*:
Let the cake **cool** for half an hour.
I **made** my sister **help** with the cooking.

▲ The passive form of *make* is followed by the *to* infinitive:
I **was made to do** my homework.

3 Verb + *-ing*

*admit	*appreciate	avoid	can't face	can't help	can't stand	carry on
*confess	*consider	delay	*deny	detest	dislike	enjoy	fancy
feel like	finish	give up	*imagine	involve	keep/keep on	*mention
(not) mind	miss	postpone	practise	put off	risk	resist	*suggest

I **enjoy making** it.
Avoid adding the eggs ...
Keep doing this ...
I **suggest adding** a little lemon juice ...

Notice how the negative is formed:
*If you don't leave immediately, you risk **not catching** your plane.*
*Can you imagine **not having** a car nowadays?*

4 Verbs + *to* infinitive or *-ing* (with no difference in meaning)

attempt	begin	can't bear	continue	hate
like	love	prefer	*propose	start

Continue adding the flour. or **Continue to add** the flour.
I **prefer using** apricots. or I **prefer to use** apricots.
I **love making** cakes. or I **love to make** cakes.

Two *-ing* forms do not usually follow each other:
*I was **starting to make** a cake when the phone rang.* (**not** ~~I was starting making a cake ...~~)

Like + *to* infinitive has a slightly different meaning from *like* + *-ing*:
I **like to catch** the early bus on Mondays. (= this is a good plan or it's a habit, but not necessarily something I enjoy)
I **like dancing**. (= I enjoy it)

▲ *Like*, *prefer*, *hate* and *love* can be followed by the *to* infinitive or *-ing*, but *would like*, *would prefer*, *would hate* and *would love* are always followed by the *to* infinitive:
She **would like to go out** but we **would prefer to stay** in.

5 Verb + *to* infinitive or *-ing* (with a difference in meaning)

The following verbs have two different meanings depending on the verb form that follows:

> *remember   *forget   *regret   try   stop   mean   go on

Verb + *to* infinitive	**Verb + *-ing***
Remember to check *whether the cake is ready.* (= an action which will be necessary)	*I* **remember checking** *that I had my keys when I left the house.* (= a memory of a past action)
Don't **forget to add** *the baking powder.* (= an action which will be necessary)	*I'll never* **forget going** *to school on my own for the first time.* (= a memory of a past action)
I **regret to inform** *you that your application was unsuccessful.* (= I am sorry to tell you ...)	*We* **regret sending** *our daughter to that school.* (= we wish we hadn't)
She **stopped to have** *a rest.* (= in order to have a rest)	**Stop beating** *when the mixture is pale and fluffy.* (= finish doing it)
They don't **mean to upset** *you.* (= they don't intend to)	*If you go by train that* **means taking** *a taxi to the station.* (= it involves)
He **went on to tell** *them how to make a different cake.* (= the next thing he did was to tell them ...)	*They* **went on cycling** *until they reached the farm.* (= they continued)
Try to ice *the cake quickly.* (= attempt to do it quickly if you can)	**Try adding** *nuts as it will improve the flavour.* (= as an experiment)

6 Verb + object + *to* infinitive or no object + *-ing*

The following verbs are followed by the *to* infinitive when they have an object and by *-ing* when they have no object:

> *advise   allow   forbid   permit   *recommend

I **recommend using** *apricots.* or *I* **recommend you to use** *apricots.*
I **advise adding** *nuts.* or *I* **advise you to add** *nuts.*

7 Verb + *-ing* or infinitive without *to* (with a difference in meaning)

The following verbs always have an object (these are mainly to do with the senses):

> *feel   hear   notice   see   watch*

Notice the difference in meaning between verb + *-ing* and verb + infinitive without *to*:

*I **watched** the boys **playing** football.* (= an activity continuing over a period of time)
*I **watched** the boy **kick** the football into the road.* (= a short completed action)

*She **heard** her mother **singing** as she came downstairs.* (= continuing action)
*She **heard** the doorbell **ring**.* (= a short completed action)

8 Verb + *that* clause

All the verbs marked * in this unit can also be followed by a *that* clause with the same meaning:

*I **suggest adding** some lemon juice.* = *I **suggest (that) you add** some lemon juice.*
*I **recommend using** sultanas and apricots.* = *I **recommend (that) you use** sultanas and apricots.*
*They **agreed to leave** early.* = *They **agreed (that) they would leave** early.*

9 Adjectives

The following adjectives are usually followed by the *to* infinitive: *afraid, cheap, *dangerous, delighted, *difficult, *easy, expensive, happy, impossible, interesting, *nice, pleased, possible, safe, sorry, surprised*:
*I'm **surprised to see** you here.*

The adjectives marked * can sometimes also be followed by *-ing* with the same meaning.
*It's **nice meeting** friends after school.*
or *It's **nice to meet** friends after school.*

> See also Unit 22, B1 for adjectives followed by a preposition + *-ing* or a noun.

17

C Grammar exercises

1 Complete this conversation using the verbs in brackets.

Andy: I've decided ..to leave.. (*leave*) **(1)** my job next month.

Sally: But I thought you enjoyed .... (*work*) **(2)** in an architect's office.

Andy: Oh, I do. But I feel like .... (*do*) **(3)** something different for a while.

Sally: Didn't you promise .... (*stay*) **(4)** there at least two years?

Andy: Yes, I did but I just can't stand .... (*work*) **(5)** with those people. One of them refuses .... (*stop*) **(6)** talking while she works, another one keeps .... (*sing*) **(7)** to himself. And then there's a man who attempts .... (*tell*) **(8)** awful jokes all the time which he always gets wrong. I detest .... (*work*) **(9)** with all that noise around me.

Sally: It sounds quite a cheerful place to me. Can't you manage .... (*ignore*) **(10)** them and get on with your work?

Andy: No, I can't. I just can't carry on .... (*go*) **(11)** there every day. I'm hoping .... (*go*) **(12)** abroad for a bit.

Sally: Well, good luck.

2 Underline the correct form of the verb.

1 I noticed the man *drop* / *dropping* / *to drop* his ticket so I picked it up for him.

2 The tour guide advised the tourists not *take* / *taking* / *to take* too much money out with them.

3 I heard the horses *come* / *coming* / *to come* down the lane so I waited for them to pass before driving on.

4 The old man said he would love *have* / *having* / *to have* the chance to fly in an aeroplane again.

5 Don't make the children *come* / *coming* / *to come* with us if they don't want to.

6 I saw the boy *jump* / *jumping* / *to jump* into the lake before anyone could stop him.

7 I recommend *phone* / *phoning* / *to phone* the hotel before you set off.

8 My father used to forbid us *play* / *playing* / *to play* in those woods.

9 The college only allows *smoke* / *smoking* / *to smoke* in the common room.

10 It was my drama teacher who encouraged me *become* / *becoming* / *to become* an actor.

3 Fill in the gaps with a suitable verb in the correct form.

1 If I go to the wedding it will mean ....*buying*.... a new dress.

2 Please try .... to the airport in good time – I'll be nervous waiting for you.

3 Will you stop .... that noise? I'm trying .... this book.

4 I forgot .... a table at the restaurant and it was full when we got there.

5 The two children went on .... their ball against the wall although they had been told several times to stop.

6 We regret .... you that the course you applied for is now full.

7 Tommy says he didn't come to the party because he didn't know about it but I remember .... him.

8 When you go out, remember .... the key with your neighbour because I haven't got one.

9 Why don't you try .... glasses? Then you might not get so many headaches.

10 I saw Philip when I was in the park so I stopped .... to him.

11 I meant .... you a postcard but I didn't have time.

12 I regret not .... to Egypt with my sister because she says it was a really great trip.

13 After getting a degree in biology, my son went on .... a book about monkeys.

14 I shall never forget .... the sun come up over the mountains when I was in the Himalayas.

4 Tony is about to go on a trip to your home town. He knows nothing about your country. Complete these sentences giving him some advice.

1 I advise you (*visit*) ...... *to visit the market in Green Street.* ......

2 You'll enjoy (*see*) ....

3 Don't miss (*go*) ....

4 Before you go, don't forget (*buy*) ....

5 While you're there, try (*eat*) ....

6 You must promise ....

7 Avoid ....

8 Remember ....

D Exam practice

Use of English Part 1

For questions **1–12**, read the text below and decide which answer (**A, B, C** or **D**) best fits each gap. There is an example at the beginning (**0**).

0 **A** round   **B** through   **C** across   **D** over

BALLOON ADVENTURE

Brian Jones is the British half of the first team to go (**0**) ..A.. the world in a balloon. He and his Swiss co-pilot have written an account of the 19-day expedition they (**1**) .... in March 1999. It was an astonishing triumph. Nobody (**2**) .... them to finish the voyage. They (**3**) .... with poisonous fumes, temperatures of minus 50 degrees Celsius and an Atlantic crossing with (**4**) .... any fuel.

Fourteen years (**5**) .... , Brian was a reasonably successful businessman, but he tired of his furniture business and (**6**) .... to buy a balloon. Before long he was one of the country's (**7**) .... balloon instructors and pilots. Why did he risk everything for one trip? He says he was not a very confident child: 'At seven a friend (**8**) .... me to go down a water slide. I still (**9**) .... being absolutely terrified. I couldn't swim and I have never learnt to swim properly.' He thinks everyone should face their greatest (**10**) .... and that is one reason why he went up in the balloon. Six of the 19 days they were (**11**) .... the air were spent staring at the Pacific Ocean – 8,000 miles of water. Brian says he won't (**12**) .... to do it again because there are so many other things he wants to do.

1 **A** followed	**B** succeeded	**C** performed	**D** completed
2 **A** expected	**B** hoped	**C** intended	**D** admitted
3 **A** did away	**B** got along	**C** kept up	**D** put up
4 **A** almost	**B** hardly	**C** quite	**D** rather
5 **A** after	**B** ago	**C** since	**D** past
6 **A** thought	**B** considered	**C** afforded	**D** decided
7 **A** unique	**B** preferable	**C** leading	**D** suitable
8 **A** demanded	**B** dared	**C** threatened	**D** wished

 9 **A** forget   **B** remind   **C** remember   **D** regret

10 **A** fears   **B** suspicions   **C** disturbances   **D** frights

11 **A** on   **B** in   **C** by   **D** to

12 **A** delay   **B** imagine   **C** attempt   **D** suggest

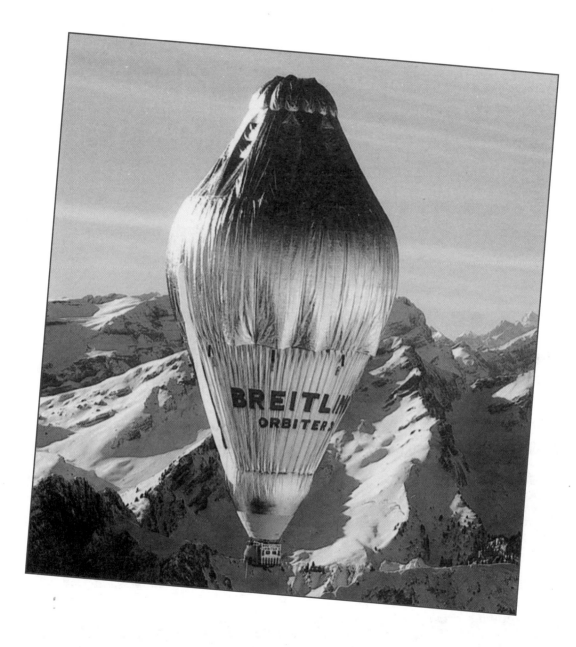

These are some words from the exam task and answers. Without looking back, put them into the right columns.

(can't) afford   admit   appreciate   attempt   consider
dare   decide   delay   demand   enjoy   expect   fancy
hope   imagine   suggest   threaten   want   wish

Verbs followed by *to* infinitive	Verbs followed by *-ing*
can't afford	admit

Writing Part 2

Your class has recently had a discussion and your teacher has asked you to write an essay giving your own views on the following statement:

Young people are given too much freedom nowadays by their parents.

Write your **essay** in **120–180** words.

This task gives you a chance to practise:
verbs followed by *-ing* and *to* infinitive.

Useful words and expressions
admit, advise, afford, agree, allow, forbid, force, give up, order, permit, persuade, promise, suggest, tell, warn
clothes, drinking, driving, parties, smoking

A Context listening

1 You are going to hear a girl called Donna talking about a pop group she
was in. Look at these pictures, which show what happened. Read the
sentences below and put them in the correct order according to the pictures.

a Bella, Jo and Zoe made plans without telling Donna. ☐

b Donna had some problems. ☐

c Donna left the group. ☐

d Donna was in a pop group with Bella, Jo and Zoe. ☐

e Donna had a row with the other girls. ☐

f One night the group didn't perform. ☐

2 ⏺18 Listen and check if you were right.

3 ⏺18 Read the definitions 1–11. They all refer to phrasal verbs which Donna uses.
Listen again and complete the phrasal verbs. Stop the recording when you need to.

1 *separate* = ...break.... up

2 *have a good relationship* = ... on with

3 *rely on* = ... on

4 *support* = ... up

5 *take care of* = ... after

6 *continue* = ... on

7 *cancel* = ... off

8 *meet* = ... together

9 *discuss* = ... over

10 *make someone leave* = ... out

11 *surrender* = ... in

18

B Grammar

1 Meaning and form

The meaning of some phrasal verbs is clear:

*I **picked up** the phone.* (*picked* and *up* have their normal meanings)

Many phrasal verbs are idiomatic and you have to learn what they mean.
They may contain the same verb but have different meanings, depending
on the preposition or adverb which follows:

*He **turned back** because he had left something at home.* (= changed direction)
*He **turned down** the invitation because he was feeling tired.* (= refused)
*They **turned up** unexpectedly.* (= arrived)

Some phrasal verbs have several meanings:

*She **put on** her clothes.* (= she got dressed)
*She **put on** weight.* (= her weight increased)
*She **put on** the light.* (= she switched the light on)
*The students **put on** a play.* (= performed)

> See Appendix 1 for a list of phrasal verbs you should understand.

The form of phrasal verbs can vary.
Some verbs have **two parts**: a verb (e.g. *do*, *go*) and another word
(sometimes called a particle) which can be an adverb (e.g. *back*, *out*) or a
preposition (e.g. *at*, *into*, *from*).
Some verbs have **three parts**: a verb (e.g. *come*), an adverb (e.g. *up*) and a
preposition (e.g. *against*).

Phrasal verbs behave differently depending on whether they are
a verb + preposition, a verb + adverb, or a verb + adverb + preposition.

2 Verb + preposition

When a phrasal verb consists of a verb and a preposition:
- it always has an object.
- the object (noun or pronoun) always goes after the preposition (the verb
  and preposition can't be separated):
  *The rest of the group **looked after** Donna.* (**not** *looked Donna after*)
  *I **counted on** them.* (**not** *counted them on*)
  *They **went over** their plans.* (**not** *went their plans over*)
  *I really **cared about** them.* (**not** *cared them about*)

3 Verb + adverb

When a phrasal verb consists of a verb and its adverb:
- it doesn't always have an object:
  *They **got together** every Monday morning.*
  *They **carried on** without me.*

- the object (when it is a noun) can come before or after the adverb (the verb and adverb can be separated):
  *They **didn't back** Donna **up** when she was in trouble.*
  or *They **didn't back up** Donna.*

  *They wanted to **throw** Donna **out** because of what she did.*
  or *They wanted to **throw out** Donna.*

  *They **called** the concert **off**.* or *They **called off** the concert.*

- the object (when it is a pronoun) must go between the verb and the adverb:
  *They **backed** me **up**.* (**not** ~~backed up me~~)
  *They wanted to **throw** me **out**.* (**not** ~~throw out me~~)
  *They couldn't do the concert without her so they **called** it **off**.* (**not** ~~called off it~~)

- the object (when it is very long) is usually put after the adverb:
  *They **called off** the concert, which had already been postponed twice.*
  (**not** ~~called the concert, which had already been postponed twice, off~~)

▲ Some phrasal verbs have two meanings and take an object with one meaning and no object with the other meaning, e.g. *give in*:
*I won't **give in** until they pay me what they owe.*
(verb + adverb + no object = surrender)
*I **gave in** my homework on time.*
(verb + adverb + object = hand it to the teacher)

▲ Most particles (e.g. *down, in, off, on, past, through, up*, etc.) can be either prepositions or adverbs:
*She **picked** the book **up**.* or *She **picked up** the book.*
(verb + adverb can be separated)
*She **went up** the stairs.* (**not** ~~went the stairs up~~)
(verb + preposition can't be separated)

You can check if a phrasal verb is a verb + preposition or a verb + adverb by looking in a good dictionary.

4 Verb + adverb + preposition

When a phrasal verb consists of three parts:
- it always has an object.
- the object (noun or pronoun) always goes after the phrasal verb (the three parts can't be separated):
  *I always **got on with** the other members of the group.*
  *... I **came up against** some problems ...*
  *I **put up with** this for a while.*
  *They're not going to **get away with** it.*

C Grammar exercises

You can use your dictionary and Appendix 1 to do these exercises if you need to.

1 Complete these sentences with words from the box to make phrasal verbs with *get*.

> at   away with   by   down   on   ~~out of~~   over   round   round to   through

1 Simon always manages to (get ......*out of*......) doing the washing-up because
  he says he has a lot of homework.

2 My grandfather (got ....) the flu very quickly because he's such a fit man.

3 Maria's daughters must be on the phone all the time because I can never
  (get ....) when I try to ring her.

4 I tried to take a message but I didn't (get ....) everything Paula said.

5 Peter hasn't had much success with jobs so far but I'm sure he'll (get ....)
  in his new one.

6 I finally (got ....) watching the video of a film I recorded two months ago.

7 People think they need lots of money but you can (get ....) with very little.

8 We don't keep things on the top shelf because we can't (get ....) them
  without standing on the table.

9 The news of Billy and Jane's engagement (got ....) the office very quickly.

10 I can never (get ....) telling a lie because my face always goes bright red.

2 Fill in the gaps with phrasal verbs from the box which mean the same as the verbs
in brackets.

> ~~care for~~   carry on   cut down   fill in   put off
> ring up   set off   take in   turn down   turn up

I had been doing the same job for years and I didn't really ......*care for*...... (*like*) (1) it
any more but it was extremely well paid. Then one day I decided to look for another
job, realising I would need to .... (*reduce*) (2) what I spent on luxuries.
I .... (*completed*) (3) lots of forms but all my applications were
.... (*rejected*) (4). I .... (*continued*) (5) looking for a job but nothing
suitable .... (*appeared*) (6) so I booked a holiday. The day before I was due to
.... (*leave*) (7) I was .... (*telephoned*) (8) by a TV company who
asked me to go for an interview the next day. I .... (*postponed*) (9) my holiday
immediately. It was the job of my dreams. I could hardly .... (*absorb*) (10)
the news when they offered it to me. And I never went on that holiday.

3 Fill in the gaps with the correct form of verbs in the box to make phrasal verbs.

> ~~break~~   come   do   fall   get   give
> go   hand   look   make   turn   work

On the Run

The film *On the Run* tells the story of three prisoners who manage to ....break.... (1) out of a jail on an island. One of the prison guards is not very honest. The prisoners .... (2) round him by offering him money and he .... (3) over some keys. They .... (4) for a nearby forest and decide to wait there for a bit because they haven't had time to .... (5) out a plan. While they .... (6) over the possibilities, a woman who is walking through the forest .... (7) across them and promises to bring them food each day if they help her to .... (8) for wood. They are hungry and are not very good at .... (9) without their dinner. She is also very beautiful so they .... (10) in with her idea. But on the third day the woman .... (11) up with a policeman. She .... (12) away their secret in order to get the reward offered.

4 **a** Look up the phrasal verbs in italics in a dictionary and decide if they are *verb + preposition* or *verb + adverb* or *verb + adverb + preposition*. Then decide if the underlined noun can go in any other place and rewrite the sentences where possible.

1 I can't *give up* <u>chocolate</u> however hard I try.
   <u>Verb + adverb: I can't give chocolate up however hard I try.</u>

2 He was so angry he *broke up* <u>the sculpture</u> into small pieces.
   ....

3 The girl *went over* <u>her work</u> several times before she was satisfied.
   ....

4 We've *run out of* <u>biscuits</u> – could you fetch some more?
   ....

5 I could tell from his expression that he'd *made up* <u>the excuse</u>.
   ....

6 I can't *put up with* that noise any longer.

....

7 I *looked after* the children while their mother was busy.

....

8 Don't forget to *put out* the lights when you leave.

....

9 With her dark eyes and hair, she *takes after* her father.

....

10 That shop *puts up* its prices every month.

....

b **Replace each of the nouns in brackets with a pronoun and rewrite the sentences with the pronoun in the correct place.**

1 I can't give up (chocolate) however hard I try.
I can't give it up however hard I try.

2 He was so angry he broke up (the sculpture) into small pieces.

....

3 The girl went over (her work) several times before she was satisfied.

....

4 We've run out of (biscuits) – could you fetch some more?

....

5 I could tell from his expression that he'd made up (the excuse).

....

6 I can't put up with (that noise) any longer.

....

7 I looked after (the children) while their mother was busy.

....

8 Don't forget to put out (the lights) when you leave.

....

9 With her dark eyes and hair, she takes after (her father).

....

10 That shop puts up (its prices) every month.

....

D Exam practice

Use of English Part 4

For questions **1–8**, complete the second sentence so that it has a similar meaning to the first sentence, using the word given. **Do not change the word given.** You must use between **two** and **five** words, including the word given. Here is an example (**0**).

0 It is essential that all library books are returned by July 5th.

BRING

You ....*must bring back*............ all library books by July 5th.

---

1 Maria had to go away unexpectedly so they postponed the wedding for a month.

OFF

Maria had to go away unexpectedly so they .... for a month.

2 It isn't worth asking Philip to tidy up.

POINT

There's .... Philip to tidy up.

3 I suggest phoning your aunt before turning up at her house.

YOU

I suggest .... your aunt before turning up at her house.

4 When I tried to make changes to the school timetable, I was faced with a lot of opposition.

AGAINST

When I tried to make changes to the school timetable, I .... a lot of opposition.

5 Dr Brown was respected by his grandchildren who all wanted to be like him.

UP

Dr Brown's grandchildren .... him and all wanted to be like him.

6 They had just started their walk when it began to pour with rain.

SET

They had just .... their walk when it began to pour with rain.

7 You'll miss your plane if you don't hurry up.

UNLESS

You'll miss your plane .... up.

8 I really can't bear to live near the railway line any longer.

PUT

I really can't .... near the railway line any longer.

18

Grammar focus task

In which of the sentences is a phrasal verb used? ....

Rewrite the following sentences using the phrasal verbs from the exam task.

1 They arrived unexpectedly while we were having dinner.
  They turned up while we were having dinner.

2 By the time we started our journey it was getting dark.

3 I really can't bear to sit in this heat any longer.

4 This desk is for books which are being returned to the library.

5 When I'd nearly finished mending the car, I was faced with a problem I couldn't solve.

6 James had always respected his boss.

7 The play was postponed for a week because the main actor was ill.

Writing Part 1

You are studying in an English-speaking country and have received this email from a hotel manager. Read the email and the notes you have made. Then write a reply using **all** your notes.

From: P Rogers
Date: 3 June
Subject: Party booking 26 June

You phoned to book a room for your end-of-term party.
I need some more information.

We have two rooms available on Friday 26th. One is free
from 5 pm till 10.30 and is on the sixth floor with a balcony. — *Say which and why*
You could have the other room between 7 pm and midnight.
That's on the ground floor and has doors to the garden, but it
is slightly smaller.

We can provide food, please let me know what you would like. — *Give details*

I assume you want music. We have equipment, but I need to
know if you want one of our staff to operate it. — *No, because …*

Do you plan to decorate the room? If so, can you tell me how
long it will take for you to do this? — *Yes! Explain*

Please let me know as soon as possible.

Regards

Peter Rogers

Write an **email** of between **120–150** words in a style appropriate for the situation.

Writing hints

This task gives you a chance to practise:
using some of the following phrasal verbs: *ask for, carry on / go on, clear up, do
without, get together, get on with, look after, put up, ring up, run out of, see about,
set up, take down, turn off, work out.*

Useful words and expressions
to hire, snacks, crisps, noise, nuts, dancing, soft drinks, waiter, disc jockey, fresh air

A Context listening

1 You are going to hear a spy, known as Double X, talking to his boss, Mr Seymour, about a photograph which Mr Seymour gives him. Mr Seymour is asking Double X to do something. Before you listen, guess what he is asking. ....

2 🔊19 Listen to the beginning of the conversation and check if you were right.

3 🔊19 Listen to the whole conversation and answer these questions.
Play the recording twice if you need to.

1 What does Mr Seymour want Double X to do? <u>To follow a man and find out all about him.</u>

2 Why doesn't Mr Seymour give Double X a better photo? ....

3 Who sent the photo to Mr Seymour? ....

4 Why is the photo fuzzy? ....

5 How is it possible to make the picture clearer? ....

6 Who is in the photo? ....

7 Can you guess who sent the photo to Mr Seymour, and why? ....

4 🔊19 Listen again and fill in the gaps.

1 If you .... him, I .... extremely pleased.

2 If we .... a better picture, we .... it to you.

3 If she .... us that, I .... to ask for your help.

4 It .... me somewhere to start if I .... where she'd phoned from.

5 It .... a bit clearer if you .... at it with your eyes half closed.

5 Look at the sentences in Exercise 4 and answer these questions.

1 Look at sentence 5. Which tense is used after *if*? ....

2 Look at sentence 1. Which tense is used after *if*? ....

3 Look at sentences 2 and 4. Which tense is used after *if*? ....

4 Look at sentence 3. Which tense is used after *if*? ....

B Grammar

Conditional sentences tell us a condition (*if ...*)* and its consequence.
The tenses we use depend on:

- whether the condition and its consequence are real or imaginary.
- whether they are generally true, or linked to a particular event.

Often the condition comes before the consequence, but sometimes the consequence comes first. When the condition comes first, it is followed by a comma. When the consequence comes first, we don't use a comma.

We can divide conditionals into four groups.

1 Zero conditional

If + present tense, + present tense	*If you're in love, nothing else matters.*
present tense (no comma) + *if* + present tense	*Nothing else matters if you're in love.*

We use this to state general truths. *If* means the same as *when* in these sentences:
If/When you're in love, nothing else matters. = *Nothing else matters if/when you're in love.*
If/When we heat ice, it melts. = *Ice melts if/when we heat it.*

2 First conditional

If + present tense, + future tense	*If you leave me, I'll die of a broken heart.*
future tense (no comma) + *if* + present tense	*I'll die of a broken heart if you leave me.*
imperative condition + *and* + future tense	*Leave me and I'll die of a broken heart.*

We use this for a condition which we believe is possible:
If you leave me, I'll die of a broken heart. (**not** *If you'll leave*) (= he hopes she won't leave)
▲ *If* does **not** mean the same as *when* in sentences like these:
When you leave me, I'll die of a broken heart (= he knows she's going to leave)

Sometimes we use the imperative to express this kind of condition (the imperative always comes first):
Leave me and I'll die of a broken heart.

3 Second conditional

If + past tense, + *would* + verb	*If you left me, I would die of a broken heart.*
would + verb (no comma) + *if* + past tense	*I would die of a broken heart if you left me.*

We use this for an imaginary condition, which we believe to be impossible or improbable. We use the past tense although the speaker is thinking about the present or future:
If you left me, I'd (would) die of a broken heart. (but I believe you won't leave me, so my heart is safe)

* For other words like *if* which introduce conditions, see Unit 20.

*All the world **would seem** wonderful **if** you **were** in love.* (but the speaker
believes you're not in love, so everything doesn't seem wonderful)
*I'd (would) love you forever **if** you **bought** me a diamond ring.* (but I don't
expect you will buy me one, so I may not love you forever!)

▲ With *I* we often use *were* instead of *was* in conditional sentences,
especially when we write. It is more formal:

*If **I was/were** you, I wouldn't phone him.*

4 Third conditional

If + past perfect tense, + *would have* + past participle	*If you **had left** me, I **would have died** of a broken heart.*
would have + past participle (no comma) + *if* + past perfect tense	*I **would have died** of a broken heart **if** you **had left** me.*

We use this to talk about past events which cannot be changed, so we know
that the condition is impossible and its consequence is imaginary:
If you'd (had) left me, I'd (would) have died of a broken heart. (but you didn't
leave me, so I was all right)
*All the world **would have seemed** wonderful **if** you'd (had) **been** in love.* (but the
speaker knows you were not in love so everything didn't seem wonderful)
*I'd (would) have loved you forever **if** you'd (had) **bought** me a diamond ring.*
(but you didn't buy me one, so I stopped loving you!)

▲ Other modal verbs like *might* and *could* are sometimes used instead of *would*
in second and third conditional sentences:
*I **might** love you if you bought me a diamond ring.*
*I **could** have loved you forever if you'd (had) bought me a diamond ring.*

5 Mixed conditionals

We sometimes meet sentences which contain a mixture of second and third
conditionals because of their particular context:
*If my boyfriend **gave** me diamonds like that, I'd **have married** him by now.*
(= my boyfriend does not give me diamonds like that so I haven't married him)
*If the weather **had been** fine last week, there **would be** roses in my garden.*
(= the weather was bad last week so there are no roses in my garden now)
*Lesley **wouldn't have missed** the bus **if** she **was** better organised.*
(= Lesley missed the bus because she is a badly organised person)

C Grammar exercises

1 Match the beginnings and endings of these sentences.

1 The house wouldn't have been such a mess ....j....   **a** if she wasn't such a jealous type.

2 If Mike had listened to his father, ...   **b** I'd probably have lots of boyfriends.

3 I would quite like Juno ....   **c** they usually wait until their parents go out.

4 If Dave didn't work so much, ...   **d** and you'll never forget his face.

5 We would have arrived early ....   **e** he wouldn't have got into trouble.

6 If I was as lovely as Nancy, ...   **f** I still wouldn't love you!

7 If teenagers want to have a party, ...   **g** she'll get a nasty surprise.

8 If Sally opens that door, ...   **h** if the roads had been less busy.

9 Take one look at Alan ....   **i** he wouldn't get so tired.

10 If you were as handsome as a film star, ...   **j** if the guests hadn't been careless.

2 Put the verbs in brackets into the correct form.

1 I won't help you with your homework if you ....*don't tidy*........ (*not tidy*) your bedroom.

2 You'll need a visa if you .... (*want*) to travel to China.

3 If he .... (*care*) about other people's feelings, he wouldn't behave that way.

4 She .... (*not be*) successful if she doesn't learn to control her temper.

5 If I'd known you were such a gossip, I .... (*not tell*) you my secret.

6 They would work harder if they .... (*not be*) so tired.

7 The boss .... (*be*) furious if he'd found out what you were up to.

8 If the temperature .... (*fall*) below freezing, water turns to ice.

9 If they .... (*not expect*) delays, they wouldn't have set off so early.

10 Open the envelope and we .... (*discover*) what John has been doing.

3 Complete the sentences for each picture using the third conditional, to show how missing her bus one day resulted in a new job for Zoe.

① I'LL GO INTO THIS CAFÉ.
ZOE MISSED HER BUS.

② I'LL SIT OPPOSITE THAT MAN.
THERE WASN'T A FREE TABLE.

③ THE SERVICE IS REALLY SLOW!
SHE HAD TO WAIT FOR HER COFFEE.

④ I'M BORED.
SHE READ THE BACK OF THE MAN'S PAPER.

⑤ I'LL APPLY FOR THAT JOB.
SHE NOTICED AN ADVERTISEMENT.

1 If she hadn't missed her bus, she wouldn't <u>have gone into the café.</u>
2 If there had been a free table, she ....
3 ...., she wouldn't have had to wait for her coffee.
4 ...., she wouldn't have read the back of the man's paper.
5 If she hadn't noticed the advertisement, ...

4 Complete these sentences, using your own ideas.

1 If I was incredibly good-looking <u>my friends would be jealous of me.</u>
2 I wouldn't have to study English if ....
3 If I pass First Certificate ....
4 I won't pass my exam if ....
5 If my teacher didn't ....
6 If I hadn't ....
7 If English grammar ....
8 You have to .... if ....
9 If you listen to English pop songs ....
10 If I complete this sentence quickly ....

169

Reading Part 2

You are going to read a magazine article about a young woman who works in a nursery school. Seven sentences have been removed from the article. Choose from the sentences **A–H** the one which fits each gap (**1–7**). There is one extra sentence which you do not need to use.

Chances – *nursery school teacher Sarah Oliver tells how a chance meeting changed her life.*

I really love my job, it makes me feel good at the beginning of every week, because I love working with small children and I enjoy the challenges that arise. But I also think what I do is something worthwhile and there was a time when I thought I would never have that sort of career.

I wasn't very good at school, I mean, I didn't like studying much, so I didn't try very hard, I thought I was the sort of person who couldn't do school work, I suppose. **1** [ ] But in my final term I started thinking what I might do and I realised that I didn't have much to offer. If I'd worked harder, I would have had better grades, but it was too late. I just accepted that I wasn't the type to have a career.

Then I thought, well, I've spent every holiday for the past five years helping my mum – I've got two brothers and a sister, all much younger than me. **2** [ ] Their father worked abroad and their mother had some high-powered job in an insurance company. I did most of the housework and I had a lot of responsibility for the children although I was only sixteen.

It wasn't too bad at first, because I was living at home and my mum gave me advice and looked after me when I got home exhausted. **3** [ ]

The problems began really when I agreed to live in, so that I would be there if my boss had to go out for business in the evening. What was supposed to happen was, if I had to work extra hours one week,

she'd give me time off the next. But unfortunately, it didn't often work out. **4** [ ] I felt trapped, because if I walked out there wouldn't be anyone to look after them.

Anyway, one Sunday, I was in the park with them, while their parents were on yet another business trip, and I met this girl Megan I used to go to school with. **5** [ ] I was telling her how I loved the kids but hated the job and she said, if you want to work with children, you ought to do a course and get a qualification.

I thought you couldn't do courses if you hadn't done all sorts of exams at school, but she persuaded me to phone the local college and they were really helpful. My experience counted for a lot and I got on a part-time course. **6** [ ] I was really short of money, I even had to get an evening job as a waitress sometimes. But it was worth it in the end.

Now I've got a full-time job. Most of the children in this school come from families where there are problems, unemployment, poor housing and so on. **7** [ ] The children benefit, but also the parents. It gives them time to sort things out, go for training, or job interviews and so on. I shall always be grateful to Megan. If I hadn't bumped into her, I would have stayed on where I was, getting more and more fed up. I wish I'd realised earlier that you can have a real career, even if you aren't top of the class at school.

A I had to leave my job with the family, but I got work helping out at a nursery school.

B I find that the work we do helps in lots of ways.

C I was getting more and more tired and fed up, because I had too many late nights and early mornings with the little ones.

D So I found myself a job as a nanny, looking after two little girls.

E And it felt great to be earning.

F We weren't particularly friendly before, but she asked me what I was doing, so we got chatting.

G The following year I gained a further certificate which meant I could apply for the post of deputy if it became vacant.

H I was just impatient to leave as soon as I could.

Grammar focus task

Without looking back at the text, match the beginnings and endings of these phrases.

1 I thought you couldn't do courses ...g..

2 If I'd worked harder, ...

3 If I hadn't bumped into her, ...
4 I could apply for the post of deputy ....
5 ... if you want to work with children, ...

6 ... if I walked out ....
7 ... if I had to work extra hours one week, ...

a there wouldn't be anyone to look after them.

b you ought to do a course and get a qualification.

c if it became vacant ...

d she'd give me time off the next.

e I would have stayed on where I was ...

f I would have had better grades ...

g if you hadn't done all sorts of exams at school ...

Writing Part 1

You have received an email from your English-speaking friend, Jessie, who is helping you to find accommodation in her city. Read Jessie's email and the notes you have made. Then write a reply, using **all** your notes.

Email
_____

There are basically two types of accommodation which might suit you, but I'm not quite sure what you want.

Do you want to be in the centre or the suburbs, or what sort of area? ——————— — Say where and why

You could have a room in a family house, where you can have breakfast and an evening meal with the family. —— No, because ...

Alternatively you can share a house with other students. —— Yes! Say why

Let me know if there's anything special you need, like parking space, internet connection etc. ——— Give details

Write back soon.

Love Jessie

Write an **email** of between **120–150** words in a style appropriate for the situation.

Writing hints

This task gives you a chance to practise:
using conditionals.

Useful words and expressions
to afford, to cost, to enjoy yourself, to get to know, to stay in / with, central, cheap, comfortable, convenient, expensive accommodation, rent, rules, freedom, responsibility

20

Conditionals 2

unless; in case; as/so long as; provided that; I wish/if only;
it's time; I'd rather; otherwise/or else

A Context listening

1 You are going to hear a man talking to a group of people about something they are going to do the next day. Here are some of the things they will take with them. What do you think they are going to do? ....

2 (🎧 20a) Listen and check if you were right.

3 (🎧 20a) Listen again and fill in the gaps. Stop the recording when you need to.

1 We're going ....*unless*............ the weather gets much worse.

2 .... that it doesn't snow too heavily tonight, I'll see you back here at six o'clock.

3 We won't reach the top of the mountain .... we set out early.

4 You need a whistle .... you get separated from the rest of the group.

5 .... you didn't bring large cameras.

6 .... we all stay together, we'll have a great time.

7 I .... you'd come a few weeks ago.

8 .... we had dinner now.

4 Look at sentences 1, 2, 3, 4 and 6 in Exercise 3. What do you notice about the tense of the verbs which follow the words in the gaps? ....

174

B Grammar

1 Unless

Unless means *if not* and is used with the present tense to talk about the future (in the same way as *if*). *Unless* can usually be replaced by *if not*:
*We're going **unless** the weather **gets** much worse.* (= if the weather doesn't get much worse)
*We won't have time to reach the top of the mountain **unless** we **set** out early.* (= if we don't set out early)
***Unless** you **drive** more slowly, I'll be sick.* (= if you don't drive more slowly)

2 In case

In case shows an action is taken because of something else that might happen.
We use the present tense after *in case* when we explain that a present action prepares us for a future event:
*Take a whistle **in case** you **get** separated.* (= there's a chance you might get separated and a whistle will help us find you)
*Take my phone number **in case** you **miss** the bus.* (= I expect you'll get the bus, but if you miss it, you'll need to phone me)

We use the past simple after *in case* to explain a past action. It often shows that you did something because another thing might happen later:
*He took his surfboard **in case** they **went** to the beach.*
(= he took his surfboard because he thought they might go to the beach)

In case can also be followed by the present perfect:
*I'll buy some extra food **in case** the visitors **have** already **arrived**.*

▲ *In case* does not mean the same as *if*. Compare:
*I'll cook a meal **in case** Sarah **comes** over tonight.* (= I'll cook a meal now because Sarah might visit me later)
*I'll cook a meal **if** Sarah **comes** over tonight.* (= I won't cook a meal now because Sarah might not visit me)

3 Provided / providing that and as / so long as

These expressions are used with a present tense to talk about the future. They have a similar meaning to *if*:
***As long as** we all **stay** together, we'll have a great time.*
***Provided** that it **doesn't snow** too heavily, I'll see you here at six o'clock.*

▲ *If, unless, in case, provided / providing that* and *as / so long as* are all followed by the present tense to talk about the future. Some adverbs (*when, until, after, before, as soon as*) are also followed by the present tense to talk about the future (➤ see Unit 6).

175

4 *I wish* and *if only*

I wish means the same as *if only*. *If only* is less common and is usually stronger.

***Wish / if only* + the past simple** is used when we express a wish:
- about a present situation:
  *I **wish** you **loved** me.* (= but you don't love me)
  *I **wish** I **knew** the answer.* (= but I don't know the answer)
  ***If only** he could drive.* (= but he can't drive)
  ⚠ Notice that we use the past tense, although we are talking about now.

We can use *were* instead of *was* after *I* and *he / she / it*:
*I **wish** I **was / were** clever like you.* (= but I'm not clever)
*I **wish** the weather **wasn't / weren't** so wet here.* (= but it is wet)

***Wish / if only* + the past perfect** is used when we express a wish or regret:
- about the past. It's like the third conditional – the event can't be changed:
  *She **wishes** she'd **(had) never met** him.* (= but she did meet him)
  *I **wish** we'd **(had) come** a few weeks ago.* (= but we didn't come)
  ***If only** I **hadn't broken** his heart.* (= but I did break his heart)

Wish / if only* + *would is used when we express a wish:
- for something to happen now or in the future:
  *I **wish** you **would stay** longer.*
  ***If only** the rain **would stop**.*

- for someone to do something (often when we are annoyed):
  *I **wish** you **wouldn't leave** your bag in the doorway.*
  *I **wish** the waiter **would hurry up**.*

⚠ Notice the difference between *I hope + will* and *I wish + would* when talking about the future:
*I **hope** he **will phone**.* (= there's a good chance he will phone)
*I **wish** he **would phone**.* (= it's unlikely he will phone)

5 *It's time* and *I'd rather*

These expressions are followed by the past tense with a present meaning:
*It's **time** we **ate** dinner now.*
*I'd **rather** you **didn't bring** large cameras.*

6 *Otherwise* and *or else*

These words mean 'because if not' and they always go in the middle of a sentence. We use them when we feel sure about something:
*I have to go to bed early, **otherwise** I get too tired.* (= if I don't go to bed early, I get too tired)
*Carry that tray with both hands **or else** you'll drop it.* (= if you don't carry it with both hands, you'll drop it)

C Grammar exercises

1 Rewrite these sentences using *unless* instead of *if not*.

1 Sam will pass his driving test if he doesn't drive too fast.
  Sam will pass his driving test unless he drives too fast.

2 They'll be here soon if their plane isn't delayed.

3 If you're not in a hurry, you could take the bus.

4 I won't be able to come to see you tomorrow if my brother can't give me a lift.

5 If the factory doesn't increase its production, it will close down.

6 If you don't write your address down for me, I'll forget it.

7 I won't stay in that hotel if it hasn't got a good restaurant.

8 If I don't hear from you, I'll meet you at six.

2 Fill in the gaps with *in case* or *if*.

1 Elaine will post the letters ....if........ she goes out.

2 I'll go for a swim .... I finish college early.

3 I'll teach you to windsurf .... you teach me to play golf.

4 I always leave the answerphone on when I go out .... I miss an important phone call.

5 I'll take Tim's address with me .... I have time to visit him while I'm in London.

6 Our team will win the match .... our goalkeeper plays like he did last week.

7 It's a good idea to have two address books .... you lose one of them.

8 I'll leave these DVDs here .... you have time to watch them.

3 Chloe is on holiday in a foreign city. She was so busy admiring the sights that she has got lost. What does she wish? Write sentences with *wish*.

1 I haven't got a map.

> I wish I had a map.

2 The streets all look the same.

> ....

3 I didn't bring my mobile phone.

> ....

4 I can't speak the language.

> ....

5 I didn't buy a phrase book.

> ....

6 I'm hot and thirsty.

> ....

7 I came here alone.

> ....

8 I need someone to help me.

> ....

9 I'm sorry I came here.

> ....

10 I want to be back in my hotel.

> ....

4 Read this email. Fill in the gaps with the correct form of the verbs in the box. You need to make some of the verbs negative.

be   be   behave   bring   can   change   finish   ~~have~~   learn   know

---

To: JOE
From: ROBIN
Subject: PARTY!

Hi Joe

I'm having a birthday party on Saturday in my uncle's flat. I wish I ....*had*........ (1) a bigger flat but I haven't. Anyway, my uncle has offered me his flat so long as there .... (2) no more than thirty people and provided that the party .... (3) by midnight. So please come and bring a friend, but I'd rather you .... (4) Matthew with you because he always causes trouble. I wish he .... (5) to behave better. I had to work hard to persuade my uncle and unless everyone .... (6) well, he won't let me do it again. I'll send you a map in case you .... (7) the street where my uncle lives. If you .... (8) find it, just ring me on my mobile. So I'll see you on Saturday unless my uncle .... (9) his mind! By the way, has Sally changed her phone number? I can't get hold of her. I wish I .... (10) rude to her last week, as she's not speaking to me now.

Bye for now.

Robin

D Exam practice

Listening Part 1

20b You will hear people talking in eight different situations. For questions **1–8**, choose the best answer (**A**, **B** or **C**).

---

1 You hear a woman telling someone about a film she has seen. What kind of film was it?

  A a thriller

  B a love story

  C a comedy

    1

2 You overhear a conversation in a restaurant. What is the man complaining about?

  A the food

  B the service

  C the noise

    2

3 You hear a woman talking to a colleague. How did the woman feel?

  A upset

  B ashamed

  C shocked

    3

4 You overhear a man talking to a friend on the phone. What was damaged?

  A a piece of sports equipment

  B a musical instrument

  C a piece of furniture

    4

5 You hear a couple planning to meet. When will the woman telephone the man?

  A about lunchtime

  B late afternoon

  C early evening

    5

6 You hear the weather forecast. What will the weather be like at the weekend?

  A foggy

  B wet

  C sunny

    6

7 Listen to a phone conversation between two women. Why is Sarah ringing Katya?

  A to make an apology

  B to offer an invitation

  C to make a request

    7

8 You overhear a woman talking to someone in a shop. Who is she talking to?

   A the shop manager

   B a customer

   C a colleague

	8

Grammar focus task

Complete these sentences about the people in the recordings.

1 The woman says she wishes *she'd persuaded her friend to go to the cinema.*

2 The man says he won't come to the restaurant again unless ....

....

3 The woman was trying not to listen to the conversation in case ....

....

4 The man wishes ....

5 The woman says they can meet that evening unless ....

....

6 Next week will be sunny as long as ....

7 Katya will lend Sarah some cutlery as long as ....

8 The woman will stand up to the manager if ....

Writing Part 2

You have decided to enter a short story competition in an English language magazine. The competition rules say that the story must be called 'A missed opportunity' and it must **begin** like this:

Last week I learned that sometimes we should listen to other people's advice.

Write your **story** for the competition in **120–180** words.

Writing hints

This task gives you a chance to practise:
joining sentences with *in case, if* and *unless*.
using *I wish* and *If only*.

Useful words and expressions
although, as, disappointed, ignored, noticed, realised, suddenly, then

21 Prepositions 1
prepositions of place and time

A Context listening

1 You are going to hear a news broadcast. Before you listen, look at the television screens and guess what the news stories are.

a ....

b ....

c ....

d ....

2 (●21) Listen and check if you were right. As you listen, put the television screens in the order you hear the stories.   1 ....   2 ....   3 ....   4 ....

3 (●21) Listen again and answer these questions. Stop the recording when you need to.

1 Where will the Prime Minister be for the next two days? <u>At a conference in Washington.</u>

2 When will he fly to Mexico? ....

3 Where did Moira MacNab's plane hit bad weather? ....

4 When does she say she will be quite well? ....

5 How far do the traffic jams stretch? ....

6 How long will the motorway remain closed? ....

7 Where was the security man? ....

8 When was the manager released? ....

4 Look at your answers to Exercise 3.

1 Which prepositions are used in answers about time? ....

2 Which prepositions are used in answers about place? ....

B Grammar

1 Prepositions of place

In, at and *on*

In is used:

- for someone or something inside a limited area (e.g. a town, a country, a garden):
  *The Prime Minister is **in** Washington ...*
  *... she is due to appear **in** Edinburgh ...*
  *There are some lovely trees **in** this garden.*

- for someone or something inside a building, room, or container:
  *... heard shouting **in** the manager's office.*
  *Do you keep your credit cards **in** this wallet?*

On is used:

- for a point on a fixed line (e.g. a road, the coast):
  *... holidaying **on** the north coast of Africa ...*
  *They were called to the bank **on** the High Street.*

- for a point on a surface:
  *... a locker **on** the wall.*

- with *floor* and *ceiling*:
  *There's a spider **on** the ceiling.*

- for public transport vehicles, such as buses, trains or planes:
  *They met **on** a plane.*
  *I can't read **on** the bus.*
  ⚠ but we use *in* for cars and taxis:
  *He came home **in** a taxi.*

At is used:

- when we think about a place in terms of its function or as a meeting place:
  *... then have talks **at** the White House.*
  *I keep my tennis racket **at** the sports club.*
  *I'll see you **at** the theatre.*

- for an event:
  *He will remain **at** the conference ...*
  *There were a lot of strangers **at** the party.*

Across and *over*

There are many places where either *across* or *over* can be used:
*... a footbridge **across** / **over** the motorway ...*

but compare:
*Their eyes met **across** the table.*
*... it was flying **across** the Mediterranean.*

across

Fred jumped over the gate.

over

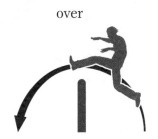

Above and *over*

Above or *over* is used if one thing is higher than another:
*They built an extra room **above** / **over** the garage.*

Over is used when one thing covers another:
*Put this rug **over** that old chair.*

Above is used when the two things are not directly on top of each other:
*The hotel is **above** the beach.*

Above is used in documents:
*Please don't write **above** the line.*

Under and below

Under or below is used if one thing is lower than another:

The garage is **below** / **under** the workshop.

Under is the opposite of over:

There's a beautiful old chair **under** that rug.

Below is the opposite of above:

The beach is **below** the hotel.

Below is used in documents:

Please don't write **below** the line.

Along and through

Along is used for something which follows a line:

There were cheering crowds **along** the route of the procession.
We strolled **along** the riverbank at dusk.

along

Through means from one side of something to the other side of it:

The motorway passes **through** Birmingham.
I struggled **through** the crowd to reach a telephone.
We could see the sea **through** the trees.

through

The train went **through** the tunnel.

By and beside

By can be used in the same way as beside, meaning 'next to':

... a security man standing **by** / **beside** the door of the bank ...
I'd love to live **by** / **beside** a lake.

Between and among

Between is used when we talk about two places, things or people:

The dictionary is **between** the grammar book and the atlas.

... the motorway **between** London and Oxford ...

Among is used to identify something as part of a group:

Is there a dictionary somewhere **among** these books?

Beyond and behind

Beyond is used for somewhere further away from us than something else. We may or may not be able to see it:

... traffic jams stretching **beyond** the beginning of the motorway.
You can't see the lake, it's **beyond** the forest.

Behind is used for somewhere which is partly or completely hidden by an object in front of it:

The robber stood **behind** the door, hoping he wouldn't be seen.

2 Prepositions of time

At, *on* and *in*

At is used:

- for a point of time:
  ... *at* the start of her tour of Europe.

- for the time of day:
  at six o'clock, *at* dawn, *at* lunchtime

- for seasonal holidays:
  at Christmas, *at* Easter

- for the following expressions:
  at the weekend, *at* first, *at* last, *at* present
  (= now), *at* the moment (= now), *at* times
  (= sometimes), *at* once (= immediately)

On is used for dates and days (including special days):

on Monday, *on* 3rd December (note that we say: *on* **the** third **of** December), *on* New Year's Day, *on* Christmas Day, *on* my wedding anniversary

In is used for all or part of a period of time:
in the afternoon, *in* winter, *in* the twenty-first century, *in* the Middle Ages

By and *until*

By means that something happens not later than, and possibly before, the time mentioned:
... she still intends to be in Chile *by* the end of the year. (= at the end of the year, or possibly before)

Can we finish this work *by* four o'clock? (= not later than four o'clock)

Until means that something continues up to, but not later than, the time mentioned:
... part of the motorway will remain closed *until* this afternoon. (= it will open this afternoon)

Until is often used with a negative, meaning 'not before':

We can't eat *until* all the guests arrive. (= we can eat when they are all here)

In, *during* and *for*

In and *during* are often used with the same meaning:

In / *During* the summer we often go for long walks.

but *during* shows a particular event against the background of a period of time:
The manager was released *during* the night ...

especially if it is an interruption:
They walked out of the hall *during* the speech.

For shows how long something lasts:
He will remain at the conference *for* two days ...
We went to Spain *for* the summer.

In shows how soon something happens:
In less than an hour we had heard all about his adventures.
I'll meet you *in* ten minutes.

21

C Grammar exercises

1 Sara is on the train and she's phoning her friend Rebecca. Complete the conversations with the prepositions in the box.

| at | at | by | by | during | for | in | in | ~~on~~ | over | until |

In Rebecca's office, 11.30 am.

Rebecca: Rebecca White.

Sara: Hi, it's Sara. I'm ....on......... **(1)** the train. Can you meet me .... **(2)** the station?

Rebecca: What time?

Sara: Three.

Rebecca: I think so. The car's got a puncture. If I can arrange to get it fixed .... **(3)** my break, I'll be there.

Sara: Thanks, that's great.

At the garage, 1.40 pm.

Rebecca: Can you fix this puncture for me?

Mechanic: Yes, probably. But my assistant won't be back from lunch .... **(4)** half an hour and I'll be working on this other job .... **(5)** then.

Rebecca: Well, I've got to collect someone from the station .... **(6)** three.

Mechanic: Oh, that's no problem. We'll have it done .... **(7)** half past two easily.

Rebecca: Thanks. I'll be back .... **(8)** an hour, OK?

Mechanic: Fine. See you then.

On the train, 2.10 pm.

Sara: Hello?

Rebecca: The car's being fixed now. I'll wait for you .... **(9)** the main door of the station, so I can help carry your stuff.

Sara: Don't worry. I haven't got anything heavy. I'll see you .... **(10)** the car park. It's just .... **(11)** the footbridge, isn't it?

Rebecca: Yes, all right. See you there.

Sara: Bye.

2 Fill in the gaps in this email with suitable prepositions.

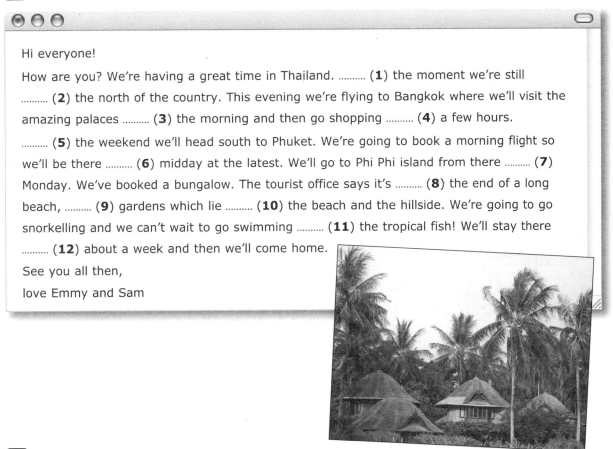

Hi everyone!

How are you? We're having a great time in Thailand. .... (**1**) the moment we're still .... (**2**) the north of the country. This evening we're flying to Bangkok where we'll visit the amazing palaces .... (**3**) the morning and then go shopping .... (**4**) a few hours.

.... (**5**) the weekend we'll head south to Phuket. We're going to book a morning flight so we'll be there .... (**6**) midday at the latest. We'll go to Phi Phi island from there .... (**7**) Monday. We've booked a bungalow. The tourist office says it's .... (**8**) the end of a long beach, ... (**9**) gardens which lie .... (**10**) the beach and the hillside. We're going to go snorkelling and we can't wait to go swimming .... (**11**) the tropical fish! We'll stay there .... (**12**) about a week and then we'll come home.

See you all then,

love Emmy and Sam

3 Choose the correct sentence from each pair.

1 a She hid below the bed until the visitors had gone.

   b She hid under the bed until the visitors had gone. ✓

2 a We arrived at our destination in dawn.

   b We arrived at our destination at dawn.

3 a During the night, we heard strange noises in the room above us.

   b During the night, we heard strange noises in the room over us.

4 a The gymnast sailed through the air and landed lightly on the mat.

   b The gymnast sailed along the air and landed lightly on the mat.

5 a The detective found an earring on the path between the pool and the house.

   b The detective found an earring on the path along the pool and the house.

6 a I need to get some cash so I'll see you at the cinema by ten minutes.

   b I need to get some cash so I'll see you at the cinema in ten minutes.

4 A hotel owner is showing some visitors round his new premises.
Fill in the gaps with suitable prepositions.

We're now standing ......in...... **(1)** the lounge, a beautiful room, with paintings
.... **(2)** the ceiling and a wonderful view .... **(3)** the park to the hills
.... **(4)** it. The cellar is being decorated .... **(5)** present, but we will open
it as a restaurant .... **(6)** a few months' time. .... **(7)** then we are serving
meals .... **(8)** the dining room only.

Do you see the trees planted all .... **(9)** the sides of the road up to the
front door? They are going to be hung with coloured lights .... **(10)** special
occasions. If we go .... **(11)** that gate, we'll reach the rose garden, where you
can see a number of interesting sculptures on display .... **(12)** the bushes.

D Exam practice

Use of English Part 2

For questions **1–12**, read the text below and think of the word which best fits each gap. Use only **one** word in each gap. There is an example at the beginning (**0**).

NEW RESIDENTS ON THE FARM

My family and I visited the new arts centre on the road between Salisbury and Winchester last week. It (**0**) ......used...... to be a farm and the new owners have really made clever use (**1**) .... the old barns and other farm buildings. There are studios which can (**2**) .... rented cheaply by local artists as well (**3**) .... workshops for people like potters and furniture makers (**4**) .... work in.

One barn has been (**5**) .... into a most attractive gallery, which displays work produced at the arts centre, in (**6**) .... to holding exhibitions by more famous artists. At (**7**) .... there is a lovely exhibition of modern glass from Scotland.

(**8**) .... the artists were in their studios when we visited so we were able to talk to them about (**9**) .... they were doing. One potter told us that it can be quite (**10**) .... lonely job at times, so she is happy to be in a place where she feels she is among people who understand her work. They can go across the yard for coffee and a chat and share their problems with (**11**) .... other.

We didn't buy anything (**12**) .... we certainly enjoyed our visit and plan to go back again soon.

After you have checked your answers to the exam task, read the text carefully once more. Then fill in the gaps with the correct prepositions without looking back at the text.

1 The arts centre is ......_on_...... the road .... Salisbury and Winchester.

2 All the artists were .... their studios when we visited.

3 The potter said it can be quite a lonely job .... times.

4 She said she was happy to be .... people who understood her work.

5 The artists go .... the yard for coffee.

Writing Part 2

Your family has received this letter from some Irish friends. Read the letter and write your reply.

... so that's some information about places you might want to go to in our area. Can you tell us about your area – the local facilities, where they are and when they're open. We're looking forward to exchanging homes with you next month.

Best wishes,

Ronan and family

Write your **letter** in **120–180** words.

This task gives you a chance to practise:
using prepositions for places and times.

Useful words and expressions
bank, gallery, local shop, museum, sports hall, supermarket, swimming pool
in the (city) centre, just up the road, not far from, on the outskirts
at weekends, on weekdays

Prepositions 2
prepositions which follow verbs and adjectives; prepositions to express *who*, *how* and *why*; expressions with prepositions

22

A Context listening

1 You are going to hear a man called Andy telling his wife, Dawn, about a fire. Before you listen, look at the pictures. What is happening in each one?

1 .... 2 .... 3 ....

2 (●22) Listen and decide which picture best fits what Andy tells Dawn. What is wrong with the other two pictures? ....

3 (●22) Listen again and fill in the gaps.

1 ... what's happened ....*to*....... your jacket?

2 ... there's no need to shout .... me.

3 ... an adventure .... the way home.

4 I called the fire brigade .... my mobile ...

5 I got in .... breaking a window.

6 ... smashed a window .... hitting it ...

7 I covered my face .... a handkerchief.

8 You could have been .... real danger.

9 ... the fire brigade were .... control ...

10 ... they thanked you .... saving their property.

11 ... do you forgive me .... being late?

12 I can't be angry .... you now.

13 I'll make a really nice supper .... you.

14 I'm looking forward .... eating it ...

4 Look at your answers to questions 5 and 6 in Exercise 3. Which preposition is used to show how something is done? ....

B Grammar

1 Prepositions which follow verbs and adjectives
Verb + preposition
Some verbs are nearly always followed by a particular preposition.
These include:

- *approve of: Yasmina doesn't **approve of** smoking.*
- *enquire about: I am writing to **enquire about** your advertisement.*
- *insist on: She **insisted on** paying for the taxi.*
- *look forward to: I'm really **looking forward to** eating it.*
- *succeed in: Did Pierre **succeed in** finding accommodation?*

Notice that prepositions are followed by a noun or by the *-ing* form:
*We enquired **about booking** a room.*
*We enquired **about our hotel** reservation.*

Verb + object + preposition
Some verbs are nearly always followed by an object and a particular
preposition. These include:

- *accuse someone of: The rock group **accused their manager of** stealing their
  money.*
- *congratulate someone on: Heidi **congratulated me on** passing the exam.*
- *forgive someone for: She can't **forgive Maurice for** all the lies he told.*
- *prevent someone / something (from): The bus strike **hasn't prevented people
  from** coming to work.*
- *suspect someone of: I **suspect Maryann of** being dishonest.*

Verb + different prepositions
Some verbs are followed by different prepositions, which change the
meaning. These include:

- *agree with someone and agree about something:*
  *I quite **agree with** you, I think you're right. (= a person)*
  *My father and **I don't agree about** politics. (= a subject)*

- *ask for something and ask about something:*
  *He **asked** me **for** some money. (= he requested)*
  *She **asked** me **about** my plans for the summer. (= she enquired)*

- *laugh about and laugh at:*
  *I was late but he wasn't angry, he just **laughed about** it. (= found it funny)*
  *I can't wear this hat. Everyone will **laugh at** me. (= make fun of – unkindly)*

- *think of* and *think about*:
  What do you **think of** my new jacket? It's great. (= what is your opinion?)
  What are you **thinking about**? Lunch – I'm hungry! (= what is in your mind?)

- *throw at* and *throw to* (also *shout at / point at* and *shout to / point to*):
  The little boy **threw** the ball **to** his father. (= part of a game)
  Don't **throw** toys **at** your sister, Harry, you might hurt her. (= probably angry or rude)

To be + adjective + preposition

Some adjectives are nearly always followed by a particular preposition. These include:

- *angry about (something)*: She**'s angry about** the theft of her purse.
- *angry with (someone)*: He**'s** very **angry with** his assistant.
- *good / bad at (something)*: She**'s good at** drawing flowers.
- *pleased about (something)*: My parents **weren't pleased about** my bad report.
- *pleased with (something or someone)*: Granny **was** very **pleased with** the book you sent her.
- *rude / polite to (someone)*: Don't **be rude to** anyone at the party.
- *(un)kind to (someone)*: The children **were** extremely **unkind to** the new boy.

2 Prepositions used to express *who, how* and *why*

By, with and *for*

We use *by* with passive verbs, for the person or thing which does the action:
*The window was smashed **by Andy**.*
*The fire was started **by an electrical fault**.*

We use *by* + *-ing* to show how something is done:
*He smashed the window **by hitting** it with a hammer.*
*He got in **by breaking** a window.*

We use *with* + noun for a tool (or other object):
*He smashed the window **with a hammer**.*
*He covered his face **with his handkerchief**.*

We use *for* + *-ing* or a noun to explain the purpose of a tool or other object:
*Hammers are normally **for knocking** in nails, not **for smashing** windows!*
*He keeps a bag of tools in his car **for emergencies**.*

We can also use *for* + *-ing* or a noun to explain the reason for something:
*The owners of the house thanked him **for saving** their property.*
*He received an award **for bravery**.*

3 Expressions with prepositions

We use prepositions in the following fixed expressions:

- ways of travelling:
  *by air, **by** plane, **by** road, **by** car, **by** bus, **by** rail, **by** train* but **on** *foot*

- ways of contacting people:
  *by post, **by** email, **by** phone* but *to be **on** the phone* (= using the phone)

- ways things can happen:
  *by chance, **by** accident, **by** mistake* but **on** *purpose*

- reasons for being somewhere:
  on *holiday,* **on** / **off** *duty,* **on** *business*

- circumstances:
  *in love, **in** secret, **in** private, **in** public, **in** / **out of** sight, **in** / **out of** debt, **in** / **out of** danger, **in** / **out of** difficulties, **in** a hurry, **in** a temper, **in** control, **in** charge of, **at** peace, **at** war, **at** work, **at** home*

⚠ Don't make mistakes with these expressions:

- *at least* and *at last*:
  *You should allow **at least** two days for visiting Ravenna.* (= no fewer than)
  *The work took a long time but **at last** it was finished.* (= finally)

- *on the way* and *in the way*:
  *I'm going to my office so I'll call and see you **on the way**.* (= between two points on a journey)
  *I can't move the table because that chair's **in the way**.* (= blocking a path between two objects / people)

- *on time* and *in time*:
  *If the train's **on time**, I'll be home at six.* (= punctual)
  *If we leave now, we'll be home **in time** to see the news.* (= at or before the correct time)

- *in the end* and *at the end*:
  *She didn't want to come with us, but **in the end** we persuaded her.*
  (= the final result)
  *It was a great show and the audience applauded loudly **at the end**.*
  (= the last thing to happen)

- *to be the matter with* and *to be about*:
  *What **was the matter with** Lesley? Why was she upset?*
  (= something wrong)
  *What's that book **about**?* (= subject)

- *to be in charge of* and *to be responsible for*:
  *She's **in charge of** the design department.*
  (= she's the boss)
  *I'm **responsible for** travel arrangements, but not accommodation.*
  (= it's my duty)

C Grammar exercises

1 Write sentences describing what happened in each of the pictures, using the words given.

1 Can you tell me what trains there are to Scotland?

(enquired)

He enquired about trains to Scotland.

2 Well done! You certainly deserved to win this tournament.

(congratulated)

....

3 No, you can't come in here.

(prevented)

....

4 I'm so sorry I forgot to phone you.   It's OK, I'm not angry.

(forgave)

....

5 You've been reading my diary!

(accused)

....

6 I didn't like that film at all.   No, I didn't either.

(agreed)

....

2 Choose the correct sentence from each pair.

1 a You know you shouldn't phone me in work!

  b You know you shouldn't phone me at work! ✓

2 a Yvonne doesn't approve of wearing real fur.

  b Yvonne doesn't approve on wearing real fur.

3 a Who is responsible of setting the burglar alarm?

  b Who is responsible for setting the burglar alarm?

4 a The mermaid was combing her hair by a silver comb.

  b The mermaid was combing her hair with a silver comb.

5 a No one's had any cake. What's the matter with it?

  b No one's had any cake. What's the matter of it?

6 a Did you drop that dish by purpose?

  b Did you drop that dish on purpose?

3 Fill in the gaps in these newspaper articles with suitable prepositions.

a

The wedding took place last Saturday of a couple who fell ......in...... (1) love through the internet. Penny and Peter communicated .... (2) email for six months until they discovered .... (3) accident that they worked .... (4) the same building. 'Actually, I had noticed her before and liked her, but I was too shy to speak to her .... (5) public,' said blushing Peter. 'When I realised she was my internet friend, at first I suspected her .... (6) laughing .... (7) me, and I was quite angry .... (8) it. But luckily she succeeded .... (9) persuading me that I was wrong. Now we're looking forward .... (10) spending our lives together.'

b

A FRENCH BANK ROBBER was arrested yesterday .... (1) Edinburgh, two years after his crime. A former cashier recognised him .... (2) chance in the hotel where she was staying .... (3) business and reported him to the security guard .... (4) duty. The guard accused him .... (5) using a false name and insisted .... (6) taking him to the hotel manager's room. The robber threw a lamp .... (7) the guard and ran out of the hotel. Fortunately, he was not very good .... (8) running, and the police soon caught him.

c

An elderly brother and sister were reunited today for the first time since they were children. Freda and Cecil Brown's parents had been .... (1) debt and the children had been put in children's homes until their family was .... (2) difficulties. But the country was .... (3) war, the children were separated, and their papers were lost. Cecil's granddaughter began trying to find Freda five years ago. 'It was hard, but .... (4) last I found the daughter of the woman who had been .... (5) charge of the home where Freda was. She said that some of the girls were sent to Canada to be .... (6) danger during the war and many of them never returned. When I thought I'd found Freda, I wanted to tell Dad immediately, but I decided to meet her .... (7) secret first, in case I was wrong. But I was right.' Two days ago, Cecil travelled .... (8) air for the first time .... (9) his life. 'We've got a lot of catching up to do,' he said.

D Exam practice

Use of English Part 3

For questions **1–10**, read the text below. Use the word given in capitals at the end of some of the lines to form a word that fits in the gap **in the same line**. There is an example at the beginning (**0**).

THE CLOTHES WE CHOOSE TO WEAR	
The clothes we wear can be a form of (**0**) _communication_ .	**COMMUNICATE**
Clothes, like a (**1**) .... language, give out a message.	**SPEAK**
This can be very simple, for example, when we wear clothing	
for keeping warm, or perhaps to attend a (**2**)	**GRADUATE**
ceremony, announce our (**3**) .... views or just look	**POLITICS**
sexy. It isn't always this simple, however. (**4**) .... ,	**FORTUNE**
as with speech, our reasons for making any statement	
have a (**5**) .... to be double or multiple. The man who	**TEND**
buys an expensive coat may simultaneously want it to offer	
(**6**) .... from bad weather, and magically surround	**PROTECT**
him with the qualities of an (**7**) .... film star.	**NATION**
(**8**) .... , people rarely succeed in satisfying both these	**NATURE**
requirements at once. Even (**9**) .... both these statements	**SUPPOSE**
could actually be made by one single coat, this (**10**)	**IDEA**
item of clothing may not be available, and if it is, we may not be	
able to afford it.	

Grammar focus task

These are some extracts from the text. Without looking back at the text, fill in the gaps with the correct prepositions.

1 The clothes we wear can be a form ...._of_....... communication.

2 ... we wear clothing .... keeping warm ...

3 ... our reasons .... making any statement ...

4 ... magically surround him .... the qualities of a film star.

5 ... people rarely succeed .... satisfying both these requirements ...

6 ... both these statements could actually be made .... one single coat ...

Writing Part 1

While studying in England, you receive a letter from the manager of a local shop asking you for information about something which you saw there. Read the manager's letter and the notes you have made. Then write a reply, using **all** your notes.

Dear Sir or Madam

I am writing to everyone who was in our shop last Wednesday afternoon. As you know, there was an unfortunate argument between a customer and one of the assistants. I would be very grateful if you could confirm the details of what you saw.

First of all, did you hear what the customer said when he first came into the shop? — *No, because ...*

Can you tell me how the argument began? — *Yes, give details*

What did the other people in the shop say or do? — *Explain*

Do you know what happened to the television in the window? — *Suggest*

I hope to hear from you soon.

Yours faithfully

Duncan Morrison

Write a **letter** of between **120–150** words in a style appropriate for the situation.

Writing hints

This task gives you a chance to practise:
describing what you did and what you could not do.
describing how you felt.
using expressions with prepositions.

Useful words and expressions
*to accuse, to be angry with, to be responsible for, to insist, to be rude to, to warn
annoyed, disappointed, satisfied, upset*

23 Relative clauses

defining and non-defining relative clauses; relative pronouns and prepositions

A Context listening

1 You are going to hear a man showing some visitors round the castle where he lives. He's talking about some paintings. Before you listen, look at each painting. Can you guess when the people lived? .... *Castle* ....
Do you think they are members of the same family? .... *yes* ....

2 🔊 23 Listen and check if you were right. As you listen, match the names to the paintings.

1 Margaret .... 2 Edmund .... 3 Henry .... 4 William .... 5 Jane ....

3 🔊 23 Listen again and complete the answers to these questions. Stop the recording when you need to.

1 What do we learn about the ship in the picture of Edmund?
It's the one <u>which he was captain of during a famous naval victory.</u>

2 Which is the picture of Henry and William?
It's the picture ....

3 How do we know who William is?
He's the one ....

4 Which side did Henry support in the Civil War?
It was the side ....

5 Which year was the picture of Jane and her children painted?
It was the year ....

4 Underline the first word in each of your answers to Exercise 3. They are all words which can introduce relative clauses. What does each word refer to?

1 .... 2 .... 3 .... 4 .... 5 ....

B Grammar

1 Defining relative clauses

Defining relative clauses tell us some essential information about the things or people they refer to:

*The picture **that hangs next to Margaret's portrait** is the one I like best.*

If we remove the words *that hangs next to Margaret's portrait* we don't know which picture Jasper is talking about.

Defining relative clauses:

- may begin with the relative pronouns *who* (for people), *which* (for things), *that* (for things and people).

- may have *who, which* or *that* as the subject or object of the relative clause:
  *... the picture **which / that** hangs next to Margaret's portrait ...* (*which / that* is the **subject** of the relative clause)
  *... the woman **who / that** he married ...* (*who / that* is the **object** of the relative clause, and he is the subject)

- very often omit the relative pronoun when it is the object of the relative clause:
  The painting we're looking at now ... or
  *The painting **which / that** we're looking at now ...*

- are never separated from the rest of the sentence by commas.

- are used in writing and speaking.

2 Non-defining relative clauses

Non-defining relative clauses tell us some extra information about the things or people they refer to:

*The next painting shows Edmund's wife Margaret, **who he married in 1605**.*

If we remove the words *who he married in 1605*, we still know who Jasper is talking about. It is *Edmund's wife, Margaret.*

Non-defining relative clauses:

- always begin with the relative pronouns *who* (for people) and *which* (for things).

- may have *who* or *which* (but never *that*) as the subject or object of the relative clause:
  *The building, **which** is very old, costs a lot of money to repair.* (**not** *that is very old*)
  *The castle's owner, **who** we've just seen, enjoys meeting visitors.* (**not** *that we've just seen*)

- never omit the relative pronoun.

- must be separated from the rest of the sentence by commas.

- are more common in writing than in speaking.

A We always omit the object pronoun (*her, him, it*, etc.) when we make a relative clause:

*We know little about **the woman that he married**.* (**not** *the woman that he married her*)

*The next painting shows Edmund's wife Margaret, **who he married in 1605**.* (**not** *who he married her in 1605*)

3 Relative pronouns and prepositions

Both **defining** and **non-defining relative clauses**:

- can begin with *whose* (instead of *his / her / their*), *when* (for times) and *where* (for places):

  *William, **whose wife Jane was a famous beauty**, had nine children.*
  *Here they are in this picture from the year **when the youngest was born**.*
  *This has been my family home, **where we've lived for over four hundred years**, since the time of Edmund Claremont.*

- can begin with *whom* (for people) as the object of a clause (this is mainly in written English, and is increasingly rare):

  *His girlfriend, **whom** he neglected, became very depressed.*

- usually have any prepositions at the end of the clause:

  *It's the one **which** he was captain **of** during a famous naval victory.*
  *I had a friend I shared everything **with**.*
  *Peter, **who** my father used to work **with**, has become a government minister.*

- in formal English, sometimes have a preposition at the beginning of the clause, followed by *which* (for things) or *whom* (for people):

  *It's the one **of which** he was captain during a famous naval victory.*
  *I had a friend **with whom** I shared everything.*
  *Peter, **with whom** my father used to work, has become a government minister.*

⚠ We cannot use *that* after a preposition in a relative clause:
*The Conference Room, **in which** the meeting was held, was not really big enough.*
(**not** ~~in that the meeting was held~~)

⚠ A defining relative clause can:

- begin with *why*, after the words *the reason*:

  *This victory was the reason **why he became a national hero**.*

- omit *why* and *when*:

  *That was the reason we went there. (= That was the reason **why** we went there.)*
  *I remember the day I met you. (= I remember the day **when** I met you.)*

C Grammar exercises

1 Fill the gaps in this letter using *who* or *which* when necessary.
If no word is necessary, write –.

Dear Mr Trotter,

I have a number of complaints about the work ....–............ (1)
your company did in my house last week.

You promised that the men .... (2) carried out the work would
arrive by 8.00. As you know, I have to catch the bus .... (3)
leaves at 8.15. On three days the men arrived after eight,
so I missed my bus and my boss, ... (4) is very strict,
was extremely annoyed. The foreman lost the written instructions
.... (5) I gave him. The paint .... (6) he used for the
hall was the one .... (7) should have been used in the kitchen.
The sitting-room wallpaper, ... (8) I had chosen with great
care, was the wrong way up. My bathroom, ... (9) you and I
agreed did not need redecorating, has been painted.

If you do not promise to put right the mistakes .... (10)
your men have made within two weeks, I will go to my lawyer.

Yours sincerely,

Cecil J. Trubshaw

2 Complete these sentences with your own ideas,
using the relative pronouns in the box.

where	when	~~which~~	which	which	who	whose	why

1 I don't really enjoy films which show a lot of violence.
2 I don't often go to parties ....
3 My teacher usually explains things ....
4 I can remember several occasions ....
5 I cannot understand the reason ....
6 Have you ever met anyone ....
7 I envy people ....
8 I would hate to have a job ....

3 Combine each pair of sentences by making the second sentence into a non-defining relative clause.

1 My brother loves chocolate ice cream.
  He is rather fat.
  <u>My brother, who is rather fat, loves</u>
  <u>chocolate ice cream.</u>

2 My uncle's cottage has been damaged by floods. We usually spend our holidays there.
  ....

3 My bicycle has been stolen. I only got it last week.
  ....

4 The chemistry exam was actually quite easy. We had been worrying about it.
  ....

5 The young man caused a fight in a bar. His girlfriend had left him.
  ....

6 During the summer there are dreadful traffic jams. Everyone goes on holiday then.
  ....

7 My parents enjoyed that film very much. They don't often go to the cinema.
  ....

4 Choose the correct sentence from each pair.

1 a Have you ever been back to the town, that you were born in?
   b Have you ever been back to the town that you were born in? ✓
2 a My left ankle which I broke last winter is still giving me trouble.
   b My left ankle, which I broke last winter, is still giving me trouble.
3 a Is that the man you were talking about?
   b Is that the man you were talking about him?
4 a I'm looking for the book you lent me last week.
   b I'm looking for the book what you lent me last week.
5 a The region, where we go for our holidays, is becoming increasingly popular.
   b The region where we go for our holidays is becoming increasingly popular.
6 a The friend that I want to introduce you to her is away this weekend.
   b The friend I want to introduce you to is away this weekend.
7 a Do you remember the name of the place in that the crime was committed?
   b Do you remember the name of the place where the crime was committed?

D Exam practice

Use of English Part 4

For questions **1–8**, complete the second sentence so that it has a similar meaning to the first sentence, using the word given. **Do not change the word given.** You must use between **two** and **five** words, including the word given. Here is an example (**0**).

0 You can only win if you enter the race.
UNLESS
You ....*can't win unless*............... you enter the race.

---

1 That's the hotel where we had lunch last Sunday.
IN
That's the hotel .... last Sunday.

2 This special offer will end on Monday!
LAST
This special offer .... Monday!

3 Being an airline employee, my girlfriend sometimes gets cheap flights.
WORKS
My girlfriend, ... , sometimes gets cheap flights.

4 He used a penknife to open the box.
OPENED
He .... a penknife.

5 I don't like Jim because he's so mean.
WHY
Jim's meanness .... I don't like him.

6 Last week Gerry borrowed a book from me and now he's lost it.
I
Gerry's lost .... last week.

7 The concert which Ben took me to wasn't very enjoyable.
WENT
I didn't enjoy .... to with Ben.

8 The mother of that boy is a well-known actress.
WHOSE
That's .... a well-known actress.

Grammar focus task

Look at your answers to the exam task.

1 Which of the sentences you have written contain relative clauses? ....

2 Are they defining or non-defining relative clauses? ....

3 How do you know? ....

Writing Part 2

You recently saw this notice in an international newspaper.

Television reviews!

Have you seen any good TV dramas this week?
Email us a review. Tell us about the characters and their
relationships. Why did you enjoy it?

The best review will win a visit to the TV studio.

Write your **review** in **120–180** words.

Writing hints

This task gives you a chance to practise:
using relative clauses to give information about people and things.

Useful words and expressions

to consist of, to recommend, to relax
actor, (latest) episode, (good) ending, plot, reason, series, storyline, suspense
amusing, gripping, witty

Linking words 1

because, *as* and *since*; *so* and *therefore*; *in order to*,
to + infinitive and *so (that)*; *so* and *such*; *enough* and *too*

24

A Context listening

1 You are going to hear two friends, Josie and Adam, talking at their sports club. Before you listen, look at the picture. Can you guess which sports they take part in? ....

....

2 (🎧 24) Listen and check if you were right.

3 (🎧 24) Listen again and fill in the gaps. Stop the recording when you need to.

1 Josie thinks Tom Castle was chosen ..*because*.. he's the coach's nephew.

2 Adam believes that Tom is certainly .... to be captain.

3 Adam suggests Josie ought to be in the team herself .... she seems to know so much about the subject.

4 Josie objects that she isn't .... to play volleyball.

5 Adam points out that Melanie is .... that she's one of the best players.

6 Josie says that going to judo once a week gives her ....

7 She thinks that volleyball would take ....

8 She adds that they have .... after school.

9 Adam says that he has been training every day .... be really fit.

10 The coach told Adam that he plays ....

11 Some of the older players may drop out .... they've got .... to do.

4 Look at your answers to questions 2, 4, 6 and 10 in Exercise 3. Why is the word order different in 6? ....

1 Expressing reason

Because, as and since

Because, *as* and *since*:

- introduce the reason for something.
- go at the beginning or in the middle of a sentence:
  *They had to choose him **as** / **because** / **since** he's the coach's nephew.*
  As / ***Because*** / ***Since*** *he's the coach's nephew, they had to choose him.*
  Notice that if they go at the beginning, there is usually a comma in the middle of the sentence.

Because is stronger than *as* and *since*, but they are often used in a similar way:
As / ***Since*** / ***Because*** *I hadn't done my homework, I didn't understand the lesson.*

⚠ *Because* (but not *as* or *since*) can be used to begin the answer to a question beginning with *why*:
Question: *Why didn't you understand the lesson?*
Answer: ***Because*** *I hadn't done my homework.* (**not** ~~As / Since I hadn't done my homework.~~)

So and therefore

So and *therefore*:

- introduce the result of something.

So usually goes in the middle of a sentence:
*They may need a new goalkeeper **so** I want to be ready.*

Therefore goes at the beginning of a new sentence:
*They may need a new goalkeeper. **Therefore** I want to be ready.*

We could also say:
*I want to be ready **because** they may need a new goalkeeper.*

Compare these sentences, which have the same meaning:
*I hadn't done my homework **so** I didn't understand the lesson.*
*I hadn't done my homework. **Therefore** I didn't understand the lesson.*
As / ***Since*** / ***Because*** *I hadn't done my homework, I didn't understand the lesson.*

So is more common in speaking.
Therefore is more common in writing.

2 Expressing purpose
(In order) to + infinitive and *so (that)* + verb
In order to, to, so that and *so*:
● link an action and its purpose.
So always goes in the middle of a sentence:
I've been training every day **so** *(***that***) I'm really fit.*

In order to and *to* go in the middle, or occasionally at the beginning, of a sentence:
*I've been training every day (***in order***) to be really fit.*
*To / ***In order to*** be really fit, I've been training every day.*

In order to and *so that* are stronger than *to* and *so* and less common in speech.

▲ Sentences with *so* can sometimes have two meanings, for example:
I've been training every day **so** *I'm really fit.*
This could mean: *I've been training every day* **in order to be** *really fit.*
or: *I've been training every day* **therefore** *I'm really fit.*
(➢ See B1)

▲ Remember, in sentences like these, we do **not** use *for* to express purpose:
(**not** ~~I've been training every day for be really fit.~~)

3 Explaining cause and effect
So and *such*
So and *such* mean 'as much as this'. We can use them to talk about cause and effect:
He walked **so slowly that** *we arrived late.* (= we arrived late because of his slow walking speed)
He was **such a slow walker that** *we arrived late.*

We often omit *that*, especially in speech:
It was **such an untidy office** *we couldn't find our books.* = *It was* **such an untidy office that** *we couldn't find our books.*

We can use *so* and *such* after *because*:
Her teachers sent her home **because** *she behaved* **so badly.**
Her teachers sent her home **because** *she was* **such a naughty child.**

So is followed by:
● an adjective or an adverb:
  Her father is **so rich** *that she's never travelled by bus.*
  He spoke to her **so rudely** *that she walked out of the room.*

● the words *many, much* and *few*, with or without a noun:
  He's invited **so many people** *to the party there's nowhere to sit down.*
  I've got **so few books** *I can keep them on one shelf.*
  You complain **so much** *that everyone gets bored.*

209

Such is followed by:

- *a(n)* (if necessary) + adjective + noun:
  *Her father is **such a rich man** that she's never travelled by bus.*
  *The café always charges **such high prices** that students can't afford to eat there.*

- *a(n)* (if necessary) + noun only:
  *They were treated with **such kindness** that they were reluctant to leave.*
  *The concert was **such a success** they decided to give another.*

- the expression *a lot (of)* with or without a noun:
  *He's invited **such a lot of people** to the party there's nowhere to sit down.*
  *I **spent such a lot** last night.*

> See Unit 8, B4 for other words which modify adjectives and adverbs.

Enough and *too*

Enough means 'sufficient, the right quantity'. *Too* means 'more than enough'.
We can use *too* and *enough* with adjectives, adverbs and nouns, followed by:

- *to* + infinitive:
  *This bag is **too heavy to carry**.*
  *I'm not **strong enough to carry** this bag.*
  *He wasn't running **quickly enough to catch** us.*

- *for* something / someone:
  *This bikini is **too small for** me.*
  *Have you got **enough money for** the car park?*

Enough:

- goes before a noun:
  *I've got **enough sandwiches for lunch**.*
  (= as many sandwiches as I need)

- goes after an adverb:
  *Are we speaking **loudly enough to be heard**?* (= Can everyone hear us?)

- goes after an adjective:
  *This room is **warm enough for me**.*
  (= the right temperature)

Too:

- goes before *many/much* + a noun:
  *I've got **too many books to carry**.* (= I can't carry all of them)
  *I've got **too much work**.* (= I can't do it all)

- goes before an adverb:
  *Are we speaking **too loudly**?* (= Are we disturbing the other students?)

- goes before an adjective:
  *This room is **too warm for us**.* (= the temperature is uncomfortably high)

⚠ *Very* does not mean the same as *too*:
*This jacket is **very** expensive, but I can afford it.*
*This jacket is **too** expensive, so I can't afford it.*

C Grammar exercises

1 Fill in the gaps, using the words and phrases in the box.

as   ~~because~~   enough   in order to   so   so   so that   too

1
> Why are you staring at me like that?

> <u>Because</u> you've got a large black mark on the end of your nose!

2
> It's only eleven o'clock. Why aren't you still at school?

> We've been sent home early .... revise for our exam tomorrow.

3
> How was the trip to the museum?

> .... several galleries were closed for repairs, it was rather disappointing.

Gallery Closed

4
> What are all those students doing in the park?

> The university term has ended .... they're having a picnic to celebrate.

5
> Why are you working late today?

> I want to finish this essay .... I'll be free to go out tomorrow.

6
> Come on! If we run fast ...., we'll catch the early train.

> Sorry, I've got .... many bags I can't run.

> Oh, never mind. If we're .... late for that train, we can have a drink while we wait for the next one.

2 For each pair of sentences, decide whether they mean exactly the same. Write S (same) or D (different).

1 a It was such a sad film I couldn't stop crying at the end.
   b The film was so sad I couldn't stop crying at the end. S
2 a We're packing our cases tonight as we're leaving very early tomorrow.
   b We're leaving very early tomorrow so we're packing our cases tonight.
3 a My father says I'm too young to have a motorbike.
   b My father says I'm very young to have a motorbike.
4 a I've lost weight so I can wear this tight skirt at my party.
   b I can wear this tight skirt at my party because I've lost weight.
5 a Since I've never been to New York, I can't tell you much about it.
   b I can't tell you much about New York as I've never been there.
6 a She's been given so much advice that she doesn't know what to do.
   b She's been given enough advice so she knows what to do.

3 Match the beginnings and endings of these sentences.

1 Tessa's got so much homework ...h...
2 Stephen's so vain ....
3 Jessie has so many hobbies ....
4 This music isn't too loud ....
5 Saskia hasn't got enough money ....
6 Keith earns so much money ....
7 I think there's enough bread ....
8 Peter has such a bad cold ....

a he should be in bed.
b to make sandwiches for us all.
c he can buy any clothes he wants.
d she neglects her schoolwork.
e for us.
f to come on holiday with us.
g he thinks every girl fancies him.
h she can't come out with us.

4 Complete these sentences using your own ideas.

1 The bus company offers cheaper fares at weekends in order to _attract more passengers._
2 The hotel dining room is closed this week. Therefore guests ....
3 We'd better phone a qualified electrician, as we ....
4 Because my brother uses a wheelchair, he often ....
5 I don't have a mobile phone so my friends ....
6 She has such beautiful clothes she ....
7 We enjoyed the party so much we ....
8 Is this box big enough to ....

D Exam practice

Use of English Part 1

For questions **1–12**, read the text below and decide which answer (**A**, **B**, **C** or **D**) best fits each gap. There is an example at the beginning (**0**).

0　Ⓐ proposed　**B** offered　**C** presented　**D** allowed

WORLD ENGLISH

The term 'World English' has been **(0)** ...A... by some people to describe the kind of English which is used and understood all around the world. It is true that if we read English language newspapers, or **(1)** .... to newsreaders who use English in different **(2)** .... of the world, we may gain the impression that one kind of English is so **(3)** .... used that it will soon unite all the different varieties which exist. Is there enough **(4)** .... to support this impression? It is in **(5)** .... misleading in several ways since a version of English which is exactly the same **(6)** .... and is equally well regarded throughout the world does not yet **(7)** .... For one thing, people whose first language is English are **(8)** .... of their particular version of the language. Therefore, they try to **(9)** .... it from the influence of other forms of English. New Zealanders, for example, do not want to speak like Australians. In addition, there are too many regional differences in **(10)** .... for the language to be the same everywhere. People need specialised words in order to **(11)** .... local politics, business, culture and natural history. Lastly, of course, learners of English may be taught American or British forms, **(12)** .... in writing and speaking.

1　**A** look	**B** listen	**C** watch	**D** hear
2　**A** divisions	**B** parts	**C** sections	**D** places
3　**A** widely	**B** extremely	**C** totally	**D** normally
4　**A** knowledge	**B** witness	**C** belief	**D** evidence
5　**A** particular	**B** fact	**C** theory	**D** danger
6　**A** always	**B** nowadays	**C** everywhere	**D** anywhere
7　**A** exist	**B** happen	**C** occur	**D** arrive
8　**A** confident	**B** jealous	**C** proud	**D** attached
9　**A** hold	**B** possess	**C** preserve	**D** insure
10　**A** pronunciation	**B** literature	**C** education	**D** vocabulary
11　**A** argue	**B** talk	**C** mention	**D** discuss
12　**A** both	**B** either	**C** or	**D** nor

These extracts are from the text. Without looking back at the text, fill in the gaps with the words in the box.

| enough | in order to | ~~so~~ | that | therefore | to | too |

... we may gain the impression that one kind of English is ......*so*...... (1) widely used .... (2) it will soon unite all the different varieties which exist.

Is there .... (3) evidence .... (4) support this impression?

For one thing, people whose first language is English are proud of their particular version of the language. .... (5), they try to preserve it from the influence of other forms of English.

... there are .... (6) many regional differences in vocabulary for the language to be the same everywhere.

People need specialised words .... (7) discuss local politics, business, culture and natural history.

Writing Part 1

You have received an email from your English-speaking friend, Catherine, who needs some advice from you. Read Catherine's email and the notes you have made. Then write a reply, using **all** your notes.

From: Catherine Palmer
Sent: 22 May
Subject: A nice problem!

Thank you for coming to my eighteenth birthday party last week. I was given quite a lot of money as presents and I'm trying to decide how to spend it. I need your advice!

My first idea was to fly to New York for a shopping trip.

No, because ...

But then I thought about buying a new computer or a motorbike and I can't decide.

Neither, because ...

Even if I buy something I'll still have some money left so I could pay to do a course but I can't decide what to study.

Yes! Say what and why

Of course, I could save it until I'm older or do you have any other exciting suggestions?

Write back soon. I need your help.

Suggest

Love,

Catherine

Write your **email** in **120–150** words in a style appropriate for the situation.

Writing hints

This task gives you a chance to practise:
making suggestions and explaining them.
using *as, because, in order to* etc. when you explain your ideas.
using *too ..., so ...,* to say why something is not a good idea.

Useful expressions
dangerous, silly, pointless, practical, sensible, fun
to have an adventure, to take risks, to use up, to run out of

25 Linking words 2

in spite of and *despite*; *but, although* and *though*; *even though* and *even if*, participle clauses; *before* and *after* + *-ing*; *when, while* and *since* + *-ing*

A Context listening

1 You are going to hear an interview with a young woman. Look at the newspaper headlines from two years earlier. One of the headlines has the correct facts, the rest are wrong.

a
New star signs contract to make three films in a year

b
15-YEAR-OLD GIVEN LEADING ROLE IN NEW FILM

c
Teenage film actor wins starring part

d
GIRL WITH NO ACTING EXPERIENCE IS NEW FILM STAR

🔊25 Listen to the interview and tick the correct headline.

2 🔊25 Listen again and fill in the gaps. Stop the recording when you need to.

1 ... you've been world famous ....*since making*........ the film *Starshine* two years ago ...

2 I got the part .... no film experience.

3 The director chose me to play the part .... several schools.

4 I had a long talk with my parents .... it.

5 I was offered two more films .... *Starshine* ...

6 ... but .... far from home, I sometimes felt very lonely.

7 I'd be happy to do another film later, ... booked up for the next few months.

8 It's actually a comedy, ... called *Dark Days*.

3 What form of the verb follows *since, in spite of, despite, after, before* and *while* in the sentences in Exercise 2? ....

216

B Grammar

1 *In spite of* and *despite*

These words:

- are used to explain an unexpected event:
  I got the part **in spite of** *having no experience.*
  We enjoyed the trip **despite** *the bad weather.*

- go at the beginning or in the middle of the sentence:
  In spite of / **Despite** *having little money, we were very happy.*
  We were very happy **in spite of** / **despite** *having little money.*
  If they go at the beginning, there is usually a comma in the middle of the sentence.

- are followed by *-ing* or a noun:
  He continued to work **in spite of** / **despite being** *ill.*
  He continued to work **in spite of** / **despite his illness**.

- are often followed by *the fact that* + subject + verb:
  I got the part **in spite of the fact that** *I had no experience.*
  Despite the fact that *I had no experience, I got the part.*

In spite of is more common in speaking than *despite*.

2 *But, although* and *though*

These words contrast two events or ideas. *Though* and *although* are slightly stronger than *but*. *Though* is weaker than *although*, and is more common in speaking.

But always goes in the middle of the sentence:
I like making films **but** *I'm really a stage actor.*

Although and *though* can go in the middle or at the beginning of the sentence:
I like making films **though** / **although** *I'm really a stage actor.*
Though / **Although** *I'm really a stage actor, I like making films.*
(notice the comma)

⚠ We can't use *though* / *although* and *but* in the same sentence.
(**not** ~~Though / Although I'm really a stage actor, but I like making films.~~)

⚠ We sometimes use *though* at the end of a sentence:
I like making films. I'm really a stage actor, **though**.

3 *Even though* and *even if*

These words emphasise a contrast. We use *even though* when we are certain about something:

*She was given the part **even though** she had no experience.* (= the speaker knows Gemma had no experience)

We use *even if* when we are not certain about our facts:

*I'll support my team **even if** they don't win the Cup.* (= I don't know whether they'll win the Cup, but I'll support them anyway.)

4 Participle clauses

The *-ing* form or the past participle:

- are used to combine two sentences when both sentences have the same subject.
- can replace the subject + verb of the first sentence:

*I **work** far from home. + **I** sometimes feel lonely. → **Working** far from home, **I** sometimes feel lonely.*
*Gemma **was asked** about the play. + Gemma → **Asked** about the play, **Gemma** said it was said it was great.*   *great.*

These structures are more common in writing than in speaking.

The *-ing* form:

- can replace an active verb:

    *We **were** short of time.*   → ***Being** short of time, **we** had to run for the bus.*
    *+ **We** had to run for the bus.*

- links two things happening at about the same time (present or past):

    *The **girl used** all her strength.*   → ***Using** all her strength, **the girl** pushed open the*
    *+ **The girl** pushed open the heavy doors.*   *heavy doors.*

The past participle:

- can replace a passive verb:

    *The **girls were refused** entry to the club.*   → ***Refused** entry to the club, **the girls** walked*
    *+ **The girls** walked slowly home.*   *slowly home.*

- links two connected events or situations:

    *'**Greensleeves**' **was written** in the*   → ***Written** in the sixteenth century, '**Greensleeves**'*
    sixteenth century.   *is still a famous song.*
    *+ '**Greensleeves**' is still a famous song.*

5 *Before* and *after* + *-ing*

Before and *after* + *-ing*:
- show the order in which things happen.
- are used to combine two sentences only when both sentences have the same subject.
- can replace the subject + verb of either sentence:

I had a long talk with my parents.   →   I had a long talk with my parents **before**
(= first event)   **accepting** the part. or
+ **I accepted** the part.   I accepted the part **after having** a long talk
(= second event)   with my parents.

These words can go at the beginning or in the middle of the sentence.
If they go at the beginning, there is usually a comma in the middle:
Before accepting the part, I had a long talk with my parents.
After having a long talk with my parents, I accepted the part.

These structures are more common in writing than in speaking.

6 *When, while* and *since* + *-ing*

We can use *when, while* and *since* + *-ing* in a similar way to *before* and *after* + *-ing*.

When + *-ing* links two actions happening at the same time:
When leaving the train, passengers should ensure that they have all their possessions with them.
It's important to make a good impression *when starting* a new job.

While + *-ing* links a longer action to an action which happens in the middle of it:
I was offered two more films *while making* 'Starshine'.
While making 'Starshine', I was offered two more films.

Since + *-ing* links an ongoing situation or action to the event or action when it began:
She hasn't been in touch once *since moving* to New York.
Since leaving school, she's completely changed.

C Grammar exercises

1 Match the beginnings and endings of these sentences.

1 I know Shanghai quite well, ...g..
2 In spite of injuring his foot, ...
3 He doesn't earn very much, ...
4 Although he's not keen on computers, ...
5 Smiling and holding hands, ...
6 When changing the torch battery, ...
7 Before signing that document, ...
8 After winning the lottery, ...
9 Despite the fact that it is very old, ...

a you should read it carefully.
b he was a very wealthy man.
c he won the race.
d in spite of being so talented.
e this book is still very useful.
f they announced their engagement.
g but I've never been to Beijing.
h Dad emails us when he's away.
i be careful not to damage the bulb.

2 For each pair of sentences, decide whether they mean exactly the same. Write S (same) or D (different).

1 a Although Sharon quite enjoys musicals, she really prefers more serious drama.
  b Sharon quite enjoys musicals, but she really prefers more serious drama. S

2 a Asking to explain his behaviour, Sam admitted that he had lost his temper.
  b Asked to explain his behaviour, Sam admitted that he had lost his temper.

3 a Brian continued to work long hours, in spite of being ill.
  b Even though he was ill, Brian continued to work long hours.

4 a Chloe's father promised her a car, even though she didn't pass her final exam.
  b Chloe's father promised her a car, even if she didn't pass her final exam.

5 a Warning of storms ahead, the mountain guide led us back to the hostel.
  b Warned of storms ahead, the mountain guide led us back to the hostel.

6 a Despite searching everywhere, I didn't find the money.
  b I searched everywhere, but I didn't find the money.

3 Combine each pair of sentences, using the *-ing* form or the past participle.

1 Arnold was faced with a difficult decision. Arnold decided to consult his boss.
<u>Faced with a difficult decision, Arnold decided to consult his boss.</u>

2 The singer waved to her fans. The singer got into her car.
<u>Waving to her fans, the singer got into her car.</u>

3 Simon grumbled about the amount of homework he had. Simon took out his grammar book.

....

4 The scientist felt very excited about her latest discovery. The scientist invited the journalists into the laboratory.

....

5 The children were puzzled by what they had heard. The children asked their teacher what it meant.

....

6 Wendy was a sensible girl. Wendy didn't panic when she cut her hand.

....

7 Paul heard cries for help. Paul dived into the water.

....

8 This CD was released only last week. This CD is already at the top of the charts.

....

4 Complete these sentences using your own ideas.

1 I quite enjoy playing tennis, in spite of the fact that <u>I usually lose.</u>
2 Although Agnes is only thirteen, she ....
3 While painting my room, ...
4 .... before attempting to run a marathon.
5 Dressed only in his underwear, ...
6 I hardly ever receive any letters even though ....
7 Waving .... the football fans cheered their team loudly.
8 They insist they'll have a barbecue even if ....
9 My grandfather swims in the lake every day despite ....
10 Since arriving in this country, ...

D Exam practice

Use of English Part 2

For questions **1–12**, read the text below and think of the word which best fits each gap. Use only **one** word in each gap. There is an example at the beginning (**0**).

ANTARCTICA

It is probable that until two hundred years (**0**) ....*ago*....... Antarctica had never been seen by any human eyes. The first people who are known to have seen it (**1**) .... hunters on ships in 1819. Two years later, one of them (**2**) .... to land there even (**3**) .... conditions prevented him from exploring very far. Larger scientific expeditions later came to the Antarctic to find out more. By the end of the nineteenth century they had succeeded in mapping the coast of the continent, in (**4**) .... of the fact that Antarctica is almost entirely covered by a thick layer of ice which in places stretches far (**5**) .... the edge of the land onto the sea.

There was something else which attracted people to Antarctica (**6**) .... scientific research. This was the South Pole. A number of attempts to reach it were made in the early years of the twentieth century, (**7**) .... the first person to get there was the Norwegian, Roald Amundsen, in 1911. Travelling with dogs (**8**) .... pull the sledges (**9**) .... carried his party's supplies, he arrived (**10**) .... the pole five weeks before his rivals, a British group (**11**) .... by Robert Scott.

(**12**) .... the terrible weather conditions, many nations now have scientific bases on Antarctica, carrying out research on a great range of subjects.

Grammar focus task

These extracts are from the text. Without looking back at the text, match the beginnings (1–5) and endings (a–e).

1 ... one of them managed to land there even though ..b...

2 ... they had succeeded in mapping the coast of the continent, in spite of the fact that ....

3 A number of attempts to reach it were made in the early years of the twentieth century, ...

4 Travelling with dogs to pull the sledges that carried his party's supplies, ...

5 Despite the terrible weather conditions, ...

a Antarctica is almost entirely covered by a thick layer of ice ...

b conditions prevented him from exploring very far.

c many nations now have scientific bases on Antarctica ...

d but the first person to get there was the Norwegian, Roald Amundsen ...

e he arrived at the pole five weeks before his rivals ...

Writing Part 2

You see the following advertisement in your university newspaper:

My hero

Which man or woman do you most admire?
Write an article explaining why you admire him/her.
We will publish the most interesting articles next month.

Write your **article** in **120–180** words.

Writing hints

This task gives you a chance to practise:
describing how someone overcame problems.
using *because, in spite of / despite, although / but, even though.*

Useful words and expressions
to accept, to bear, to carry on, to cope with, to put up with, to refuse, to succeed

223

Key

Entry test

If you have the wrong answer, see the units indicated for more information.

1	A	(➤ Unit 1)
2	B	(➤ Unit 1)
3	C	(➤ Unit 2)
4	B	(➤ Unit 2)
5	A	(➤ Unit 3)
6	B	(➤ Unit 3)
7	B	(➤ Unit 4)
8	C	(➤ Unit 4)
9	B	(➤ Unit 5)
10	A	(➤ Unit 5)
11	A	(➤ Unit 6)
12	B	(➤ Unit 6)
13	A	(➤ Unit 7)
14	C	(➤ Unit 7)
15	A	(➤ Unit 8)
16	C	(➤ Unit 8)
17	A	(➤ Unit 9)
18	C	(➤ Unit 9)
19	A	(➤ Unit 10)
20	C	(➤ Unit 10)
21	A	(➤ Unit 11)
22	B	(➤ Unit 11)
23	C	(➤ Unit 12)
24	B	(➤ Unit 12)
25	C	(➤ Unit 13)
26	B	(➤ Unit 13)
27	A	(➤ Unit 14)
28	C	(➤ Unit 14)
29	C	(➤ Unit 15)
30	A	(➤ Unit 15)
31	B	(➤ Unit 16)
32	C	(➤ Unit 16)
33	B	(➤ Unit 17)
34	A	(➤ Unit 17)
35	A	(➤ Unit 18)
36	C	(➤ Unit 18)
37	C	(➤ Unit 19)
38	B	(➤ Unit 19)
39	C	(➤ Unit 20)
40	B	(➤ Unit 20)
41	C	(➤ Unit 21)
42	B	(➤ Unit 21)
43	A	(➤ Unit 22)
44	B	(➤ Unit 22)
45	A	(➤ Unit 23)
46	A	(➤ Unit 23)
47	A	(➤ Unit 24)
48	B	(➤ Unit 24)
49	A	(➤ Unit 25)
50	B	(➤ Unit 25)

Unit 1

A: Context listening

2 1 in her room / at home
   2 in a shopping centre / outside a shop
   3 Millie is phoning to ask Lisa if she wants her to buy a bag.

3 2 She buys new clothes.
   3 She's looking for a new skirt / one of those new skirts.
   4 She's wearing a pair of old jeans.
   5 She's cleaning her room.
   6 She looks for a bag.
   7 She's looking at a blue bag (that Lisa wants).
   8 She wants Millie to buy the bag.

4 1 The present simple.
   2 The present continuous.
   3 2 and 6.
   4 1, 3, 4, 5 and 7.
   5 No. It is in the present simple but is not a regular action.
   (➤ see B3)

C: Grammar exercises

1 2 a 3 a 4 a 5 b (➤ B1–3)

2 2 are you wearing; looks 3 smells 4 like; don't fit 5 are you thinking 6 have; means; don't understand 7 Do / Can you see; 're (are) looking; Do you recognise; seem; 're (are) coming 8 are you doing; 'm (am) just making; don't want; are waiting; 're (are) getting (➤ B1–3)

3 2 are enjoying 3 cost 4 are staying 5 have 6 don't like 7 serve 8 never eat 9 don't feel 10 have 11 are having 12 are visiting 13 love 14 behave 15 smile 16 says 17 is always showing (*shows* is correct but does not make clear that she is criticising) 18 come 19 realise 20 are taking (➤ B1–3)

4 *Sample answers:*
   2 I listen to pop music every day.
   3 My aunt's visiting us at the moment.
   4 I have a shower before breakfast, but I don't get dressed.
   5 We're revising for our exams this term.
   6 I go on holiday once a year.
   7 I play squash or go swimming most weekends.
   (➤ B1–3)

D: Exam practice
Listening

1 B 2 A 3 C 4 A 5 B 6 C 7 A

Grammar focus task

2 think 3 he's actually doing 4 enjoy 5 goes 6 do you do 7 form

Writing *Sample answer:*

Dear Charlie,

Thanks for your letter. Yes, it's summer holiday time here. Not many people go abroad, because there are good beaches and mountain resorts in my country. Usually families go to the seaside for a few weeks, but some prefer to spend time in the mountains. It's cooler there and you can explore in the forests or go rock-climbing. My family stay with my uncle's family in a house near the sea. We swim and go out in my uncle's boat. We're at the beach house now, in fact.

You want to know what I'm doing this afternoon. Nothing adventurous! I'm lying on the sofa writing to you. My cousins are watching TV, but it's not very good. They're always watching silly films, but I don't like doing that. Most people stay indoors during the afternoon in summer, because of the heat. In the evening we play volleyball or some other games on the beach, and sometimes we eat at a typical local restaurant with other families.

When does your holiday start?

Write soon,

Fernando

Unit 2

A: Context listening

2   2 J   3 G   4 M   5 J

3   1 He went to London, went to the cinema, saw a famous footballer and went to a club.

2 a We caught the coach … it was only ten pounds return.

b … we went to see a film.

3 The past simple.

4 Collect autographs, go up to town alone, scream at pop concerts.

5 a I used to collect all the autographs …

b I used to scream at pop concerts.

6 No.

7 Yes.

4   1 were travelling 2 were queuing
3 was buying; were walking

5   The past continuous.

C: Grammar exercises

1   2 found 3 explained 4 was 5 knew 6 wrote 7 seemed 8 ate
9 drank 10 got 11 learnt / learned 12 found 13 fed 14 gave
15 tied 16 went 17 spoke 18 met 19 read 20 had 21 spread
22 came (➤ B1)

2   2 travelled; always kept 3 saw; was waiting; did not / didn't
see 4 filled; gave 5 was working; met; looked 6 finished;
was always cancelling (*always cancelled* is also possible but it
doesn't emphasise that Simon was annoyed by her behaviour)
7 was hoping; didn't get (➤ B1–2)

3   2 used to feel 3 met 4 was walking 5 told 6 were breaking
7 were sitting 8 realised 9 didn't want 10 moved
11 am not used 12 thought (➤ B1–3)

4   2 are used to 3 is used to 4 isn't used to / wasn't used to
5 Are you getting used to / Have you got used to / Are you
used to 6 got used to (➤ B3)

5   *Sample answers:* 3 I used to be afraid of the dark. 4 I used to
study French. 5 I used to play football with my father.
6 My sister and I used to share a room. (➤ B3)

6   *Sample answers:* 2 I didn't finish till ten. 3 ran out of the
room. 4 spend a whole morning climbing trees. 5 we saw a
teacher from our school. 6 travelled by train / used to travel
by train / would travel by train 7 was revising for my exams.
8 borrowing his brother's car. (➤ B1–3)

D: Exam practice
Use of English

1 A 2 B 3 C 4 C 5 A 6 D 7 C 8 B 9 D 10 C 11 B 12 C

Grammar focus task

2 became 3 began 4 came 5 fell 6 found 7 went 8 held 9 led
10 made 11 rang 12 spent

Writing *Sample answer:*

When I was quite young, I did something silly one day. It was soon after my family moved from the country to the city. In those days, there was little traffic in the countryside. My friends and I used to play on the open ground between the houses. In the city we had a garden, and my mother said to me, 'You must play in the garden. Don't go outside.' I didn't understand why she said this, but I obeyed.

One day I was playing in our garden when I saw one of my friends. She was walking along the other side of the road with her father. I rushed out of the garden to meet them. A lorry was coming down the road and it nearly hit me. Luckily, I wasn't hurt. But I was very frightened.

I now realise that I forgot my mother's instructions because I didn't understand the reason for them. I clearly remember thinking about this at the time. Now I always give an explanation when I tell young children to do something.

Unit 3

A: Context listening

2   They live next door to each other. Mike plays a saxophone and Lucy can't concentrate on her work.

3   2 I've been at the gym.
3 I still haven't finished it.
4 I started it last week.
5 I never enjoyed studying history.
6 I've lived next door since June.
7 I've lived here for two years.
8 Nobody's ever complained before.

4   1 The past simple.
2 The present perfect.
3 3, 6 and 7.
4 1, 4 and 5.

C: Grammar exercises

1　2 h　3 d　4 f　5 c　6 b　7 i　8 e　9 a　10 g (➤ B1)

2　2 slept　3 has grown　4 sent; hasn't replied　5 Did you learn
　6 bought; 've (have) used　7 have you had　8 's (has) just
　arrived　9 've (have) never seen　10 dreamt　11 met
　12 did you get; haven't noticed (➤ B1)

3　2 arrived　3 felt / was　4 have already made　5 took / drove
　6 went / swam　7 enjoyed / loved / liked　8 've (have) learnt
　9 haven't been　10 've (have) had　11 went　12 played
　(➤ B1)

4　2 have you been playing　3 We've played　4 we haven't
　finished　5 you've been playing　6 We've read
　7 Have you tried　8 we've already started　9 we've booked
　(➤ B2)

D: Exam practice
Reading

1 A　2 C　3 B　4 B　5 C　6 C　7 D　8 B　9 A　10 C　11 D　12 C　13 A
14 B　15 D

Grammar focus task

1　've always spent
2　intended
3　've enjoyed
4　didn't own
5　bought
6　walked
7　fell
8　hasn't happened
9　've worn
10　worked
11　was
12　've been

Writing *Sample answer:*

Dear Sir

　I would like to apply for a job at a Mulberry seaside camp. I
would prefer to be by the sea as I have been living in a big city
for five years and now I would like to swim and do sport by
the sea. I am not free in July because I am visiting relatives in
Australia then. However, I am available in August. I have been
studying English since I was ten and I have spent some time in
Australia, so I am fluent in speaking, and my teachers say I have
a good accent.

　I have been in my school swimming team for two years and I
have taken part in national competitions. I have always enjoyed
all kinds of sport and I like helping younger children. I have also
helped with school drama productions although I do not act.

　I hope you will consider my application.

　Yours faithfully,

　Nika Tabakova

*Note: As this is a letter of application the verbs are all in
their full forms (I have, not I've). We use the full forms of
verbs when we write formal letters.*

Unit 4

A: Context listening

2　He's been painting his room. His mother is angry because
　there is paint on the carpet.

3　2 'd painted　3 ran out of　4 was　5 'd been　6 'd done
　7 'd finished　8 'd been driving　9 broke down

4　1 3 happened after 1 and 2. He uses the past perfect for 1 and
　　2, and the past simple for 3.
　2 4 happened after 5, 6 and 7. He uses the past simple for 4,
　　and the past perfect for 5, 6 and 7.
　3 8 happened first. She uses the past perfect continuous for 8,
　　and the past simple for 9.

C: Grammar exercises

1　2 hadn't been learning / studying　3 had been planning
　4 'd (had) been worrying　5 'd (had) been waiting　6 'd (had)
　been sending　7 hadn't been playing　8 'd (had) been saving
　9 had they been looking (➤ B2)

2　2 No　3 Yes: it had been snowing　4 No　5 No　6 No
　7 Yes: they'd been arguing　8 No (➤ B1–2)

3　2 came; fainted; hadn't (had not) seen　3 had begun; arrived
　4 had you been applying; got　5 Had you ever done; built
　6 didn't (did not) see; 'd (had) gone　7 sat; 'd (had) left
　8 'd (had) been driving; realised　9 went; stopped; looked
　10 'd (had) washed; hung　11 discovered; 'd (had) believed
　(➤ B1–2)

4　2 'd (had) been playing　3 'd (had) ever had　4 'd (had) been
　practising　5 'd (had) been moving　6 had gone
　7 'd (had) arranged　8 didn't (did not) answer　9 came
　10 banged　11 'd (had) been phoning　12 hadn't (had not)
　heard　13 arrived　14 'd (had) forgotten (➤ B1–2)

D: Exam practice
Reading

1 C　2 A　3 B　4 C　5 A　6 D　7 D　8 B

Grammar focus task

2 was　3 'd been writing　4 had just sent　5 had　6 'd heard
7 gathered

Writing *Sample answer:*

The house was empty but I could see that someone had been
there and had only just left. I had been walking in the forest and
I had lost my way so I had come to the house to ask directions.
To my surprise I noticed that the table had been laid ready for
a meal with glasses and plates and somebody had been cooking
because there was a lovely smell coming from the kitchen. I ate a
few spoonfuls from a saucepan and it was delicious so I had a few
more. I looked round the house but there was nobody there.

　Suddenly there was a loud noise from the back of the house.
I held my breath and tiptoed towards the door. I was too late. A
large angry man appeared in front of me at the door. He shouted
at me. I tried to explain that I had found the door open and
wanted to ask for directions. He came towards me and I thought
he might hit me so I ran away as fast as I could. But at least I had
tasted his dinner.

Unit 5

A: Context listening

2   1 c 2 b 3 d 4 a   Tom is a journalist.

3   2 starts 3 arrives 4 'm playing 5 'm flying 6 'm having
7 won't be 8 'll get 9 'll have 10 will be 11 won't be
12 will live

4   1 1, 2 and 3; the present simple.
2 7, 8 and 9; the *will*-future.
3 4, 5, and 6; the present continuous.
4 10, 11 and 12; the *will*-future.

C: Grammar exercises

1   2 doesn't leave 3 stops 4 doesn't arrive 5 are staying
6 are spending 7 doesn't go 8 are having 9 leaves 10 arrives
(➤ B1–2)

2   2 is leaving 3 'm (am) giving; are you giving; 'll (will)
probably get 4 're (are) moving; 'll (will) come 5 will not
continue; will not recover 6 'll (will) have 7 is staying
8 'll (will) have 9 Are you doing; is arriving; 'm (am) driving
10 'll (will) get (➤ B2–3)

3   *Sample answers:*
1 Rebecca Jones will be pleased that Anna has invited her
to visit.
One of the cousins will reply to Anna and she will realise
her mistake.
Anna will be angry with herself when she finds out what
she has done and she will have to explain what happened to
her cousins.
2 There will be an argument. The teachers will insist that
the hotel manager finds them rooms. The hotel manager
will apologise.
The hotel manager will offer to find them rooms in another
hotel. He will order taxis to take them there.
The teachers and teenagers will be angry because they are
tired. (➤ B3)

4   2 is going to see / is seeing the doctor 3 will be 80 4 starts
5 'll (shall / will) be a teacher 6 'll (will) be flying / sitting in
an aeroplane 7 ends / finishes 8 'll (will) be skiing 9 're (are)
going 10 will lend / give me (➤ B1–4)

D: Exam practice
Listening

1 coffee bar 2 order / ask for 3 7.15 / (a) quarter past seven
4 deputy manager 5 waterfall 6 (flour) mill 7 (coal) mine
8 lamps 9 windsurfing 10 strong boots

Grammar focus task

1   2 're going 3 're travelling 4 'll probably eat 5 're making
6 'll be 7 won't be able to 8 'll probably stop 9 'll need

2   The verbs in 2, 3 and 5 are in the present continuous because
these things have already been arranged.

Writing *Sample answer:*

Dear Alison

I'm looking forward to seeing you too, and showing you round
here. I'll meet you at the station at 11.30. You needn't bring any
food because there's a good café near there, where we can have
a coffee and catch up on all our news. You can meet some of my
friends there too. I think you'll like them.

My mother will make you a typical meal of our region for
lunch and you'll see my home.

In the afternoon we'll go to the old part of the town, which
has lots of good shops for souvenirs and a great café where they
sell local ice cream. The last train leaves at 7.30 so we'll have
plenty of time to look round.

I'm sorry you can't stay overnight, but perhaps you'll be able
to come again soon.

Love from

Tanya

Unit 6

A: Context listening

2   Simon has come to interview the people on the island. Life on
the island is very tough.

3   2 Because they're fed up with the cold, the wind, the mud and
the rain.
3 As soon as possible.
4 They'll have survived longer than anyone else in a place like
Wildrock.
5 For nearly six months.
6 As soon as they find a restaurant.
7 Simon stays because the other people take his boat and
leave him!

4   1 2, 3, 6 and 7.
2 1.
3 4 and 5.

C: Grammar exercises

1   *Sample answers:*
2 're (are) going to / about to arrest him.
3 's (is) going to / about to score a goal.
4 's (is) going / about to to sink.
5 's (is) going to / about to crash.
6 's (is) going to / about to kiss him. (➤ B1 and 5)

2   2 The world's population will have doubled. 3 Computers will
have replaced most manual workers. 4 We will have used all
the oil resources on Earth. 5 Doctors will have discovered a
cure for AIDS. 6 Scientists will have invented new sources of
energy. 7 Sea temperatures will have risen by several degrees.
(➤ B4)

3   2 b 3 b 4 a 5 b (➤ B2)

4   2 The secretary will have been typing letters for four hours.
3 The manager will have been interviewing new staff for five
and a half hours.
4 The waitress will have been standing in the dining room for
three hours.

5 The cleaner will have been vacuuming floors for seven hours.
(➤ B4)

5 2 's (is) going to be 3 're (are) going to stay 4 finds out
5 was going to wash 6 'm (am) going to look round
7 're (are) going to miss 8 gets 9 will have taken
10 'll (will) have been working
11 'm (am) going to start / 'm (am) about to start
(➤ B1–5)

D: Exam practice
Reading

1 E 2 A/C 3 A/C 4 B 5 C 6 A/E 7 A/E 8 D 9 A 10 D 11 B
12 D 13 C 14 E 15 A

Grammar focus task

2 starts 3 do 4 will have taken 5 'm (am) 6 go 7 've (have) had
8 get

Writing *Sample answer:*

Dear Class 10B

We are all looking forward to meeting you. This is the plan for the visit.

When you arrive, we're going to show you round the school in groups. You're going to spend the morning in our normal lessons every morning from Monday to Friday. We finish school at 2.30. You're having lunch with us and then you're going to do a variety of activities. On Monday we're going to take you to the swimming pool near the school. So swimming things are essential, but we will provide towels. On Wednesday you can do sport with us. You need football boots and shorts.

On the other days we're going to take you to places like museums and so on. In the evenings we're going to take you to our homes and we can accompany you if you want to go out. There's going to be a party for you at our school on Thursday evening.

We hope you like our plan.

Best wishes,

Georg Schmidt

Unit 7

A: Context listening

2 1 fitness centre 2 wildlife park 3 cleaner 4 music shop
3 1 Stronger, slimmer and more self-confident.
   2 The fiercest lions, the funniest monkeys you've ever seen.
   3 Tired trying to keep the house clean.
   4 The greatest variety of CDs ever.
4 1 sensible; friendly; excellent 2 wonderful; the best; amazing; special 3 fresh; shining; (no) sticky; reasonable
   4 astonishing; the latest; traditional; the most beautiful

C: Grammar exercises

1 2 as / so spacious as 3 more expensive than 4 worse
   5 the smartest 6 the loveliest 7 the poorest 8 the most exhausted 9 the best 10 younger 11 as cheap as
   12 nearer (➤ B1–2)
2 2 depressed 3 amazing 4 annoying 5 bored 6 interesting
   7 excited 8 disgusting 9 relaxed (➤ B3)
3 2 beautiful blue Chinese silk 3 magic gold 4 elegant long leather riding 5 tight yellow silk (➤ B5)
4 2 a 3 b 4 b 5 b 6 a (➤ B1–5)

D: Exam practice
Use of English

1 A 2 B 3 C 4 D 5 A 6 B 7 B 8 D 9 C 10 B 11 A 12 D

Grammar focus task

2 old 3 school 4 good 5 different 6 long 7 few 8 university
9 main 10 leisure

Writing *Sample answer:*

My room is quite small. I have a special bed which is high up. I have to go up a little ladder to reach it. Under the bed I have a desk, where I do my homework, and a small bookshelf for reference books. There are two cupboards, one quite small, and one bigger one, where I keep all my clothes and other things.

The best improvement would be to have a bigger room, but that's not possible. So, I would like to have some new shelves with plenty of space for my DVDs and a small TV. I'd also like to have a giant noticeboard above my bed. I have lots of posters of my favourite singers and sports champions and I'd like to display them properly.

Lastly, I'd like to have my room painted in a better colour. It's pale blue at the moment. I'd like a more exciting colour, like red or purple. But it may be difficult to persuade my parents about that.

Unit 8

Context listening

2 1 stadium 2 spectators 3 whistle 4 ball 5 ground 6 quickly
   7 goal 8 scored 9 loudly
3 2 in the city today; late 3 patiently in their seats 4 happily
   5 steadily 6 heavily on the ground 7 rarely 8 quickly 9 well
   10 Last week 11 often
4 *When:* finally; today; late; last week
   Where: in the city; in their seats; on the ground
   How: patiently; happily; steadily; heavily; quickly; well
   How often: rarely; often

C: Grammar exercises

1 2 gratefully 3 anxiously 4 easily 5 sincerely (➤ B1)
2 2 complete 3 well 4 hard; fluent 5 awful 6 efficiently
   7 normal 8 badly (➤ B1–2)

3   2 Nowadays they rarely eat steak because it is so expensive /
    They rarely eat steak because it is so expensive nowadays. /
    They rarely eat steak nowadays because it is so expensive.
    3 My grandfather used to take us swimming in the lake in the
    summer holidays. / In the summer holidays my grandfather
    used to take us swimming in the lake.
    4 There is usually a good film on TV on Sunday evenings.
    5 My mother insisted that good manners are always terribly
    important. / My mother always insisted that good manners are
    terribly important. (➤ B5)
4   2 earlier 3 always 4 very / rather 5 skilfully 6 rather / very
    7 hardly 8 stiffly 9 now 10 warmly (➤ B1–5)
5   2 b 3 b 4 a 5 a 6 b (➤ B1–5)

D: Exam practice
Use of English

1 scientific 2 equipment 3 qualification 4 extremely
5 dangerously 6 calmly 7 unusually 8 announcement 9 luckily
10 amazing

Grammar focus task

2 extremely, extreme 3 well, good 4 dangerously, dangerous
5 calmly, calm 6 hard, hard 7 unusually, (un)usual
8 luckily, lucky

Writing *Sample answer:*

Last week I saw two films. One was an adventure film called
Speed Robber. I usually enjoy films with lots of action and car
chases, especially when they are cleverly filmed. I was looking
forward to sitting nervously on the edge of my seat for an hour,
because I'd seen other films by the same director. But the story
was disappointingly slow, the actors weren't performing as well
as usual, and the car chase was only a few minutes in a city. It's
certainly the worst film I've seen for a long time.

The other film I saw was completely different. It was a
comedy called *The Last Word*. It was about some students
trying unsuccessfully to write a play. The actors all performed
brilliantly, the dialogue was extremely original, and the plot was
more interesting than *Speed Robber*. My friends and I thoroughly
enjoyed it and we recommend everyone to see it.

Unit 9

A: Context listening

2   Because Mina wasn't at home when he phoned.
3   2 Three. 3 Mina. 4 Peter. 5 By the college gate.
4   2 Have you been checking up on me? No, I haven't.
    3 You said you'd be in tonight, didn't you? Yes, I did.
    4 You know I love you, don't you? Of course I do.
    5 And do you love me? You know I do.
    6 And you'll always love me, won't you? Of course I will.
    7 Let's meet by the college gate, shall we? Yes, let's.

C: Grammar exercises

1   2 b 3 b 4 a 5 b 6 a (➤ B1–4)
2   *Sample answers:*
    3 How long do you spend on your homework?
    4 Have you ever tried windsurfing?
    5 What do you usually do on Sunday evenings?
    6 How often do you see your grandparents?
    7 Did you enjoy the party last weekend?
    8 Why were you late for school this morning?
    (➤ B1 and 3)
3   2 Where was he born?
    3 Who did he telephone?
    4 When did he telephone her / Shirley?
    5 How many children do they have / have they got?
    6 Why is she really pleased?
    7 Who is looking forward to welcoming them back to Farley?
    (➤ B3)
4   2 did they 3 wouldn't you 4 haven't I 5 shall we
    6 could it 7 didn't they 8 won't she 9 can we
    10 don't you (➤ B4)
5   2 c 3 h 4 g 5 a 6 f 7 b 8 e (➤ B5)

D: Exam practice
Listening

1 B 2 C 3 A 4 A 5 C 6 B 7 A 8 C

Grammar focus task

2 did I 3 don't you 4 doesn't it 5 wasn't it 6 can't you 7 aren't I

Writing *Sample answer:*

Dear Michael,

I was very happy to get your letter. I'm seventeen and I live in
Verona with my parents, my two brothers and my grandmother.
My older brother is called Carlo, he's twenty-two and he is at
university. My younger brother is only eleven. He's very naughty.
My mum is a teacher at my brother's school, and he's always in
trouble. My dad works for the tourist office. We have two cats but
no other pets. We live in a flat near the edge of the city.

All my family are crazy about football except for my mum. We
go to a match every weekend. My grandmother watches sport on
television every day.

I'm interested in films, specially horror films, and I like
dancing and going to parties. What sort of films do you like? Do
you do any sport? Have you visited Italy?

I'm interested in travelling but I've never been abroad. I hope
to go to England or Scotland next year with Carlo and some
friends.

Write back to me soon.

Best wishes,

Luisa

Unit 10

A: Context listening

2 *Sample answers:*
  1 She's a sales executive. 2 He works for a garage. / He's a mechanic. / He drives a recovery truck. 3 He delivers pizzas. He's a pizza delivery man. 4 She's a taxi driver.

3 2 Travel. 3 Her health. 4 Fruit. 5 When they run out of petrol. 6 The police. 7 Insurance. 8 He needs cash. 9 Chemistry. 10 The traffic. 11 Food and clothing. 12 There's a lot of unemployment.

4 1 Biscuits or sweets. 2 At a garage. 3 Pizzas. 4 Traffic jams. 5 A job with a reasonable salary. 6 For three years. 7 She's got three children / kids.

5 The nouns in Exercise 3 are uncountable; the nouns in Exercise 4 are countable.

C: Grammar exercises

1a 2 cards 3 paper / glass 4 shoppers 5 glass 6 meat 7 tools 8 clothes 9 rice 10 books / paper / luggage / clothes
 b *Sample answers:*
  1 loaf / slice 2 lump / sheet / block 3 drop / litre 4 plank / splinter / block 5 speck (➤ B1)

2 *Always countable:* experiment; hobby; journey
 Always uncountable: accommodation; advice; homework; information; leisure; luck; scenery; traffic
 Can be countable or uncountable: cheese; coffee; experience; glass; meat; time
 (➤ B1)

3 2 the 3 the 4 the 5 the 6 a 7– 8 the 9 the 10 the 11– 12 – (➤ B2)

4 1 Birmingham Airport 2 the Mediterranean; Naples; Corsica 3 the Sahara; the Andes; Paris 4 a ski instructor; Switzerland 5 a terrible journey; Peterborough station
 (➤ B3)

5 We had *a* great trip to ~~the~~ France last weekend. We went to *the* little hotel that you recommended and it was very pleasant. *The food* at the hotel *wasn't* so good, as you warned us, but we strolled down to *the* city centre on Saturday evening and had *a* lovely meal there. In fact, we ate so much for ~~the~~ dinner that we didn't want *a* breakfast on Sunday!
 Thanks again for the advice and *information.* Now I must unpack and do the *washing.*
 Here is *a* photo of the hotel to remind you. (➤ B1–3)

D: Exam practice
Use of English

1 allowed to play tennis
2 takes pleasure in buying / gets pleasure from buying
3 gave me (some) advice about/on
4 the exact sum/amount of money
5 item of clothing
6 'm/am about to go to / leave for
7 will have been waiting for
8 but/although he hardly ever

Grammar focus task

2 B 3 U 4 U 5 C 6 U 7 C 8 B

Writing *Sample answer:*

  Many people nowadays are worried about their figures, so lots of us want to lose weight. Unfortunately, this is not always easy because so much of our food is not really good for us. For example, fast food, such as burgers and crisps, contains lots of fat.

  Some people think that the best way to control your weight is to eat only lettuce and be miserable! In fact this is not at all good for you. It's much better to eat a diet which consists of lots of different sorts of food.

  You should choose good quality bread, rice, pasta and potatoes for energy. Make sure you eat lots of delicious fruit and vegetables. Meat, fish, cheese and eggs are also good but you don't need so much of these. If you eat well, you'll stay healthy and you'll have plenty of energy for studying and for having fun.

Unit 11

A: Context listening

2 The woman went to the beach last year (picture *a*). The man would probably prefer the quiet mountain holiday (picture *c*).

3 2 myself; of mine 3 Neither 4 by myself 5 each other 6 somewhere 7 None

C: Grammar exercises

1 2 there is 3 It is 4 there are 5 There are 6 there are 7 It is 8 It is 9 there is 10 it is (➤ B5)

2 2 b 3 a 4 a 5 b (➤ B1–3)

3 2 each other 3 every 4 Each 5 everyone 6 Everyone 7 all the 8 one another 9 The whole 10 nobody
 (➤ B2, 4, 6–8)

4 2 Both John and Rob have an earring.
  3 Neither Pete nor John has a moustache.
  4 All of them have short hair / wear glasses.
  5 They all have short hair / wear glasses.
  6 None of them has / have a beard / is bald.
 Sample answers:
  7 Both my mother and my sister have dark hair.
  8 Neither my father nor my grandfather is bald.
  9 All of my family/friends live quite nearby.
  10 None of my family wears/wear glasses.
 (➤ B7 and 9)

D: Exam practice
Use of English

1 everyone / everybody 2 own 3 there 4 mine 5 the 6 else 7 it / mine 8 when / if / whenever 9 than 10 Every 11 Neither 12 both

Grammar focus task

2 a name of my own 3 a close friend of mine
4 somebody else 5 all kinds of 6 neither of them seemed to
mind 7 they both agreed

Writing *Sample answer:*

People travel nowadays from one side of the earth to the other. It
is possible to go anywhere you want and it only takes a few hours
because of aeroplanes. This is good for tourists because they can
visit places which are very different to their own countries and
have a good holiday.

On the one hand, most countries welcome tourists because
they bring money, and tourism gives people jobs so both the
visitors and the local people benefit. On the other hand, there
are some places which have been completely spoilt and this is
not good for the people who live there. Travelling also brings
pollution and damages the environment.

International travel helps trade between countries and makes
the world a smaller place. This is very important for business
and the economy of most countries. By trading with one another,
people from different countries get to know one another and
learn one another's languages.

Unit 12

A: Context listening

2 He's a chef at the Grand Hotel.

3 2 None. 3 It's his day off. 4 He has two days off every week
instead of one. 5 He offers to show Alice the kitchens.

4 2 c 3 a 4 g 5 i 6 j 7 b 8 f 9 h 10 d

5 *Needn't* and *must* aren't followed by *to*.

C: Grammar exercises

1 2 doesn't have to 3 mustn't 4 'll (will) have to 5 has to
6 didn't have to 7 must 8 Do you have to 9 mustn't
10 must 11 had to 12 have to 13 must 14 don't have to
(➤ B1–2)

2 2 f 3 e 4 d 5 a 6 h 7 c 8 b (➤ B2–3)

3 2 worn his latest designer clothes.
3 stand in the queue.
4 carry his luggage.
5 walk from the car park.
6 got angry with his driver.
(➤ B3)

4 2 You needn't / don't need to / don't have to phone me before
you come.
3 Students must / need to buy a good dictionary.
4 You shouldn't have taken money from my purse without
asking.
5 I didn't need to drive to the station to pick up my sister.
6 You should help me (to) do the washing-up.
7 Students mustn't smoke in the canteen.
8 She needn't have turned the music down

9 She shouldn't make promises which she doesn't keep.
10 You don't have to / don't need to / needn't give the tour guide
a tip.
(➤ B1–3)

D: Exam practice
Reading

1 E 2 H 3 B 4 G 5 A 6 F 7 C

Grammar focus task

2 The first thing you must address is tiredness.
3 You should also do a session of exercise once or twice a week in
the evenings.
4 ... walking or tennis have to be kept up for at least an hour ...
5 ... you should choose something which you like doing.
6 ... you must keep doing it until you get really used to it.
7 ... you need to keep reminding yourself of the advantages.
8 ... you don't need to behave in the same way.

Writing *Sample answer:*

Dear Megan

You want to know about our school. We don't have many
rules but we have to arrive by 8.15 every morning. The younger
students have to wear uniform but we needn't. We mustn't wear
jeans, that's all. We mustn't take mobiles into classrooms, we
have to leave them in our lockers during lessons. We have to wear
correct footwear in the sports hall, so you need to bring soft shoes
for that. And of course you'll need your swimming things, but
you won't need your tennis racket, because we've got several. And
you should bring a bag to carry your things in.

What else? You don't need to bring your laptop, because we
can't take them into school and at my house you can use our
computer for email. Older students used to take laptops into
school, but some of them were stolen so we have to leave them at
home now.

That's all the school rules I can think of.

Let me know if you need any more information. It'll be great
to see you!

Viera

Unit 13

A: Context listening

2 2 Can you lend me your new jacket?
3 Can you give me a lift to town now?
4 Will you get me some new batteries?
5 Can you collect me from the city centre at midnight
tonight?

3 2 ✗ 3 ✗ 4 ✗ 5 ✓

4 Would you please give me a lift? Could you collect me?
She asks differently the second time because she wants to be
more polite.

C: Grammar exercises

1   2 May / Could 3 How about / What about 4 could
    5 Will / Can (*Could* is more formal) 6 can / could / 'll (will)
    7 shall / why don't 8 could / would (*can* is less polite)
    9 Can / May 10 Can / Will (➤ B1–4)

2   *Sample answers (other versions possible):*
    2 You should empty the wastepaper bin.
    3 You ought to tidy the filing cabinet / put the papers in the filing cabinet.
    4 You could buy a lampshade.
    5 You'd better take the coat off the chair.
    6 You shouldn't leave the telephone there.
    7 You should repair (the glass in) the window.
    8 You'd better wash the coffee cups.
    (➤ B5)

3   2 Can I do 3 Could I see 4 I'm afraid 5 You can't have
    6 Would you exchange 7 You shouldn't have done 8 You should ask 9 Shall I ask 10 You'd better not 11 You could give
    (➤ B1–5)

4   *Sample answers:*
    2 Shall I / I could / I'll / I can help you clean the flat.
    3 You could buy her some perfume or a CD.
    4 You shouldn't put so much salt on your food.
    5 Could / Can you order this book for me, please?
    6 Can I pay by credit card?
    7 You should buy a watch.
    8 Shall I / I'll / I can help you clear up.
    9 Can you get me a battery for my camera?
    10 Could / Would you give me a lift home?
    (➤ B1–5)

D: Exam practice
Listening

1 F 2 D 3 A 4 E 5 C

Grammar focus task

2 O 3 A 4 F 5 F 6 O 7 A 8 A

Writing *Sample answer:*

Tate Modern gallery
The trip last term was successful. Twelve people came and we travelled by minibus. The gallery had a lot of interesting paintings in it and we enjoyed seeing the ones we had been learning about. There were a few problems on the journey home, but luckily no disasters.

My advice for future trip organisers:

1   You must make sure everyone knows the time and place to meet the bus. On the journey, you ought to check that they all know where they can buy lunch and you should also ask them if they remember what time the bus will leave in the afternoon. Some people are very forgetful!

2   You should allow extra time for the journey home. The traffic may be heavy in the afternoon. If you've got a mobile phone, you'd better take it with you. If there are delays, you could phone to say that the bus will be late.

Unit 14

A: Context listening

2   The woman isn't his mother, but she could be his sister or his girlfriend – Fiona and Clare aren't sure.

3   1 His mother.
    2 The young woman can't be his mother because she's much too young.
    3 To walk across together and pretend they're looking in the shop window.
    4 Because the young woman could be Danny's new girlfriend.
    5 She used to be Danny's girlfriend and she still likes him.

4   2 must be 3 can't be 4 might see 5 could be

5   1 Sentences 2 and 3. 2 Sentences 1, 4 and 5.

C: Grammar exercises

1   2 couldn't / wasn't able to 3 can 4 was able to 5 will be able to
    6 have never been able to 7 to be able to 8 could
    9 couldn't / wasn't able to 10 can't 11 could / can
    (➤ B1 and 2)

2   *Sample answers:*
    2 must
    3 might/could
    4 can't/couldn't
    5 might/could
    6 must
    7 can't/couldn't
    (➤ B2)

3   a 5, 6, 10
    b 2, 3, 4, 7, 8, 9 (➤ B2)

4   2 should be swimming / must be swimming 3 can't / couldn't have left 4 might not / may not have listened 5 might / may / could be 6 must be doing 7 should be 8 must have grown
    9 must be 10 might not / may not come (➤ B2 and 3)

5   *Sample answers:*
    2 can't have stolen; she was with the other cleaners after 6.00.
    3 could have stolen; he was there until 7.15 and alone after his phone call.
    4 must have stolen; he stayed after the gallery was shut and he bought an expensive car.
    5 may have stolen; she was alone there between 6.05 and 6.15 and nobody saw her leave.
    6 couldn't have stolen; she was with the cleaners and they left together.
    (➤ B2)

D: Exam practice
Use of English

1 occasionally 2 confidently 3 assistants 4 delivery
5 instructions 6 attractive 7 fashionable 8 impression
9 actress / actor 10 unlikely

Grammar focus task *Sample answers:*

2 She can't be / couldn't be / might not be / may not be
3 She must be 4 She can't have / might not have 5 She could be / might be / may be 6 She might have / may have / could have

Writing *Sample answer:*

We found the car with its doors open and a briefcase full of money on the back seat. We looked around. We couldn't see anyone. There was a high wall on one side of the road.

'There must have been several people,' I said. 'All the doors are open.'

'Do you think it could be a kidnap? We may be in danger if the kidnappers are nearby,' said my brother.

It was very mysterious. 'I suppose so,' I answered. 'The money might be the payment. But where are they? They can't have left all this money. Anyone could just walk away with it!'

We looked at each other and moved closer to the car. I looked at the money. There was something strange about it. My brother picked up a note. He turned it over. There was nothing on the back.

We had just decided that it must be a game when we saw a television camera on top of the wall. Then we realised a television company was making a film! We spent the rest of the afternoon watching them. It was a great day.

Unit 15

A: Context listening

2 1 d 2 b 3 a 4 c

3 2 were being 3 had been 4 is 5 were being 6 was 7 is 8 was 9 had been 10 to be 11 has been 12 is

4 All of them.

C: Grammar exercises

1 2 b 3 a 4 b 5 a 6 a 7 a (➤ B1)

2 2 had been done 3 are made / have been made / were made 4 to be made 5 are being counted 6 to have been opened; was delivered 7 had been sacked 8 will be awarded (➤ B1)

3 2 has been (completely) crushed 3 has been destroyed 4 was captured 5 was broadcast 6 had been liberated 7 were called on 8 have been arrested 9 are being taken 10 will be put (➤ B1)

4 2 c; have it fixed 3 g; have it cleaned 4 a; 've (have) had it coloured. 5 d; have it redecorated 6 b; to have them taken in 7 h; had it designed 8 f; 're (are) having it serviced (➤ B2 and 3)

D: Exam practice
Use of English

1 was given by the 2 in addition to going 3 flat was looked after by 4 was not passed 5 was accused of cheating by 6 we (often) used to make 7 been promised his 8 to have / get my computer mended

Grammar focus task

Questions 1, 3, 4, 5, 7 and 8 test the passive.

Writing *Sample answer:*

Hi Robbie

You asked about our local celebration. Well, every summer a festival of art and music is held in the village at the beginning of July. The streets are decorated with little flags and things, and coloured lights are hung all round the square. All the shops put flowers in their windows. Some children are made to wear traditional costumes by their parents. Luckily, I'm too old for that!

Most of the concerts are held in the open air. The art exhibitions are in the old market house and sometimes sculptures are displayed in the park.

On the Saturday night, there is a parade through the streets, with music and dancing. The usual sleepy atmosphere is completely changed and everyone feels as if they are at a party. When it is over, everyone is exhausted, but plans are soon being made for the next year.

Perhaps you'll come and stay with me this July, then you can join in. What do you think?

Giorgio

Unit 16

A: Context listening

2 She's asking him about the race and what it's like on the yacht.

3 2 haven't seen 3 think I might 4 was 5 didn't sleep 6 's; 's shining 7 can 8 'll spend 9 must get my

4 1 are you 2 think you're going 3 's the weather 4 Can you see

5 When one speaker uses a present tense, the other reports with a past tense. When they use a past tense or the present perfect, it is reported with the past perfect.

C: Grammar exercises

1 2 could easily find another one.
3 was going to travel round Africa.
4 had lived there as a child.
5 might get a part-time job there.
6 was packing his bag.
7 was really excited.
8 would be away for a year.
9 might stay longer.
10 could come / go too.
(➤ B1)

2 2 e 3 a 4 d 5 b 6 f (➤ B3 and 5)

3 2 how old I was 3 I was studying 4 I came from 5 whether / if I had worked 6 I played 7 whether / if I would work 8 whether / if I could start 9 whether / if I needed 10 whether / if I would like (➤ B1 and 5)

4 2 me (that) I could do well.
  3 if I studied every evening. / what time I went to bed. / if I had decided on a career yet.
  4 what time I went to bed. / if I studied every evening. / if I had decided on a career yet.
  5 (me) (that) I wouldn't get good marks.
  6 (that) I spent too much time with my friends.
  7 (me) if I had decided on a career yet. / what time I went to bed. / if I studied every evening. (➤ B1, 3 and 5)

5 *Woman:*   The same thing happened to me yesterday.
  Suzie: What did you do?
  Woman: Someone lent me the fare and I'm going to give it back today on the bus, so I'm happy to do the same for you. You can give the money back to me tomorrow.
  Suzie: Thank you very much. I'm very glad you're here.
  (➤ B1 and 3–6)

D: Exam practice
Use of English

1 made no attempt to 2 sun will shine 3 told me (that) he hadn't
4 don't we go 5 if she had booked 6 will we leave tomorrow
7 I can dress myself 8 whether they / we were meeting David

Grammar focus task

Questions 0, 2, 3, 5, 6, 7 and 8 test reported speech.
1 The weatherman predicted (that) there would be sunshine all day. (question 2)
2 Paul complained (that) he hadn't heard from Helen for a long time. (question 3)
3 The little boy insisted (that) he could dress himself without any help. (question 7)

Writing *Sample answer:*

Place and time
At the beginning of the meeting we discussed when we would hold the Film Club meetings and where. Everybody said that the hall would be the best place and most people agreed that after school on Friday would be the best time.

Choosing films
We decided that we would make a list of films at the beginning of each term. Emma said that each class could choose one film and there would be a committee to check there was a good variety.

Cost
Some people said they couldn't come every week so they didn't want to pay a membership fee for the whole term. Kerry suggested that we had a lower membership fee and then charge a small amount to see each film.

Reviews
Tom suggested that it might be a good idea to have a discussion after each film and then someone could write a review for the school magazine.

Unit 17

A: Context listening
2 He is making a fruit cake.
3 2 adding 3 beating 4 to add 5 using 6 to use 7 to add
  8 to use 9 to check 10 adding 11 to ice 12 to have
4 Some of the verbs are *to* infinitive and some are *-ing* form.

C: Grammar exercises
1 2 working 3 doing 4 to stay 5 working 6 to stop 7 singing
  8 to tell 9 working 10 to ignore 11 going 12 to go
  (➤ B1 and 3)
2 2 to take 3 coming 4 to have 5 come 6 jump 7 phoning
  8 to play 9 smoking 10 to become (➤ B1, 2, 4, 6 and 7)
3 *Sample answers (other verbs are also possible as long as they are in the right form):*
  2 to get 3 making; to read / to finish
  4 to book 5 throwing 6 to inform / to tell 7 inviting
  8 to leave 9 wearing 10 to talk / to speak / to chat 11 to send
  12 going / travelling 13 to write 14 watching / seeing (➤ B5)
4 *Sample answers:*
  2 You'll enjoy seeing the paintings in the museum.
  3 Don't miss going on a river boat.
  4 Before you go, don't forget to buy a sun hat.
  5 While you're there, try eating the sausages.
  6 You must promise to visit my family.
  7 Avoid travelling on the buses at night.
  8 Remember to take your credit card.
  (➤ B1–9)

D: Exam practice
Use of English

1 D 2 A 3 D 4 B 5 B 6 D 7 C 8 B 9 C 10 A 11 B 12 C

Grammar focus task

Verbs followed by to *infinitive:* attempt; dare; decide; demand; expect; hope; threaten; want; wish

Verbs followed by -ing: appreciate; consider; delay; enjoy; fancy; imagine; suggest

Writing *Sample answer:*

Young people have more freedom today than they did one hundred years ago but it depends on the family.

Sometimes parents are too busy to make their children tell them where they are going and they allow them to stay out all night. This isn't a good idea because young people can easily get into trouble by drinking too much or mixing with the wrong people. Parents should warn their children not to drink and smoke too much and definitely not to drink and drive. On the other hand, young people must learn how to be adults. If their parents don't encourage them to do anything on their own they will never manage to be independent.

I don't think parents in most families give their children too much freedom but it is important that parents and children discuss everything, and that there are some rules which the young people agree to keep to.

Unit 18

A: Context listening

2 1d 2b 3f 4a 5e 6c

3 2 get 3 count 4 back (me) 5 look 6 carry 7 call 8 get 9 go
10 throw (me) 11 give

C: Grammar exercises

1 2 over 3 through 4 down 5 on 6 round to 7 by 8 at
9 round 10 away with (➤ B1–4)

2 2 cut down 3 filled in 4 turned down 5 carried on
6 turned up 7 set off 8 rung up 9 put off 10 take in
(➤ B1–4)

3 2 get 3 hands 4 make 5 work 6 are going 7 comes
8 look 9 doing (*going* is also possible) 10 fall 11 turns
12 gave / had given (➤ B1–4)

4a 2 verb + adverb: broke the sculpture up 3 verb + preposition:
no 4 verb + adverb + preposition: *no* 5 verb + adverb: made
the excuse up 6 verb + adverb + preposition: *no* 7 verb +
preposition: *no* 8 verb + adverb: put the lights out 9 verb +
preposition: *no* 10 verb + adverb: puts its prices up
(➤ B1–4)

 b 2 broke it up 3 went over it 4 run out of them 5 made it up
6 put up with it 7 looked after them 8 put them out 9 takes
after him 10 puts them up (➤ B1–4)

D: Exam practice
Use of English

1 put the wedding off / put off the wedding 2 no point (in) asking
3 (that) you (should / could) phone 4 came up against
5 looked up to 6 set out on / for / set off on / for
7 unless you hurry 8 put up with living

Grammar focus task

There are phrasal verbs in sentences 0 (*bring back*), 1 (*put off*),
4 (*come up against*), 5 (*look up to*), 6 (*set out / set off*), 7 (*hurry up*)
and 8 (*put up with*).

2 By the time we *set out / set off* on our journey it was getting
dark.

3 I really can't *put up with* sitting in this heat any longer.

4 This desk is for books which are being *brought back* to the
library.

5 When I'd nearly finished mending the car, I *came up against* a
problem I couldn't solve.

6 James had always *looked up to* his boss.

7 The play was *put off* for a week because the main actor was ill.

Writing *Sample answer:*

Dear Mr Rogers

  We have decided to book the ground floor room from 7 pm to
midnight because we would like to go into the garden for fresh air
if the weather is hot.

  Please can you provide snacks such as nuts, crisps and so on,
at 7.30 pm and pizzas at 9 pm? Can you work out how much food
we need for fifty people?

We would like to use your equipment for music. Can your
staff set it up before the party starts? One of us will be the disc
jockey, so we don't need anyone else.

  We plan to put up some balloons and other decorations. We
can do that in half an hour so the party can start at 7.30. Can
we have some time to take them down after midnight or will the
hotel staff do that when they clear up?

  Thank you.

  Kai Jansen

Unit 19

A: Context listening

2 Seymour wants Double X to find the man in the photo.

3 2 Because he doesn't have a better one. 3 A woman.
4 Because the woman faxed it to them.
5 If you look at it with your eyes half closed. 6 Double X.
7 *Sample answer*: Double X's former girlfriend sent it, because
she was angry with him and wanted to cause trouble!

4 1 find; 'll be 2 had; 'd give 3 'd told; wouldn't have needed
4 would give; knew 5 's; look

5 1 The present simple. 2 The present simple. 3 The past
simple. 4 The past perfect.

C: Grammar exercises

1 2 e 3 a 4 i 5 h 6 b 7 c 8 g 9 d 10 f (➤ B1–4)

2 2 want 3 cared 4 won't be 5 wouldn't have told
6 weren't 7 would have been 8 falls 9 hadn't expected
10 'll (will) discover (➤ B1–4)

3 2 wouldn't have sat opposite that man. 3 If the service hadn't
been really slow 4 If she hadn't been bored 5 she wouldn't
have applied for that job. (➤ B4)

4 *Sample answers (notice the commas):*
2 it wasn't spoken in so many countries.
3 , I'll go out and celebrate with all my friends.
4 I don't study really hard.
5 give us so much homework every day, we'd be able to go
out more often.
6 forgotten my book, I would have done better in the test.
7 wasn't so different from my own language, I wouldn't
make so many mistakes.
8 revise regularly if you want to pass an exam.
9 , it really helps to improve your English.
10 , I'll have time for a coffee.
(➤ B1–4)

D: Exam practice
Reading

1 H 2 D 3 E 4 C 5 F 6 A 7 B

Grammar focus task

2 f 3 e 4 c 5 b 6 a 7 d

Writing *Sample answer:*

Hi Jessie

Thanks for your email. I'd prefer to live in the city centre. If I'm somewhere central, I can go out to cinemas and other places easily, but if I'm in the suburbs, I'll have a long journey at the end of the day. I don't want to be in a family home because I want to go out and eat with other students in the evenings. If I share a house with other students it will be a good chance to get to know people of my own age out of college and I'll have more freedom. I would probably only meet children and older people if I lived with a family. It would be convenient if the house had wireless internet, but that sort of house may be expensive. I can't spend all my money on rent! Provided the house is warm and comfortable, I'm sure I'll be fine.

I really appreciate your help with this.

See you in September – I'm getting excited already.

Alessandro

Unit 20

A: Context listening

2 They're going to climb a mountain.

3 2 Provided 3 unless 4 in case 5 I'd rather 6 As long as 7 wish 8 It's time

4 The verbs are in the present tense.

C: Grammar exercises

1 2 They'll be here soon unless their plane is delayed.
3 Unless you're in a hurry, you could take the bus.
4 I won't be able to come to see you tomorrow unless my brother can give me a lift.
5 Unless the factory increases its production, it will close down.
6 Unless you write your address down for me, I'll forget it.
7 I won't stay in that hotel unless it's got a good restaurant.
8 Unless I hear from you, I'll meet you at six.
(➤ B1)

2 2 if 3 if 4 in case 5 in case 6 if 7 in case 8 in case (➤ B2)

3 *Sample answers:*
2 I wish the streets didn't all look the same.
3 I wish I'd brought my mobile phone.
4 I wish I could speak the language.
5 I wish I'd bought a phrase book.
6 I wish I wasn't / weren't hot and thirsty. / I wish I had a drink.
7 I wish I hadn't come here alone. / I wish I'd come here with someone else.
8 I wish someone would help me.
9 I wish I hadn't come here.
10 I wish I was / were back in my hotel.
(➤ B4)

4 2 are 3 finishes 4 didn't bring 5 would learn 6 behaves 7 don't know 8 can't 9 changes 10 hadn't been
(➤ B1–5)

D: Exam practice
Listening

1 A 2 C 3 A 4 B 5 A 6 B 7 C 8 C

Grammar focus task

2 the manager does something about the noise. 3 it was about someone she knew. 4 he had been more careful. 5 she has a meeting. 6 the morning fog clears. 7 she has it back on Sunday. 8 he embarrasses her again.

Writing *Sample answer:*

Last week I learned that sometimes we should listen to other people's advice. I was going to the science museum to see some exhibits about space exploration. As I was leaving the house, my brother said, 'You'd better take your autograph book in case you meet someone famous in London.' Although I'm quite keen on collecting autographs, I ignored him. I wouldn't need it unless I saw someone famous in the museum, and I didn't want to have a lot of things to carry.

When I got to the museum I spent three hours looking at the rockets and other interesting exhibits. Then I had lunch. In the café I noticed that people were looking at the table next to mine. It was a family with some children. Suddenly I realised it was the Prime Minister! Several people spoke to him and asked for his autograph. I was still looking for a piece of paper when they got up and left. I was really disappointed. I wish I'd had my autograph book with me.

Unit 21

A: Context listening

2 1 d; (Prime Minister in Washington)
2 a; (pop singer)
3 c; (traffic jam)
4 b; (bank robbery)

3 2 At the weekend. 3 As it was flying across the Mediterranean. 4 By the weekend. 5 Beyond the beginning of the motorway. 6 Until this afternoon. 7 By the door of the bank. 8 During the night.

4 1 at; by; until; during 2 at; across; beyond; by

C: Grammar exercises

1 2 at 3 during 4 for 5 until 6 at 7 by 8 in 9 by 10 in 11 over (➤ B1–2)

2 1 At 2 in 3 in 4 for 5 At 6 by 7 on 8 at 9 in 10 between 11 among 12 for (➤ B1–2)

3 2 b 3 a 4 a 5 a 6 b (➤ B1–2)

4 2 on 3 across 4 beyond 5 at 6 in 7 Until 8 in 9 along 10 on 11 through 12 among (➤ B1–2)

D: Exam practice
Use of English

1 of 2 be 3 as 4 to 5 made/turned/converted 6 addition 7 present 8 All 9 what 10 a 11 each 12 but

Grammar focus task

1 between 2 in 3 at 4 among 5 across

Writing *Sample answer:*

Dear Ronan,

Here's some information which I hope will be helpful.

There is an excellent local shop just up our road, or the supermarket on the outskirts of town, which isn't bad. The swimming pool is just by the supermarket. On weekdays you can use the free car park at the supermarket if you go for a swim, but not at weekends.

The bank is open from 9.30 to 4.00 on weekdays, but it shuts at 12.30 on Saturdays. It's on Market Street, between the big hotel and the museum. The museum's worth visiting, although it's only open in the afternoon.

The market is held on Tuesdays and Saturdays. You need to go early in the morning to buy fresh food, but there are also stalls with second-hand books and so on. I sometimes find good bargains among the rubbish! Those stalls are there until dusk.

Have a great time. We look forward to hearing all about it.

Love from

Nika and Peter

Unit 22

A: Context listening

1 1 A man is breaking a window. Fire is coming from the door.
2 A man is taking a toolbox out of a car. Fire is coming from an upstairs window.
3 A man is looking out of an upstairs window. Smoke is coming from downstairs.

2 Picture 2 fits best. Picture 1 shows the fire and the man in the wrong place, and Andy didn't put his handkerchief over his face until he was inside the house. Picture 3 also shows the fire in the wrong place, and there is someone upstairs, but Andy didn't go upstairs and there was no one else in the house.

3 2 at 3 on 4 on 5 by 6 by 7 with 8 in 9 in 10 for 11 for 12 with 13 for 14 to

4 by

C: Grammar exercises

1 *Sample answers:*
2 She congratulated her on winning the tournament.
3 They prevented him from entering the disco.
4 She forgave him for not phoning her.
5 She accused him of reading her diary.
6 She agreed with him about the film.
(➤ B1)

2 2 a 3 b 4 b 5 a 6 b (➤ B1–3)

3 a 2 by 3 by 4 in 5 in 6 of 7 at 8 about 9 in 10 to
b 1 in 2 by 3 on 4 on 5 of 6 on 7 at 8 at
c 1 in 2 out of 3 at 4 at 5 in 6 out of 7 in 8 by 9 in
(➤ B1–3)

D: Exam practice
Use of English

1 spoken 2 graduation 3 political 4 Unfortunately 5 tendency
6 protection 7 international 8 Naturally 9 supposing 10 ideal

Grammar focus task

2 for 3 for 4 with 5 in 6 by

Writing *Sample answer:*

Dear Mr Morrison

I was in your shop last Wednesday afternoon and saw the argument you mention. However, I did not hear what the customer said when he came in because I was talking to the friend who was with me.

Suddenly, I heard the customer say 'Are you accusing me of lying?' in a loud voice and the shop assistant seemed very upset. All the customers were watching by this time. Another shop assistant warned the customer that he was being rude. The customer insisted on speaking to the manager and he wasn't satisfied when he heard that you were out. He was so annoyed he ran out of the shop. I think he knocked over the television in the window by accident as he passed it. Nobody else was near it, so he was responsible for the damage.

I hope this is helpful.

Yours sincerely

K. Lee

Unit 23

A: Context listening

1 They lived around 1600. They were all members of the same family.

2 1 b 2 a 3 c (boy on horse) 4 c (boy with book) 5 d

3 2 that hangs next to Margaret's portrait. 3 who's holding the book. 4 which lost. 5 when the youngest son was born.

4 1 *Which* refers to *the one (ship)*. 2 *That* refers to *the picture*. 3 *Who* refers to *the one (William)*. 4 *Which* refers to *the side*. 5 *When* refers to *the year*.

C: Grammar exercises

1 2 who 3 which 4 who 5 – (*which* is not necessary)
6 – (*which* is not necessary) 7 which 8 which 9 which
10 – (*which* is not necessary) (➤ B1–2)

2 *Sample answers:* 2 where people wear designer clothes.
3 which we don't understand. 4 when I felt embarrassed by my family. 5 why some people dislike cats. 6 who was very famous? 7 whose parents buy them cars. 8 which involved working at weekends. (➤ B1–3)

3 2 My uncle's cottage, where we usually spend our holidays, has been damaged by floods.
3 My bicycle, which I only got last week, has been stolen.
4 The chemistry exam, which we had been worrying about, was actually quite easy.

5 The young man, whose girlfriend had left him, caused a fight in a bar.

6 During the summer, when everyone goes on holiday, there are dreadful traffic jams.

7 My parents, who don't often go to the cinema, enjoyed that film very much.
(➤ B2–3)

4 2 b 3 a 4 a 5 b 6 b 7 b (➤ B1–3)

D: Exam practice
Use of English

1 in which we had lunch / which we had lunch in
2 will (only) last until / till 3 who works for an airline
4 opened the box with / by using 5 is (the reason) why
6 the book I lent him 7 the concert (which / that) I went
8 the boy whose mother is

Grammar focus task

1 Sentences 1, 3, 5, 6, 7 and 8.
2 Sentence 3 is non-defining, all the others are defining.
3 You can tell by the punctuation. If you remove the words between the commas in sentence 3, it still makes sense.

Writing *Sample answer:*

The Parsons Family

This is a great series to watch when you get home from school and want to relax. It's about a family who have lots of problems, but it is also very amusing. The family consists of a mother, who can't cook, and a father, who can't drive, and their three teenage children, who run the house and organise their parents. In the latest episode, the oldest boy had a pet snake, which was always escaping, and he and his brother had to find it before their mother saw it. She'd told him to take it back to the shop where he bought it but he didn't. The brother who owned the snake had made a secret place for it in the boys' bedroom. Their mother was really pleased because they were keeping their room really clean and tidy, which was unusual. Of course the reason was that they didn't want her to look under the bed. The story goes fast and the actors who play the boys are really funny.

I recommend this series to all teenagers.

Unit 24

A: Context listening

2 Josie does judo and Adam plays volleyball.
3 2 good enough 3 since 4 tall enough 5 so quick
6 enough exercise 7 too much time 8 too many practice
games 9 in order to 10 well enough 11 as; so much revision
4 *Exercise* is a noun. *Good* and *tall* are adjectives, and *well* is an adverb.

C: Grammar exercises

1 2 in order to 3 As 4 so 5 so that 6 enough; so; too
(➤ B1–3)

2 2 same 3 different: In *a* we understand that his father doesn't allow him to have a motorbike, but in *b* he may have one although he's unusually young. 4 same 5 same
6 different: In *a* we understand that she's confused by too much advice, but in *b* she's had as much advice as she needs, no more, no less. (➤ B1–3)

3 2 g 3 d 4 e 5 f (*b* is also possible, though less likely)
6 c (*g* is also possible, though less likely) 7 b 8 a
(➤ B1–3)

4 *Sample answers:* 2 have to eat at a local restaurant.
3 can't fix this ourselves. 4 has problems with public transport. 5 sometimes have difficulty contacting me.
6 always looks elegant. 7 didn't notice the time.
8 hold all your books? (➤ B1–3)

D: Exam practice
Use of English

1 B 2 B 3 A 4 D 5 B 6 C 7 A 8 C 9 C 10 D 11 D 12 A

Grammar focus task

2 that 3 enough 4 to 5 Therefore 6 too 7 in order to

Writing *Sample answer:*

Hi Catherine

My advice is that you should spend the money on travelling, but not on a shopping trip in New York because you wouldn't enjoy being in such a big city on your own and I can't afford to go with you now. Therefore I think you should save it until we can go round Europe together as I'll have earned some money by August. Motorbikes are so dangerous that I'm sure your family wouldn't like you to buy one, and you already have a computer which is good enough for email and homework and things, haven't you? Actually, if you've got enough money to do a course, I suggest you spend a month in Italy or Spain and do a language course. I'm sure you'd have fun and it would also be useful for later. Then we could travel together afterwards.

Well, let me know what you decide!

Love

Saskia

Unit 25

A: Context listening

1 b (*a* is wrong because she didn't sign a contract to make more films; *c* is wrong because Gemma was not a film actor before she got the part; *d* is wrong because Gemma was already at theatre school, it was only in films that she had no experience)
2 2 in spite of having 3 after visiting 4 before accepting
5 while making 6 working 7 but I'm 8 despite being
3 The *-ing* form.

C: Grammar exercises

1 2 c 3 d 4 h 5 f 6 i 7 a 8 b 9 e (➤ B1–2 and 4–6)

2 2 different: In *a* Sam asked for the chance to explain his behaviour and admitted losing his temper, but in *b* someone else asked him to explain his behaviour and he answered that he'd lost his temper.
3 same
4 different: In *a* Chloe's father promised her a car after she'd failed the exam, but in *b* he promised it before she took the exam.
5 different: In *a* the mountain guide warned us, but in *b* the guide received the warning from someone else.
6 same
(➤ B1–6)

3 3 Grumbling about the amount of homework he had, Simon took out his grammar book.
4 Feeling very excited about her latest discovery, the scientist invited the journalists into the laboratory.
5 Puzzled by what they had heard, the children asked their teacher what it meant.
6 Being a sensible girl, Wendy didn't panic when she cut her hand.
7 Hearing cries for help, Paul dived into the water.
8 Released only last week, this CD is already at the top of the charts.
(➤ B4)

4 *Sample answers:* 2 has appeared on television several times.
3 I accidentally spilt paint on the rug. 4 You must train seriously 5 Christopher ran along the hotel corridor. 6 I write lots. 7 their scarves in the air, 8 it rains. 9 being over 80.
10 I have been working for an international company.
(➤ B1–6)

D: Exam practice
Use of English

1 were 2 managed 3 though 4 spite 5 beyond 6 besides 7 but
8 to 9 which / that 10 at 11 led 12 Despite

Grammar focus task

2 a 3 d 4 e 5 c

Writing *Sample answer:*

My hero is my cousin Benjamin despite the fact that he's only eighteen, which is quite young to be a hero. I have chosen him because about six years ago he made a difficult decision and carried on without complaining.

Unfortunately, Ben's parents divorced when he was about ten. He has a younger sister, Emily, who was nearly six then. Ben and Emily lived with their mother, although they saw their father regularly, and everything seemed to be going quite well for them. Then their mother became very ill.

Advised that he and Emily should go to live with their father, Ben refused. From the age of 12, he was in charge of his home. Helping his mother and looking after Emily, he had little time for himself. But he always seemed cheerful and made us all laugh at family parties, even though he was missing so much of the fun that most teenagers have.

Last year, a new treatment meant that his mother's health began to improve. Now, Ben's life is easier. But he will always be our family's hero.

Recording scripts

Lisa: Hello?

Millie: Hi, Lisa – I'm in the shopping centre.

Lisa: Hi, Millie. What are you doing?

Millie: I'm looking round the shops. It's Saturday.

Lisa: Yeah, of course. Honestly, you buy new clothes every Saturday!

Millie: Well, nearly every Saturday.

Lisa: You're always buying new clothes! So, what are you looking for today?

Millie: One of those new skirts. You know, like everyone's wearing this autumn.

Lisa: Well, I'm not wearing one, I'm wearing a pair of old jeans. Is there anything special you want to talk about? Because actually, I'm cleaning my room.

Millie: Yes, there is, only you're being so impatient, you don't deserve to hear it.

Lisa: OK, sorry. I'm listening.

Millie: Well, you know that leather bag you want like the blue one you lost?

Lisa: None of the shops have one. Whenever I go into town I always look, but I never find a blue one.

Millie: Well, I'm in front of a shop window and I'm looking at a blue bag right now. Do you want it? I can buy it for you.

Lisa: Oh, yes. Those bags sell really fast because everyone thinks they're really cool as well as useful.

Millie: Yeah, and blue bags are getting really fashionable.

Lisa: I know. It'll be gone if I wait till Monday. I'll pay you when I see you.

Millie: OK.

Lisa: Oh, thank you, Millie. Sorry I was cross.

Millie: That's OK. Bye.

Lisa: Bye.

Jed: Hi everybody, this is Jed Jones, and welcome to *Study Talk*, our weekly look at news from universities around the country. And today, someone is sitting beside me to give us some info on a course he's doing. It gives people the chance to study a subject not traditionally associated with university. In fact there are some people who think it's not really a subject for serious study at all, but is only a hobby. So, I've got here with me Ellis Graham who says he's actually doing a degree in something I enjoy from time to time – now this isn't for real, is it Ellis – in surfing? Tell me you're a mathematician who goes surfing in his free time, aren't you?

Ellis: Sorry to disappoint you, Jed, it's for real.

Jed: So what do you do? You have classes on the beach?

Ellis: Well, that's possible sometimes, 'cause there is a practical element to the course, but most of it is indoors, with our books or computers. We have to study a very wide range of things.

Jed: Like where the best waves are?

Ellis: Well, yes, that's one way of describing it. We learn about weather and geographical influences on coastal regions, for example. And how waves form and grow. In fact there is quite a bit of mathematics in the course.

Jed: But, I don't want to sound rude here, but, surely surfing isn't a very academic subject, is it?

Ellis: You mean, surfers don't have very big brains?

Jed: I guess I do –

Ellis: Actually, you need really good exam results from school to be accepted on this course, because so many people want to do it, so there are many more applicants than the university has places for.

Jed: Oh, I see. So, OK, I've got to take the whole business a bit more seriously. But what I'm not clear about, is what can you do when you graduate? I mean, a degree won't make you a better surfer than if you just spend your time hanging about on the beach, will it?

Ellis:	Probably not. If that's what you want, it's the practice that matters. But that's not my aim. You see, surfing is a big part of the commercial life of some parts of the world, south-west England, for example, or parts of the US and of course Australia. There are hundreds of business opportunities, some of them well known, but plenty of others are just waiting for the right person to come along and get going to make a living out of them. And a very good living.
Jed:	So you're not just talking about sitting in a beach hut hiring out a few surf boards?
Ellis:	By no means. But that's just my idea. Some of my fellow students will go into research and so on. There are all sorts of possibilities.
Jed:	Well, I wish you all the best, Ellis. But just one last question – if I want advice on a new place to go for some really good surfing away from the crowds, would your department be able to tell me?
Ellis:	That's a bit of a tricky one, actually, Jed. You see, we're looking into this for a package holiday company, so I'd be giving away confidential commercial information!
Jed:	Oh, dear. I might have known! Well, thank you very much, Ellis, for filling us in ...

Recording 2

Gran:	Hello, Jack! Come in.
Jack:	Hello, Gran. How are you?
Gran:	Fine, thanks Jack. What about you?
Jack:	Oh, you know, too much college work. We had an exam on Thursday. But I went to London last Saturday with some mates. We had a great time.
Gran:	Oh, yes? I suppose you spent all your money.
Jack:	No, it wasn't really expensive. We caught the coach, so it was only ten pounds return.
Gran:	But isn't it slow?
Jack:	Well, we did some revision for our exams while we were travelling, so it didn't matter.
Gran:	Well done. And where did you go?
Jack:	Oh, you know, round the shops.
Gran:	That's what I did too, but not in London. I was hoping to find a new jacket. But there wasn't anything I liked.

Jack:	And then we went to see a film. But the brilliant thing was, when we were queuing for the cinema, we saw a really famous footballer. He was buying a burger from a stall near us like an ordinary person and all the crowds were walking past but nobody noticed him except me.
Gran:	So did you get his autograph?
Jack:	No, I didn't want to embarrass him.
Gran:	Ooh, when I was your age, I used to collect all the autographs of film stars and singers and so on. I would go up to town on my own and wait outside the theatre till they came out.
Jack:	Really?
Gran:	Yes. And I used to scream at pop concerts. I really enjoyed myself when I was a teenager. But don't tell your mother. She never used to do anything like that. She was always worrying about her homework.
Jack:	OK. So do you want to hear about the club we went to after the cinema?
Gran:	You bet!
Jack:	Well, it was really ...

Recording 3

Lucy:	Can you hold the doors a minute, Mike? I've got a big bag here.
Mike:	Hi, Lucy. Nice to see you. Up to the fourth floor?
Lucy:	Yes, please. Have you just finished work, Mike?
Mike:	Actually, I finished at lunchtime today because they're replacing our computers. So I've been at the gym this afternoon.
Lucy:	Are you going out tonight?
Mike:	No I don't think so. Why? Are you inviting me somewhere?
Lucy:	Oh no, I've got lots of work to do. I've actually spent all day trying to write a history essay and I still haven't finished it. I have to hand it in tomorrow. I started it last week ...
Mike:	Well, sorry, I can't help you with that ... (After you.) ... I never enjoyed studying history at school and I wasn't very good at it either.
Lucy:	I don't need any help with the essay. But you can help me by not playing your saxophone.
Mike:	Huh?

Lucy:	I'm sorry, I just can't stand it any more. I've lived next door since June and you've played the saxophone every night for at least an hour.
Mike:	But I thought you liked it. I've lived here for two years. Nobody's ever complained before so I'm really surprised. This is the first time anyone has asked me not to play. Why haven't you told me this before?
Lucy:	I've tried lots of times but I was afraid of sounding rude.
Mike:	So would you like me to play more quietly?
Lucy:	No, Mike. I don't want you to play at all. Tonight and ideally never again.
Mike:	I tell you what. I'll learn some new tunes. Why don't you suggest some?
Lucy:	Ohhhhhhh ...

Recording 4

Mother:	Hi, Richard. I'm home. Where are you?
Richard:	Upstairs, Mum. In my room.
Mother:	... Oh, Richard. Whatever have you been doing?
Richard:	I've been painting my room, Mum.
Mother:	Yes, I can see that. But why did you change colour halfway through?
Richard:	Well I'd done the ceiling, and I'd painted one wall, when I ran out of paint, so I went to the shop for some more. But then I realised the second pot was a slightly different colour. That's why it looks a bit odd.
Mother:	But why were you painting anyway? I thought you'd planned lots of things to do with your friends.
Richard:	Oh, they were all busy in the end. And yesterday afternoon I was bored. I'd been to town for a few hours – you know round the centre. I'd done the shopping – everything on your list – and I'd finished all my homework so I decided to paint my room.
Mother:	Mmm. Well, I suppose you can put some posters up. But look at the carpet. Why didn't you cover it up?
Richard:	Oh, yes, I see what you mean.

Mother:	Well, I can't think about all this now. I've had such a hard day.
Richard:	Why? What happened?
Mother:	Well, the meeting was difficult and then I had such a long journey home. I'd been driving for only an hour when the car broke down.
Richard:	Oh no.
Mother:	Anyway, it took me much longer than normal. So I'm just going into my room to have a lie down.
Richard:	Don't go in there just yet Mum. Let me tell you about ...
Mother:	Well, come and tell me in my room so I can sit down.
Richard:	That's what I wanted to tell you. I've painted your room too. And it was quite difficult so you might not be too pleased ... It was supposed to be a surprise ...

Recording 5a

Conversation 1

Tom:	Hello?
Claire:	Hello, Tom. It's Claire.
Tom:	Hi, Claire. How are you?
Claire:	Fine. Are you reporting on the conference in Amsterdam? I thought maybe we could travel together.
Tom:	That would be good but I've already booked my flight. People are travelling from all over the world so I decided to book early.
Claire:	Well, maybe I can get on the same one.
Tom:	I'm flying with British Airways and my plane leaves Edinburgh on Tuesday at 11.05. It arrives at Amsterdam airport at 13.40.
Claire:	It's quick, isn't it? When does the conference actually begin?
Tom:	It starts on Wednesday at 9.30 so you need to get there on Tuesday. The main speaker arrives at the conference on Tuesday afternoon and I'm interviewing him at 6.30.
Claire:	OK, I'll let you know what I arrange. See you.
Tom:	Bye.

Conversation 2

Steve: Tom, hello.

Tom: Hi, Steve. How are you? Oh ... you're in a hurry. Where are you going?

Steve: I'm playing badminton in a few minutes with Paul. But what about me and you? We haven't played for ages. What are you doing tomorrow evening? I usually play at about seven.

Tom: Oh, sorry. I'll be working then. I'm flying to a conference in Amsterdam tomorrow morning. But what about the weekend? I'm not working then. I'm having my eyes tested on Saturday afternoon but I'm free the rest of the weekend.

Steve: OK. Let's make it Sunday morning? About ten at the sports centre?

Tom: Fine. See you there.

Steve: Bye, then.

Tom: Bye.

Conversation 3

Woman: Good afternoon, sir. What name is it please?

Tom: Tom Hughes.

Woman: Ah yes. Room 341. Are you having dinner here tonight?

Tom: I haven't decided yet. I'm interviewing someone at 6.30 so I probably won't be back in time. I think I'll get a meal in town.

Woman: And breakfast?

Tom: Err ... oh, I'll have breakfast in my room please.

Woman: Here's the key then, sir. Take the lift to the third floor and turn left.

Tom: Thank you.

Woman: Oh, just a minute. There's a message for you, sir. It's from your newspaper office in Edinburgh.

Tom: Oh, thanks. I'll ring them now.

Conversation 4

Tom: So, you got here in the end, Claire.

Claire: Yes, but your flight was full and I couldn't get on a plane till Wednesday so I missed the first day of the conference.

Waiter: Eherm, what would you like to drink, sir?

Tom: I'll have some fizzy water, please. Claire?

Claire: I'll have the same, please. Anyway, what did I miss, Tom?

Tom: Well, the first day was mainly about the future of the planet, you know in a hundred years' time the world will be a very different place. There'll be millions more people but there won't be much oil available for energy. And people will live much longer. You know, that kind of thing. I've interviewed the main speaker and I've written my article about him. It'll be in the newspaper tomorrow.

Claire: I'll read all about it there then. And I need to write my article about the rest of the conference tonight so I mustn't spend too long having dinner.

Tom: Oh, right. OK then.

Recording 5b

Good morning. I hope you slept well and are ready to start exploring South Wales on the first day of our holiday here. Before I tell you what we are doing today, the hotel has asked me to mention a few things. Meals are served in the dining room, except breakfast which is served in the coffee bar – any time between 6.45 and 9.15. We won't actually be here to have lunch because we are going out on trips every day, so you need to order sandwiches for the next day's lunch before seven each evening from reception. Collect your lunch from the dining room in the morning. In the evening the dining room is open from 7.00p.m. until 9.30. I shall see you all in the dining room at a quarter past seven each evening because the hotel has asked if we can eat together as a group and be finished by 8.45 so please try to get there on time. There's still time to go out into town afterwards if you want to as long as you're back for breakfast the next morning!

I'm your tour guide in charge of all the trips and am looking after you while we're out. While you're in the hotel, however, if you have any problems you should talk to the deputy manager. The manager himself is off sick at the moment. The receptionist will show you where the office is.

In about ten minutes the coach is picking us up to take us on a tour of the valleys of South Wales. You may know that the area is famous for its industry but you may not realise what a lot of natural beauty there is too. Last year I visited a wonderful waterfall near here with a group and we didn't have time to explore properly so we're going back there today to have a better look. Because it rains a lot here it's quite a sight. During the 1700s, the waterfall was used to power a mill which produced flour and you can see what's left of the building and imagine what it was like.

Then we're travelling a bit further up the valley to visit a museum which has been built where there used to be a huge coal mine. They don't mine coal there any more but the museum is fascinating. There's a video you can watch and in the souvenir shop, as well as buying all the normal souvenirs, you can buy lamps which are exactly like the ones the miners carried to light their way.

We'll probably eat our lunch up there near the museum, in the coach if the weather's bad.

Then we're making our way back south to the coast to admire some more beautiful scenery. There'll be time for a walk along the cliffs or if any of you are feeling energetic you can try a bit of windsurfing. Sailing, canoeing and fishing are also popular sports in the area but we won't be able to do those today. We'll probably stop at a café on the way back to have a cup of coffee and a snack and we arrive back at the hotel by five o'clock. You'll need a coat or something to keep you dry, some strong boots because our walk might be muddy and don't forget your cameras. Now if anyone has any questions ...

Recording 5c

In about ten minutes the coach is picking us up to take us on a tour of the valleys of South Wales. You may know that the area is famous for its industry but you may not realise what a lot of natural beauty there is too. Last year I visited a wonderful waterfall near here with a group and we didn't have time to explore properly so we're going back there today to have a better look. Because it rains a lot here it's quite a sight. During the 1700s, the waterfall was used to power a mill which produced flour and you can see what's left of the building and imagine what it was like.

Then we're travelling a bit further up the valley to visit a museum which has been built where there used to be a huge coal mine. They don't mine coal there any more but the museum is fascinating. There's a video you can watch and in the souvenir shop, as well as buying all the normal souvenirs, you can buy lamps which are exactly like the ones the miners carried to light their way.

We'll probably eat our lunch up there near the museum, in the coach if the weather's bad.

Then we're making our way back south to the coast to admire some more beautiful scenery. There'll be time for a walk along the cliffs or if any of you are feeling energetic you can try a bit of windsurfing. Sailing, canoeing and fishing are also popular sports in the area but we won't be able to do those today. We'll probably stop at a café on the way back to have a cup of coffee and a snack and we arrive back at the hotel by five o'clock. You'll need a coat or something to keep you dry, some strong boots because our walk might be muddy and don't forget your cameras. Now if anyone has any questions ...

Recording 6

Simon:	Good afternoon, my name is Simon Trite and I'm here from Hightime Radio Corporation to interview you! Now that you've had time to settle in, we're going to do a series about your adventures here on Wildrock. So, er, how are you finding life here in the wild? Pretty exciting, huh?
Woman 1:	Actually, we're about to leave.
Simon:	What? You can't be! You were going to stay here for at least a year.
Man 1:	Look, we're fed up. We're fed up with the cold.
Woman 2:	And the wind.
Woman 1:	And the mud.
Man 2:	And the rain.
Simon:	It's not raining now.
Man 2:	But it's going to rain soon. See those clouds over the hill?
Simon:	Huh?
Man 2:	So, we know it's going to rain.
Woman 1:	And it's the same almost every day. So, we're going to pack up our stuff, we're going to send a message to the mainland, and we're going to leave.
Woman 2:	As soon as possible.
Simon:	Everyone's going to be very surprised when you arrive. Aren't you embarrassed to let the weather defeat you?
Man 1:	By the end of this week, we'll have survived longer than anyone else in a place like this.

Man 2:	By the end of this week we'll have been living here for nearly six months. And that's enough.
Simon:	But surely it's not really that bad?
Woman 2:	No?
Man 2:	Tell you what, why don't you try it?
Simon:	What?
Man 2:	Yes, you can stay here. We're going to go to the mainland.
Woman 1:	We're going to eat a big hot meal as soon as we find a restaurant.
Man 1:	And we're not going to talk to any reporters until we've had a long sleep in warm, dry beds.
Simon:	Wait for me!
	You aren't going to leave me here all alone, are you?
	Hey! That's my boat! Oh no. Now what am I going to do?

Recording 7

1 Look in your mirror – is it time for a change? Come and work out at Transformers Fitness Centre. Together, you and Transformers can make you a stronger, slimmer and more self-confident person. Our professional advisers will help you to plan a sensible route to better health. Call in this weekend for a friendly welcome and see our excellent facilities. We're at 25 Market Street and we're open from eight in the morning till eight in the evening.

2 Looking for a really wonderful day out next summer? Come to the best wildlife park in the country. We've got the fiercest lions here at the Animal Wonder Park, in addition to the funniest monkeys you've ever seen. Phone 273156 for our amazing brochure and take advantage of our special offers for families.

3 Do you have a full-time job? Do you feel tired all the time, trying to keep the house clean as well? Don't wear yourself out – call The Sparklers. You'll come back to fresh carpets, shining sinks and surfaces and no sticky finger marks on the paintwork. Phone 273989. You'll be surprised by our reasonable prices.

4 Hurry, hurry, hurry! There's something for everyone at the Music Store in Spice Lane. We've got the greatest variety of CDs ever! And astonishing bargains! The Music Store has thousands of special deals – the latest rock and pop, traditional jazz, the most beautiful classical music. Come to the Music Store today!

Recording 8

And here I am at the city stadium and the sun is shining. And finally the players are coming onto the pitch. As I was saying earlier there were such terrible traffic jams in the city today that the match is starting late. Most of the spectators have been waiting patiently in their seats since two o'clock but now as the players come out they're cheering happily. And the whistle goes. Rossi has the ball and is running steadily down the pitch but, oh no, the game has hardly started – only two minutes have gone – and he's fallen heavily on the ground. He's so experienced in these kinds of conditions that he rarely falls. But he's OK and he has the ball. Now Parker is running quickly towards the goal to take the ball from Rossi. Parker is playing incredibly well. But of course that's what we expect from him. Last week he scored the winning goal to take this team into the semi-final. It's often Parker who shoots that important goal. And he has, he's scored! And the crowd are roaring really loudly so it's difficult to make myself heard. That was a marvellous goal by Parker.

Recording 9a

Mina:	Hello?
Peter:	Are you home at last?
Mina:	Yes, I am. Why?
Peter:	You've been out all evening, haven't you?
Mina:	What are you talking about?
Peter:	I phoned three times and you didn't answer.
Mina:	Have you been checking up on me?
Peter:	No, I haven't. I was just worried. You said you'd be in tonight, didn't you?
Mina:	Yes, I did. But I had a change of plan, OK?
Peter:	Of course. I'm sorry.
Mina:	So am I. I don't want to quarrel.
Peter:	Neither do I. You know I love you, don't you?
Mina:	Of course I do.
Peter:	And do you love me?
Mina:	You know I do.
Peter:	And you'll always love me, won't you?
Mina:	Of course I will. You can meet me tomorrow, can't you?
Peter:	Sure. Let's meet by the college gate, shall we?

Mina: Yes, let's. We'd better say goodnight, then.

Peter: OK. Goodnight. Love you.

Mina: Love you. Bye.

Peter: Bye.

Recording 9b

1 *You hear a man talking to some tourists.*
   Who is he?

   A *a café owner*

   B *a tourist guide*

   C *a street trader*

   This is a good place to sit and drink a coffee when you
   want a break and if you like you can watch the street
   market just across the way, where there's lots going on,
   plenty of local colour. Now, everybody's here I think, so
   let's order some drinks, shall we?

2 *You hear a woman and her friend in an airport.*
   What has the woman lost?

   A *her handbag*

   B *her passport*

   C *her boarding pass*

   Man: It leaves in five minutes and we can't get all
             the way back to the check-in – surely you put
             it inside your passport, like you usually do.

   Woman: And that's right where I always keep it, in the
             side of my handbag, but the boarding pass
             isn't there. I didn't give it to you to hold,
             did I?

3 *You hear a man talking about his holiday.*
   Which place did he enjoy most?

   A *the seaside*

   B *Bangkok*

   C *the north*

   We went on a sort of tour, you know the sort of thing I
   mean, don't you? We had a week by the coast to start
   with, then four days in Bangkok, and three days seeing
   something of village life in the north, which was all
   fascinating, I admit – but I get a bit tired of moving
   about, so to be honest the first week was the real holiday
   as far as I was concerned.

4 *You hear a girl talking about choosing a coat.*
   Whose advice did she follow?

   A *her mother's*

   B *her sister's*

   C *the shop assistant's*

   Well, my mum had said I ought to get a really warm
   coat, so that's why I tried on this long one first of all,
   but my sister said the short one was more fashionable
   and so did the shop assistant. But it was much more
   expensive, that's why she said that. And I think my
   sister was right in a way, but then she'd want to borrow
   it. In the end I went for the long one, and, well, it looks
   OK, doesn't it?

5 *In an office, you hear a man talking on the telephone.*
   Where is Mr Richardson?

   A *in a hotel*

   B *in America*

   C *at home*

   I'm afraid Mr Richardson isn't available today ... no, he
   took a short holiday after he got back from the States,
   and now he's home sick this week because he picked up
   a tummy bug at the hotel he stayed in. It was unlucky,
   wasn't it? Shall I get him to call you when he's back?

6 *You overhear a man telling a friend about a trip to a gym.*
   How does the man feel?

   A *ashamed*

   B *determined*

   C *angry*

   Woman: Have you joined that new gym?

   Man: I've decided against it. When I went along
             there – they have these fitness trainers
             who talk to you before they let you use the
             equipment – well, he looked about fourteen
             to me – he told me I could only use their
             equipment if I went away and lost ten kilos –

   Woman: You can do that, can't you?

   Man: He was trying to tell me I was too old to use
             a gym really. I had to laugh because there
             was someone who looked like my son telling
             me how to organise my life. But because of
             what he said I've made up my mind that I
             really will get fit this time.

7 *You hear a woman talking to a doctor's receptionist. Why does she want an early appointment?*

A *because she mustn't eat before she comes in*

B *because she's having problems eating*

C *because she wants to see the doctor without taking time off work*

Woman: But I have to have an appointment first thing in the morning. The doctor wants to do some tests and I mustn't eat for twelve hours before that – I am right, aren't I?

Receptionist: Yes.

Woman: So, she said the best way is to go without breakfast and come in early.

Receptionist: Yes.

Woman: Then I can have a snack and not miss too much time at work.

8 *You hear a man talking about selling his bicycle. How did he do it?*

A *He paid for an advertisement in the newspaper.*

B *He told all his friends about it.*

C *He advertised it at work.*

Yeah – you know me, I never pay much attention to advertisements myself, you know, in the papers or in shops or whatever, so I didn't think of it. But I was talking to this colleague over the coffee break and he said, what about putting one on the notice board in the staff cloakroom? And I got three enquiries straight off! Sold it yesterday.

Recording 10

1 I'm Angela, and I'm a sales executive for a company which makes furniture. An important part of my work is travel. I drive thousands of miles every year and that can make it quite hard to get exercise. I do care about my health though, and when I stop I usually buy fruit to eat rather than biscuits or sweets. If there's any available, that is.

2 I'm Ken and I work at a garage. I mainly drive the recovery truck – that's the vehicle that helps motorists when they break down. Some people just keep driving without thinking ahead. It's the phone calls from drivers who've run out of petrol that really annoy me. Or, the other thing is, I'm called out by the police after an accident. Some firms charge a lot of money for that, but

I don't think we're too bad. Anyway, motorists have got insurance – or they should have!

3 I'm Charlie and I've got this job delivering pizzas for a fast food restaurant on a motorbike. It's OK, I can usually get round the traffic jams. I got my motorbike licence last year and I need cash. I'm a student. My subject's chemistry. I hope I won't need a job like this after I've graduated. I want to find a job with a reasonable salary.

4 I'm Hazel and I've been driving a taxi now for three years. I can't say I enjoy this sort of work. The traffic's terrible here. But I've got three kids and I've got to pay for food and clothing and so on. There's a lot of unemployment round here, so I mustn't grumble, really, I suppose.

Recording 11

Woman: Hello. How can I help?

Man: I want to go on a week's holiday. Somewhere sunny but not too …

Woman: Have you looked at any of our brochures? Do help yourself. Are you interested in anywhere in particular?

Man: Well, I was wondering …

Woman: The resorts in this one, look, are all near the airport and on the coast. In fact, I went to this place myself last year with some friends of mine to see what it was really like. It's got discos, nightclubs, restaurants and it's only a few metres from the hotel to the beach. Or this place, look, has even more entertainment. Everyone's going there this year.

Man: Neither of those would suit me. I was looking for something a bit …

Woman: I know, maybe you'd prefer some of the places on this island. My brother's friend had a holiday in this place, look, so I can really recommend it. Are you going on your own?

Man: Yes, by myself.

Woman: Well, we can book apartments which you share with three other people. That's better because you get to know each other really well. You'd have fun there. And each apartment has its own balcony with a view.

Man:	I'd rather have my own apartment. I've looked at this brochure. I'm interested in either this holiday or this one on the next page.
Woman:	Mmm, oh I'm sorry that's last year's brochure. It must have got on the shelf by mistake. But look at this one. The hotel itself is quite old but they are modernising it at the moment.
Man:	Sounds a bit noisy. All I want is somewhere quiet – anywhere that I can relax. Maybe in the mountains. All the places near the coast seem rather busy.
Woman:	Well, most of our holidays are by the sea. But here's one for you: a camping holiday in the countryside. You'd be staying in a big campsite with really good facilities.
Man:	I don't think you quite understand. Every brochure you've shown me contains the kind of holiday I would hate. None of the holidays look enjoyable at all.
Woman:	Well, you just can't please some people ... Hello madam, can I help?

Recording 12

Chris:	Hi Alice. What are you doing walking on the beach? Shouldn't you be at school?
Alice:	Oh, I've left school. I'm going to college next month. I'm hoping to train to be a chef.
Chris:	Really? Well you know I've worked as a chef for the last five years and I work at the Grand Hotel now. In fact I'm head chef there so you need to talk to me if you want to know what the job is really like.
Alice:	Well, what is it really like then? I'd like to work in a hotel like the Grand. I'm sure it's really exciting and you get to meet all kinds of rich and famous people.
Chris:	Actually no. Chefs have to spend their time in the kitchen. Rich and famous people don't go there.
Alice:	But you get lots of time off, don't you? Look, you're walking on the beach now at lunchtime.
Chris:	Yes, but it's my day off today. I needn't think about the hotel kitchen today.
Alice:	Well, normally then, what's it like? You don't have to work all day, do you?

Chris:	I have a break in the afternoon but I need to get up early. I have to start work at 6.30 in the morning and I have to stay until all the food is cooked and served in the evening. It's late by then.
Alice:	Mmm, sounds like hard work. How many days off do you get?
Chris:	In my last job, I had to work every day except Monday. At least here I have two days off every week. In the summer I'll have to work longer hours. That's because the hotel is busier. Listen, I must go now. You must come to the hotel one day. You can have a look around. I can show you the kitchens and you can see what we do.
Alice:	Mmm, thanks. I'm not so sure any more about being a chef.
Chris:	Well, come and see me and we'll have another chat.

Recording 13a

Sophie:	Mum ...
Mum:	Yes Sophie?
Sophie:	Will you lend me ten pounds?
Mum:	What for?
Sophie:	And can you lend me your new jacket?
Mum:	My new one?
Sophie:	Yes, and ...
Mum:	And what?
Sophie:	Can you give me a lift to town now?
Mum:	Start again. You want to borrow ten pounds, you want to borrow my new jacket and you want me to give you a lift to town now? Anything else?
Sophie:	Oh ... will you get me some new batteries?
Mum:	Well ...
Sophie:	And can you collect me from the city centre at midnight tonight?
Mum:	Right. Shall we go through them one by one? You can borrow ten pounds, but you already owe me ten pounds, so you'd better not spend too much. You definitely can't borrow my new jacket.
Sophie:	Oh Mum ...

Mum:	I will give you a lift to town, but not till four o'clock, because I'm busy right now.
Sophie:	But I need to go now.
Mum:	You could walk of course, or take the bus. You should get more exercise anyway. You'll go past a shop that sells batteries then. I haven't got time to do that. And you really ought to be more polite. I feel like saying no to everything when you speak to me like that.
Sophie:	OK, sorry, I'll wait till you're ready. So would you please give me a lift? And could you collect me from the city centre at midnight, do you think?
Mum:	Yes, I will ... but you'd better leave me to finish what I'm doing now or I'll change my mind.
Sophie:	OK then.

Recording 13b

Speaker 1: It's difficult to imagine that you'll ever be able to wear it, isn't it, when it's freezing cold here? But it's perfect for the kind of holiday you've described. And it's very reasonable too, of course. It'll be cool during the day when you're travelling around and in the evening you could put a jacket on top and wear it in the hotel for dinner. I have one very similar myself. Shall I leave you to think about it for a moment or two?

Speaker 2: You'll be surprised how cold it gets up in the mountains when it's so warm down here. I forgot to remind last week's group and it was much colder than they expected. You must bring something warm to put on when we get up there. You may not need it, of course, but you'd better all go and get a pullover or jacket or something from your rooms now before we leave. I don't want any complaints later on that someone's cold.

Speaker 3: I took all the wrong clothes of course when I went. I just didn't realise it would be so cool in the evenings. It was lovely and hot during the day but in the evenings I really needed a jacket or something. I had to go and buy one in the end. In fact I could lend it to you if you want. Why don't I pop across the road and get it? It'll only take a minute. I know exactly where it is in the wardrobe.

Speaker 4: Don't do what I did last year and sit out in the sun too long. It made me ill actually. In fact, when I got back here everyone said I looked worse than when I left, that I should have spent my holiday here at my desk. But you're more sensible than me. You'll have the right clothes, hats and things. So have a good time – don't even think about us back here looking at a computer screen all day. Oh, and don't forget what I said about the shops – you must bring one of those wonderful shirts back.

Speaker 5: At least you've been there before so you won't waste your time finding your way around. Have you got all the right clothes? You ought to take things for the daytime when it's warm and things for the evening. It can get quite cold, you know. You remember when we all went together as a family, we enjoyed walking in the evenings. I know you'll be in a group and you'll probably do different things from us. And you'd better not spend all your money in the airport shop because there are lovely things to buy when you get there.

Recording 14

Fiona:	Hey look, Clare. Isn't that Danny over there?
Clare:	I can't see him, Fiona. Where?
Fiona:	Sitting at a table in that café over there.
Clare:	It might be Danny.
Fiona:	But who's that he's with?
Clare:	Oh she must be his mother. He said she was coming to visit him for a few days but not till next week. They must have changed their plans.
Fiona:	Look Clare, she can't be his mother. She's much too young. Could you get a bit closer and see who he's with?
Clare:	Why don't you?
Fiona:	He might see me ... OK. We'll walk across together. We'll pretend we're looking in that shop window over there.
Clare:	OK ... No, you're right Fiona. She's much too young. Hey, we ought to get back to college now – our lecture starts in ten minutes. Shall we just go and say hi as we go past?

| Fiona: | I don't think so. She could be his new girlfriend and I'd be embarrassed. Anyway, Clare, I'm not interested. |
| Clare: | Oh no? You must forget about him Fiona, you know. You two broke up ages ago. He's really boring anyway. Come on. We need to get back ... |

Recording 15

Four burglars have escaped from custody only hours after being sentenced to ten years in prison. They were being transferred from the law courts in Manchester to Strangeways Prison. They had been found guilty of stealing electrical goods and money from shops in the Manchester area. It is thought that they were all members of the same gang. They escaped from the van in which they were being transported, when the driver was forced to stop because of a tree across the road. It is believed that the tree was placed there by other members of the gang, who had been informed of the route to be taken by the van. A full investigation of the events leading to the escape has been ordered and anyone with information is asked to contact the police to help with their inquiries. And now over to Simon for the weather forecast ...

Recording 16

Rachel:	Hello James. Are you there? Can you hear me?
James:	Hi, Rachel. Yes, I can hear you very well.
Rachel:	How do you feel?
James:	I'm fine.
Rachel:	Where are you now, James?
James:	I'm about 100 kilometres off the coast of Australia. So it's not far to the finish.
Rachel:	Do you think you're going to win, James?
James:	Well, I haven't seen another boat for a few days. It's a really amazing feeling to be alone in the middle of the ocean. I think I might win.
Rachel:	Could be that you're last, James, and the others have all finished! Just joking, of course! What's the weather like?
James:	Last week there was a terrible storm. It was really loud and quite frightening and I didn't sleep for three days but now the weather's completely different, the sea's calm, so beautiful, the sun's shining, it's almost too hot.
Rachel:	Can you see dolphins there?

James:	I can sometimes see sharks and dolphins swimming in the distance as well as so many different kinds of birds.
Rachel:	I'm on my way to join you, out of this noisy studio! And what's the first thing you'll do when you get to Australia?
James:	I'll spend two hours in a hot bath I think – oh, and I must get my hair cut. But the very first thing is to ...
Rachel:	Hello, James, are you still there? ... Oh, we've lost him, I think. Hope one of those sharks hasn't come to visit! We'll talk to James again ...

Recording 17

Today I'm going to explain how to make one of my own favourites – I think I enjoy making it as much as eating it. You need a large cake tin and I'll give you a complete list of ingredients at the end. First of all, beat the butter and sugar together. Continue doing this until the mixture begins to look pale and fluffy. Then pour in the eggs. Avoid adding the eggs all at the same time, you should add them slowly and keep beating all the time. Next, add the flour, and don't forget to add the baking powder, or you'll end up with a biscuit rather than a cake. Now for the fruit. I recommend using sultanas and apricots but if you prefer to use dates or raisins that's fine. Some people like to add some nuts too but you needn't include them if you prefer not to. If you decide to use nuts, chop them up small. Mix everything together and pour the mixture into the tin. Bake in the oven for about one-and-a-quarter hours. Remember to check if the fruit cake is ready after about an hour as everyone's oven is slightly different. Let the cake cool for about half an hour. If you want to ice the cake, mix up some icing sugar with water. I suggest adding a little lemon juice as well. Don't try to ice the cake until it's completely cold. If you decide not to ice it, just sprinkle some sugar on top. One word of warning, don't expect to have much fruit cake left after a couple of hours – it's delicious. My family can't resist it. And now here is the list of ingredients you need ...

Recording 18

People are saying that I caused the group to break up and I want everyone to know the truth. It really wasn't my fault. I'd always got on with the other members. We'd been together for more than five years and I thought I could count on them as friends as well as work colleagues. I thought they would always be there to back me up when I was in trouble. I had expected them to look after me when I needed them as I would always be there for them. But last year when I came up against some problems at home I wasn't able to perform in a couple of concerts. Instead of carrying on without me – they could have managed on their own – they called the concerts off and said it was my fault. And they stopped talking to me. They would get together every Monday morning and sit round the table. They would then go over plans for the next week and not tell me anything. I put up with this for a while, then we had a big argument. They said they wanted to throw me out of the group because of what I'd done. I was so upset because I really cared about them but I don't any more. Now I'm determined that they're not going to get away with it. They're not going to treat me like that. I won't give in until they've paid me every penny they owe me. Anyway, enough of all that. Now let me tell you about my plans for ...

Recording 19

Double X: You wanted to see me, Mr Seymour?

Seymour: Yes, come in, Double X. I have an important mission for you. I want you to follow a man and find out all about him. If you find him, I'll be extremely pleased.

Double X: Who is he, sir?

Seymour: If I knew that, I wouldn't be giving you this job! Here's a photo of him.

Double X: But this is all fuzzy. It's impossible to tell what he looks like.

Seymour: If we had a better picture, we'd give it to you. Anyway, we've had an anonymous tip-off, so we know he's a spy, and we know he works in London.

Double X: Didn't your source tell you who he works for?

Seymour: If she'd told us that, I wouldn't have needed to ask for your help.

Double X: So the source is a woman?

Seymour: Yes. She telephoned and then faxed us the photo. But we couldn't trace the number.

Double X: That's bad. It would give me somewhere to start if I knew where she'd phoned from. It's a pity we haven't got a better photo – it's just a man standing in front of a door.

Seymour: It is a bit clearer if you look at it with your eyes half closed.

Double X: Hmmm. Wait a minute. There's a number on the door. Forty-two. Oh no! It can't be. But it is.

Seymour: What? What is it?

Double X: Well, sir, this is very embarrassing. But I'm afraid that's my front door. And the man standing outside it is – me!

Recording 20a

Is everybody here? Good. Now listen carefully. I hope you've all had a good day today. I wish the weather were better here for you. It's very unusual to have so much snow and rain here at this time of year.

Some of you were asking about tomorrow. Well, we're going unless the weather gets much worse during the night. OK? So, provided that it doesn't snow too heavily tonight, I'll see you back here at six o'clock. Set your alarms for 5.30. We'll take our breakfast with us because we won't reach the top of the mountain unless we set out early, before it's light. So be here tomorrow morning with everything you need. You've all got a list – you need a whistle in case you get separated from the rest of the group, warm waterproof clothes and gloves, and a good pair of boots. Don't forget the maps I gave you. I'd rather you didn't bring large cameras and video cameras as they'll be a nuisance.

Now, is everyone happy and looking forward to tomorrow? You all look rather worried. There's really no need. As long as we all stay together and you follow my instructions, we'll have a great time. I've never lost anyone up there yet! I wish you'd come a few weeks ago when the weather was better because we could've done so many more walks then. Never mind, there's always next year. It's time we had dinner now so if anyone has any questions, you can ask me on the way to the dining hall. Let's go in.

Recording 20b

1 *You hear a woman telling someone about a film she has seen. What kind of film was it?*

   A a thriller

   B a love story

   C a comedy

   I wish I'd persuaded you to come with me. I must admit I really wasn't sure whether I was going to enjoy it or not so I didn't want to drag you along too but I could go again if you want to see it – although I know the ending, I'd still enjoy watching that car chase again. Someone had told me it was a romantic comedy but it's not how I would describe it. There was certainly nothing in it that made me laugh. I would have liked a bit of romance actually because it was rather exhausting sitting on the edge of your seat all the time.

2   *You overhear a conversation in a restaurant. What is the man complaining about?*

   A   *the food*
   B   *the service*
   C   *the noise*

   Man: I've been coming here for years and I've always recommended it to people. But I really haven't enjoyed my meal today.

   Manager: I'm sorry, sir. Can I get you something else?

   Man: The food is up to its usual standard, thank you. I just can't understand why you've removed the carpets and curtains from the restaurant and put down these tiles. I've brought my colleague here to discuss important business and I've only caught half of what he's said. All I can hear is other people's conversations. I complained to the waiter but of course it's not his fault. You'll have to do something about it, otherwise I shan't come here again.

   Manager: Well, I'm afraid there's not much I can do …

3   *You hear a woman talking to a colleague. How did the woman feel?*

   A   *upset*
   B   *ashamed*
   C   *shocked*

   I was standing in the queue in the canteen and there were a couple of people in front of me. They were talking about someone and I thought – Oh dear, that person's got quite a few problems. I was trying not to listen actually because I thought they might be talking about someone I knew. Then I realised they were talking about me. They turned round and they were quite embarrassed. The only person who knows all those things about me is Andrea and she must have told them. I tried not to be bothered about it but I had trusted her so it's really hurtful. I wasn't really surprised though because she never could keep a secret, could she?

4   *You overhear a man talking to a friend on the phone. What was damaged?*

   A   *a piece of sports equipment*
   B   *a musical instrument*
   C   *a piece of furniture*

   I was really cross with myself for being so careless. I was in a hurry and as I opened the car boot it just fell out. I'd got a little table in the boot too so it was probably because there wasn't enough room in there. I couldn't have my lesson – it's no good if you haven't got anything to play. I just hope it will sound all right when I've had it repaired. It'll probably cost a lot too.

5   *You hear a couple planning to meet. When will the woman telephone the man?*

   A   *about lunchtime*
   B   *late afternoon*
   C   *early evening*

   Man: You know we said we'd have a game of badminton one evening? How about today? Let's meet after work, shall we?

   Woman: Um, I'm not sure about today. I may have a meeting and if I do it'll run late this afternoon, but I'm not sure yet.

   Man: Well, I'm going out to do some deliveries now, but I'll have my mobile with me.

   Woman: Well, I can phone you then, can't I? I should know by around lunchtime whether I'll be able to get away early enough, then we can fix a time for the evening.

   Man: OK.

6   *You hear the weather forecast. What will the weather be like at the weekend?*

   A   *foggy*
   B   *wet*
   C   *sunny*

   And here is the weather forecast for today, Friday. There's quite a lot of fog about this morning but it should clear to give a fine day with just the odd cloud in the sky. It'll be cold though. Then a change as we move into the weekend. On Saturday and Sunday we can expect heavy rain as the clouds move in. Next week there should be more sunshine – that is if the early morning fog clears. That's all from me. I'll be back at midday.

7 *Listen to a phone conversation between two women. Why is Sarah ringing Katya?*

A *to make an apology*

B *to offer an invitation*

C *to make a request*

Katya: Three – four – two – seven – five – nine.

Sarah: Hi, Katya. This is Sarah.

Katya: Hi Sarah.

Sarah: Look, I know you can't come to the party on Friday and I'm really sorry about that but I wondered if I could borrow some of your cutlery. You see, there are far more people coming than I expected. Don't worry if it's not possible. I'll ask someone else.

Katya: That should be fine, Sarah, but I'll need it back on Sunday.

Sarah: No problem.

Katya: You'll come and get it then? And maybe we could go to the cinema next week?

Sarah: Fine.

8 *You overhear a woman talking to someone in a shop. Who is she talking to?*

A *the shop manager*

B *a customer*

C *a colleague*

Well, I was serving at the time and there was a woman waiting in the queue looking very impatient. Mr Reynolds came across the shop and said to me: 'Hurry up, look, there's someone waiting. Why are you so slow?' In front of a customer too. Just like he did to you the other day. Next time he embarrasses us, we've got to stand up to him you know ... We've worked there longer than he has and we know most of the customers anyway so we have to stop and have a chat with them, don't we?

Recording 21

Good morning. Here is the news for Wednesday the fifth of September.

The Prime Minister is in Washington to attend an international trade conference. He'll spend two days at the conference and after that he'll have talks at the White House with the President. At the weekend he'll fly to Mexico.

Singer Moira MacNab has suffered problems at the start of her tour of Europe with the cancellation of her London concert. She had been holidaying on the north coast of Africa before her tour and was injured on the plane coming to England. Her flight hit bad weather as it was flying across the Mediterranean and she was hurt by a case which fell from a locker on the wall. However Ms MacNab says that she will be quite well by the weekend when she is due to appear in Edinburgh.

A footbridge over the motorway between London and Oxford has collapsed, causing serious delays, with traffic jams stretching beyond the beginning of the motorway. Emergency services are at the scene but part of the motorway will remain closed until this afternoon.

And the local news:

Police have arrested a man who was holding a bank manager hostage. They were called to the bank on the High Street late yesterday afternoon when a security man standing by the door of the bank heard shouting in the manager's office. The manager was released during the night and the gunman gave himself up early this morning.

And now back to Annie for some more music.

Recording 22

Andy: Hi, Dawn! I'm home.

Dawn: Andy! Where have you been? And what's happened to your jacket? It's filthy!

Andy: OK, OK, there's no need to shout at me. Actually I had a bit of an adventure on the way home.

Dawn: What happened?

Andy: Well, I was driving up Wellbourne Road when I saw flames coming out of an upstairs window. I called the fire brigade on my mobile and then I thought I'd better see if I could do anything. I decided I'd better try and go in. I thought perhaps someone was in there. I got in by breaking a window.

Dawn: What! How?

Andy: I remembered the toolbox I keep in the car for emergencies –

Dawn: Oh, yes.

Andy: – and smashed a window by hitting it with a hammer. The room was full of smoke, so I covered my face with a handkerchief. There wasn't anyone on the ground floor, and I was just wondering if I could go upstairs, when a neighbour arrived and the fire brigade. They said the house was empty – the owners work in town.

Dawn: Thank God. You could have been in real danger.

Andy: Oh not really. Well, anyway, then the fire brigade were in control, so I went to my car. Then the owners arrived.

Dawn: Poor things.

Andy: Well, it wasn't so bad because luckily, I'd called the fire brigade before the fire had spread too far.

Dawn: I hope they thanked you for saving their property.

Andy: Oh, yes.

Dawn: Do they know how it was started?

Andy: By an electrical fault, they think. Anyway, do you forgive me for being late?

Dawn: Don't be silly! I can't be angry with you now. Go and have a shower and I'll make a really nice supper for you.

Andy: Great. I'm looking forward to eating it already.

Recording 23

Welcome, everybody, to Claremont Castle. I'm Jasper Claremont and this has been my family's home, where we've lived for over four hundred years, since the time of Edmund Claremont, who first lived here in 1600. This room is the great hall and the paintings you can see here are our oldest portraits. The painting we're looking at now shows Edmund himself. Do you see the ship in the background? It's the one which he was captain of during a famous naval victory. This victory was the reason why he became a national hero. He was given the piece of land where Claremont Castle now stands as a reward. The next painting shows Edmund's wife Margaret, who he married in 1605. She's wearing all the family jewels. And now let's move on to the picture of Henry and William, their two sons. It's the picture that hangs next to Margaret's portrait, and it's the one I like best. The one who's sitting on the horse is Henry, and William's the one who's holding the book. William, who was his mother's favourite, became a poet, while Henry, who his father preferred, was more of a man of action. He fought in the Civil War, which broke out in

1642. Unfortunately, he supported the side which lost. We don't know much about the woman he married, and he had no heirs, but William, whose wife Jane was a famous beauty, had nine children, who all survived. Here they are in this picture from the year when their youngest son was born. Now, if I can lead you into the dining room, where we'll see some more recent pictures ...

Recording 24

Adam: Hi, Josie, what's up?

Josie: Adam, have you heard? Tom Castle's the new captain of the volleyball team!

Adam: Tom Castle?

Josie: Yeah, and it's really bad.

Adam: Why?

Josie: They only chose him because he's the coach's nephew.

Adam: That's not fair. Tom's certainly good enough to be captain. I think he's an obvious choice.

Josie: Well, I still think it's wrong.

Adam: What do you mean?

Josie: Look, he's captain of the team. Why? Because of his uncle.

Adam: Perhaps you ought to be in the team yourself since you seem to know so much about the subject.

Josie: I'm not tall enough to play volleyball.

Adam: Nonsense – several people your size are in the team. Melanie, for example. She's so quick that she's one of the best players.

Josie: You know I'm not into team games. Going to judo once a week gives me enough exercise. Anyway, volleyball would take too much time. They have too many practice games after school.

Adam: Well, I've been training every day in order to be really fit. They may need some new people so I want to be ready.

Josie: You? You're joking.

Adam: No, I'm not. The coach said that I play well enough. And the exams start next term. Some of the older players may drop out as they've got so much revision to do.

Josie: Really? Oh. Well, good luck then. But I won't be with you.

Recording 25

Paul: Hello there. I'm Paul Dadley and this is Studio One with all your favourite music and entertainment news. And first off, I'm very happy to welcome actor Gemma Lewis to the studio.

Gemma: Thank you.

Paul: Actually, shouldn't I call you a film star rather than an actor? After all, you've been world famous since making the film *Starshine* two years ago, haven't you?

Gemma: Well, yes, I suppose so. I enjoyed making that film but I really want to be a stage actor.

Paul: It was quite a surprise to get the lead in *Starshine*, wasn't it?

Gemma: Yes. I got the part in spite of having no film experience.

Paul: How was that?

Gemma: I was at a theatre school. I was fifteen and I'd only acted small parts in some stage plays. The director chose me to play the part after visiting several schools. I still don't really know how he guessed I would be right for it.

Paul: And you had no hesitation in accepting?

Gemma: Oh, yes. I had a long talk with my parents before accepting it. In the end, I went for it, even though I knew I would have to spend a year away from home. It was a chance I couldn't afford to miss.

Paul: But you didn't make any more films after finishing *Starshine*. Why is that? You must have had plenty of offers.

Gemma: Yes I did. In fact I was offered two more films while making *Starshine*, but working far from home, I sometimes felt very lonely, and I wanted to develop a stage career. So I came back to England.

Paul: So, no more films?

Gemma: Oh, I don't know. I'd be happy to do another film later, but I'm booked up for the next few months.

Paul: Well, Gemma, that's good news for your fans. Now, what about the play you're appearing in at the moment?

Gemma: It's great. It's actually a comedy, despite being called *Dark Days*. It's really funny.

Paul: And it's at the Arts Theatre. So, everybody, don't miss the chance to see Gemma Lewis live! Gemma, thank you for coming to talk to us.

Gemma: Thank you.

Paul: And now some music ...

Note: *Although actress means female actor, the word actor is increasingly used for both men and women in modern English.*

Appendix 1: Phrasal verbs

These are some of the most common phrasal verbs. Many phrasal verbs have more than one meaning. Check them in a good dictionary and study Unit 18 before using this list.

ask after	come up against	get on with	keep back	pay off	stand up to
ask for	count on	get out	keep down	pay up	stay in
back out of	count up	get out of	keep off	pick out	stay out
back up	cross out	get over	keep on	pick up	stick out
be away	cut across	get round	keep out	point out	stop off
be in	cut back	get round to	keep up	pull down	stop over
be into	cut down	get through	keep up with	pull in	switch on
blow up	cut in	get together	knock down	pull off	switch off
break down	cut out	get up	knock out	pull out	take after
break in	cut up	get up to	leave in	pull up	take away
break off	deal with	give away	leave on	put aside	take back
break out	do away with	give back	leave out	put away	take in
break up	do out of	give in	let down	put by	take off
bring about	do without	give out	let in	put down	take on
bring back	draw in	give up	let off	put off	take over
bring in	draw out	go after	let out	put on	take to
bring out	draw up	go by	let through	put out	take up
bring round	drop back	go down with	live on	put through	talk over
bring up	drop by	go for	live through	put up	think about
build up	drop in on	go in for	live up to	put up with	think of
burst in	drop off	go off	lock up	ring back	think out
burst out	drop out	go on	look after	ring off	think over
call for	face up to	go out	look at	ring up	throw away
call in	fall back on	go over	look back on	rub out	throw out
call off	fall behind	go through	look for	run away with	try on
call on	fall for	go with	look forward to	run down	try out
care about	fall in with	go without	look in	run into	turn back
care for	fall out	grow out of	look into	run out of	turn down
carry off	fall through	grow up	look on	run over	turn into
carry on	feel like	hand in	look out	see about	turn off
carry out	feel up to	hand on	look over	see off	turn on
catch on	fill in	hand out	look through	see through	turn out
catch up with	fill out	hand over	look up	see to	turn over
check in	find out	hang about	look up to	send for	turn up
check out	fit in	hang on	make for	send out	wash up
check over	get across	hang up	make up	set back	watch out
check up	get along with	have back	make up for	set in	wear off
clear out	get around	have on	miss out on	set off	wear out
clear up	get at	have round	mix up	set out	wipe off
come across	get away	hold back	move in	set up	wipe out
come down	get away with	hold in	move out	show off	wipe up
come forward	get back	hold on	own up	show up	work out
come off	get by	hold on to	pass away	stand by	work up
come on	get down	hold out	pass off	stand for	write down
come out	get in	hold up	pass out	stand in for	write in
come round	get off	join in	pay back	stand out	write off
come up	get on	join up	pay in	stand up for	write up

Appendix 2: Irregular verbs

Verb	Past simple	Past participle
arise	arose	arisen
be	was / were	been
beat	beat	beaten
become	became	become
begin	began	begun
bend	bent	bent
bite	bit	bitten
bleed	bled	bled
blow	blew	blown
break	broke	broken
bring	brought	brought
broadcast	broadcast	broadcast
build	built	built
burn	burnt	burnt
burst	burst	burst
buy	bought	bought
catch	caught	caught
choose	chose	chosen
come	came	come
cost	cost	cost
creep	crept	crept
cut	cut	cut
deal	dealt	dealt
dig	dug	dug
do	did	done
draw	drew	drawn
dream	dreamt	dreamt
drink	drank	drunk
drive	drove	driven
eat	ate	eaten
fall	fell	fallen
feed	fed	fed
feel	felt	felt
fight	fought	fought
find	found	found
fly	flew	flown
forbid	forbade	forbidden
forget	forgot	forgotten
forgive	forgave	forgiven
freeze	froze	frozen
get	got	got
give	gave	given
go	went	gone
grow	grew	grown
hang	hung	hung
have	had	had
hear	heard	heard
hide	hid	hidden
hit	hit	hit
hold	held	held
hurt	hurt	hurt
keep	kept	kept
kneel	knelt	knelt
know	knew	known
lay	laid	laid
lead	led	led
lean	leant	leant
learn	learnt	learnt
leave	left	left
lend	lent	lent
let	let	let
lie	lay	lain

Verb	Past simple	Past participle
light	lit	lit
lose	lost	lost
make	made	made
mean	meant	meant
meet	met	met
pay	paid	paid
put	put	put
read	read	read
ride	rode	ridden
ring	rang	rung
rise	rose	risen
run	ran	run
say	said	said
see	saw	seen
sell	sold	sold
send	sent	sent
set	set	set
sew	sewed	sewn
shake	shook	shaken
shine	shone	shone
shoot	shot	shot
show	showed	shown
shrink	shrank	shrunk
shut	shut	shut
sing	sang	sung
sink	sank	sunk
sit	sat	sat
sleep	slept	slept
slide	slid	slid
smell	smelt	smelt
sow	sowed	sown
speak	spoke	spoken
spell	spelt / spelled	spelt / spelled
spend	spent	spent
spill	spilt	spilt
spit	spat	spat
split	split	split
spoil	spoilt	spoilt
spread	spread	spread
spring	sprang	sprung
stand	stood	stood
steal	stole	stolen
stick	stuck	stuck
sting	stung	stung
strike	struck	struck
swear	swore	sworn
sweep	swept	swept
swell	swelled	swollen
swim	swam	swum
swing	swung	swung
take	took	taken
teach	taught	taught
tear	tore	torn
tell	told	told
think	thought	thought
throw	threw	thrown
understand	understood	understood
wake	woke	woken
wear	wore	worn
weep	wept	wept
win	won	won
write	wrote	written

Grammar glossary

adjective
A word which tells us about a noun:
*a **new** house; a **boring** film*

or a **pronoun**:
*She's **tired**.*
*They're **beautiful**.*

adverb
A word which tells us about a verb:
*They talked **quietly**.*
*We'll meet our friends **tomorrow**.*

or an **adjective**:
*a **very** expensive computer*

or a **sentence**:
***Luckily**, we knew all the answers.*

auxiliary verb
A **verb** (like *be, do, have*) which we use with a
main verb in some tenses:
*She **is** talking.*
*You **do** not understand.*
***Have** they arrived?*

conjunction
A word that connects clauses or phrases in a
sentence:
*Paul read a magazine **while** he was waiting for
Tina.*
***Although** Karen worked hard, she didn't pass
her history exam.*

determiner
A short word which goes in front of a **noun**:
***some** people; **each** person*

imperative
A **verb** which gives an order:
***Leave** your tray here, please.*
***Open** the door!*

infinitive
The basic form of a **verb** which we can use
after other verbs, often with *to*:
*I want **to see** you.*
*This is difficult **to understand**.*
*We must **leave** early.*

main verb
The part of a **verb** which gives its meaning
(compare **auxiliary verb**):
*She is **talking**.*
*You do not **understand**.*
*Have they **arrived**?*

modal verb
A special kind of **verb** which we use with an
infinitive to give extra meaning:
*You **can't** sit here.*
*He **must** hurry.*
***May** I help you?*

noun
A word for a person or thing:
*a **child**; a **group** of **people**; the **place** where I
keep my **books***
*I felt great **anger** when I heard the **news**.*

object
The **noun** or **pronoun** (with other words like
determiners etc.) which follows a **verb**:
*He's drinking **some hot chocolate**.*
*They don't like **us**.*
*Did you solve **your problem**?*
*She gave **me a present**. (= two objects)*

participle

The *-ing* form (e.g. *working, eating*) or the **past participle** (e.g. *worked, eaten*) of a **verb**. We use them with **auxiliary verbs** to make **tenses**:
*The boys are **working** hard.*
*We had **eaten** our meal.*

The *-ing* form and the past participle can sometimes be used as an **adjective**:
*an **exciting** story; a **frightened** animal*

The *-ing* form can sometimes be used as a noun:
***Swimming** is good for you.*

phrasal verb

A **verb** made up of two or three words (verb + adverb / preposition):
look after; give away; look forward to

preposition

A short word which usually goes in front of a **noun** or **pronoun** and links it to other words:
*Please speak **to** her.*
*He fell **off** his chair.*
*What's the meaning **of** this word?*

pronoun

A word used in the place of a **noun**:
*The girls like volleyball so **they** play **it** every week.*
*Are **you** hungry?*

sentence

A group of words in which there is usually a **verb** and its **subject** or **object**. In writing, sentences begin with a capital letter. A sentence can:

- make a **statement**:
  My name is John.

- ask a question:
  Do you enjoy learning English?

- give an instruction (see **imperative**):
  Study this page.

- be an exclamation:
  You're very beautiful!

statement

A **sentence** which tells us some information:
I like chocolate.
My brother doesn't live here.

subject

The person or thing which does the **verb**:
***My family** comes from London.*
***Smoking** is not good for your health.*
*Do **your friends** have any money?*
*Where are **they**?*

tense

The form of a **verb** which gives extra information, for example, about the time it happens:
*She **lives** there. (= present tense)*
*She **lived** there. (= past tense)*

verb

A word which describes what happens:
*The boy **wrote** a letter.*
*We **thought** about you.*

CD Tracklisting